REALITIES OF FREE TRADE: TWO INDUSTRY STUDIES

Edited by Harry G. Johnson

NEW TRADE STRATEGY FOR THE WORLD ECONOMY

by Harry G. Johnson, Gerard and Victoria Curzon, Lionel Gelber, Maxwell Stamp and Harry Cowie, David Robertson

Second impression

Edited by Hugh Corbet

TRADE STRATEGY AND THE ASIAN-PACIFIC REGION

by Hugh Corbet, G. C. Allen, Sir Robert Scott, Leonard Beaton

Edited by Harry G. Johnson

TRADE STRATEGY FOR RICH AND POOR NATIONS

by Harry G. Johnson, David Wall, Hans Liesner, M. D. Steuer

Realities of Free Trade

Two Industry Studies

BY

DUNCAN BURN

AND

BARBARA EPSTEIN

WITH AN INTRODUCTION BY

Harry G. Johnson

London

GEORGE ALLEN & UNWIN LTD

RUSKIN HOUSE · MUSEUM STREET

First published in 1972

ISBN 0 04 382016 6

Printed in Great Britain
in 10 point Baskerville type
by Redwood Press Limited
Trowbridge & London

ATLANTIC TRADE STUDY PROGRAMME

The Atlantic Trade Study Programme was initiated in December, 1966, by a private group in London for the purpose of exploring the implications for Britain of participating in a free trade treaty among developed countries as the framework within which might be pursued the further liberalisation of international commerce. It has been financed by contributions from a wide range of British banks and industrial companies and some firms overseas.

The committee responsible for the research project is under the chairmanship of Sir Michael Wright, formerly Permanent Head of the British Delegation to the Geneva Disarmament Conference, while the research director is Professor Harry G. Johnson, of the London School of Economics and the University of Chicago. The programme is being administered by the Trade Policy Research Centre (see below). The full committee is as follows:

SIR MICHAEL WRIGHT
Chairman

PROFESSOR HARRY G. JOHNSON
Director of Studies

PROFESSOR H. C. ALLEN	PROFESSOR JAMES MEADE
SIR GEORGE BOLTON	HUGH MULLENEUX
SIR DOUGLAS BUSK	W. G. PULLEN
HUGH CORBET	TIMOTHY RAISON
SIR ROY HARROD	

As a basis on which to proceed with research, the proposed free trade association was defined as initially embracing the United States, Canada, Britain and other member countries of the European Free Trade Association; open to the European Communities and to Japan, Australia and New Zealand, as well as other industrially advanced nations; and affording less developed countries greater access to their markets.

Several proposals along these lines had already been receiving serious attention at academic, business and official levels in North America. The project was in fact a British response to a new trade strategy proposed in May, 1966, by the Canadian-American Committee, a non-official group sponsored by the Private Planning Association of Canada and the National Planning Association in the United States.

With the expiry on June 30, 1967, of President Johnson's authority under the Trade Expansion Act of 1962 to negotiate trade agreements with other countries, and the completion of the so-called Kennedy Round of multilateral tariff negotiations, made possible by the Act and conducted under the auspices of the General Agreement on Tariffs and Trade, the United States Administration and Congress was expected to embark upon a thorough reappraisal of trade policies and practices with a view to formulating a fresh negotiating authority. The proposal for a multilateral free trade association initiated by North Atlantic countries has been one of the policy options to have subsequently come under consideration.

Meanwhile, the British Government had made a second application for United Kingdom membership of the European Communities. But whether Britain gained admission or not, the concept of a potentially world-wide free trade association was deemed, in either eventuality, as likely to prove of large significance. For in the event of membership being negotiated it was considered that the United Kingdom would then require an informed policy for the development of closer commercial and political relations between Western Europe and North America. If, on the other hand, the European Communities rejected Britain again, even if only temporarily, it was considered important to have examined beforehand whether there existed a viable alternative.

That assessment still held when, a few years after the failure of the second application, the British Government made a third attempt to negotiate Common Market membership. Indeed, at its ministerial council meeting in June, 1971, the Organisation for Economic Co-operation and Development authorised a high-level study group to examine the consequences for the world economy of *inter alia* the enlargement of the European Communities and to advise on appropriate courses that might be taken by the international community.

TRADE POLICY RESEARCH CENTRE

The Trade Policy Research Centre, London, was established in 1968 to promote independent analysis and public discussion of commercial and other foreign economic policy issues. It is a privately-sponsored non-profit organisation, financed by foundations and corporate donations, and is essentially an entrepreneurial centre under the auspices of which are conducted a variety of activities.

Intense international competition, technological advances in industry and agriculture and new and expanding markets, together with large-scale capital flows, are having profound and continuing effects on international production and trading patterns. With the increasing integration of the world economy there is thus a growing necessity to increase public understanding of the problems now being posed and the kind of solutions that will be required to overcome them.

The Centre is managed by a Council, the Chairman of which is Mr Frank McFadzean, a Managing Director of the Royal Dutch/Shell Group of Companies. Professor Harry G. Johnson, of the London School of Economics and the University of Chicago, is the Director of Studies. The Director is Mr Hugh Corbet.

The principal function of the Centre is the sponsorship of research programmes on policy problems of national and international importance. Specialists in universities and private firms are commissioned to carry out the research and the results are published and circulated in academic, business and government circles throughout Britain and in other countries. The Centre also organises seminars and meetings and publishes occasional papers under the omnibus heading of *Thames Essays* and a general series of books on *World Economic Issues* is in preparation.

CONTENTS

Part II

CHEMICALS UNDER FREE TRADE

by

DUNCAN BURN

Chairman, Centre for the Study of Industrial Innovation, London; Visiting Professor of Economics, University of Manchester, 1967–69, and University of Bombay, 1971; formerly a leader writer on The Times, *London; author of* The Economic History of Steelmaking, 1867-1939 (*1940*), The Steel Industry, 1939-59 (*1961*) *and* The Political Economy of Nuclear Energy (*1967*)*; and author of* The Structure of British Industry (*1958*).

TABLES

Part I

Part II

FIGURES

Part I

Part II

ABBREVIATIONS

ELECTRIC POWER COMPANIES

BPA	(United States)—Bonneville Power Administration
CEGB	(United Kingdom)—Central Electricity Generating Board
EdF	(France)—Electricité de France
ENEL	(Italy)—Ente Nazionale per l'Energia Elettrica
RWE	(West Germany)—Rheinisch-Westfälische Elektrizitätswerke AG
TVA	(United States)—Tennessee Valley Authority

MANUFACTURERS

ACEC	(Belgium)—Ateliers de Constructions Electriques de Charleroi
Adda	(Italy)—Adda Officine Elettrotechniche e Meccaniche
AEG	(West Germany)—Allgemeine Elektricitäts-Gesellschaft
AEI	(United Kingdom)—Associated Electrical Industries Ltd
ASEA	(Sweden)—Allmänna Svenska Elektriska Atiebolaget
ASGEN	(Italy)—Ansaldo San Giorgio and Compagnia Generale de Elettricita
BBC	(Switzerland and West Germany)—Brown Boveri and Company
BP	(United Kingdom)—British Petroleum Co Ltd
CEM	(France)—Compagnie Electro-Mécanique
Delle	(France)—Delle-Alsthom, a subsidiary of Alstrom
EE	(United Kingdom)—English Electric Company, now part of the General Electric Company Ltd
Galileo	(Italy)—Officine Galileo Elettromecanniche
GE	(United States)—General Electric Company
GEC	(United Kingdom)—General Electric Company Ltd
ICI	(United Kingdom)—Imperial Chemical Industries Ltd
Magrini	(Italy)—Fabbriche Riunite Magrini-Scarpa and Magnano MSM
M·A·N	(West Germany)—Maschinenfabrik Augsburg-Nürnberg AG
M and G	(France)—Merlin and Gerin
TIBB	(Italy)—Tecnomasio Italiano Brown Boveri

Technical Terms

ASP	American Selling Price system of customs valuation
EHV	extra high voltage: ratings 345 kilovolts and higher
HP	high pressure: cylinder of a turbine
Hv	high voltage: ratings from 110 to 345 kilovolts
IP	intermediate pressure: cylinder of a turbine
KA	kilo ampere: measure of current used for circuit breaker ratings
KV	kilovolt: measure of transmission line capacity (1 kilovolt = 1,000 volts)
LP	low pressure: cylinder of a turbine
MVA	megavolt ampere: measure of transformer capacity (1 megavolt-ampere = 1,000 kilovolt-amperes = 1,000,000 volt-amperes)
MW	megawatt: measure of power output of a turbine (1 megawatt = 1,000 kilowatts = 1,000,000 watts)
psi	pounds per square inch
SF6	sulphur hexafluoride

Organisations

ANIE	(Italy)—Associazione Nazionale Industrie Elettrotechniche ed Elettroniche
BEAMA	(United Kingdom)—British Electrical and Allied Manufacturers' Association
EAEA	(United States)—Electrical Apparatus Export Association
EEC	European Economic Community
EFTA	European Free Trade Association
GATT	General Agreement on Tariffs and Trade
IEA	International Electrical Association
INCA	International Notification and Compensation Agreement
MITI	(Japan)—Ministry of International Trade and Industry
NEMA	(United States)—National Electrical Manufacturers' Association
OECD	Organisation for Economic Co-operation and Development
OEEC	Organisation for European Economic Co-operation

PREFACE

This is the fourth volume of studies to be published under the Atlantic Trade Study Programme. The project, which has been administered by the Trade Policy Research Centre, has been concerned with exploring the implications and possibilities of a free trade treaty among developed countries as the framework within which might be pursued the next phase in the liberalisation of world commerce. What the proposal would amount to is the formation of a multilateral free trade association open to all developed countries and providing for (a) an across-the-board elimination of tariffs over an agreed transition period, (b) rules of competition for dealing with non-tariff barriers to trade, (c) non-reciprocal tariff preferences in favour of less developed countries during the transition period and (d) commitments towards the expansion of commercial trade in agricultural products. Some such broad strategy is required to counter effectively the protectionist trends that have been developing on both sides of the Atlantic since the conclusion, in the middle of 1967, of the Kennedy Round of tariff negotiations.

The basic concept has not altered much since it was first proposed in 1966 by a group of business, trade union and university leaders comprising the Canadian-American Committee, sponsored by the National Planning Association, in the United States, and the Private Planning Association of Canada. But the presentation of the concept has had to take into account each change in the circumstances of international trade. For the proposal was put forward at a time when the Kennedy Round negotiations were making little progress and there seemed little prospect of negotiations being resumed on the enlargement of the European Community. The former were eventually brought off successfully, but the second attempt by Britain to join the Common Market was vetoed by France almost from the outset. Then it was the turn of international trade relations to go into decline and heaven smiled on Britain's third attempt to come to terms with the original Rome Treaty countries which, even before the departure of President de Gaulle from the French political scene, had begun to adopt more flexible approaches towards European integration.

In *New Trade Strategy for the World Economy*, published in 1969, four Atlantic Trade Study Papers were brought together which had previously been published as individual monographs. The volume was edited by Harry G. Johnson, of the London School of Economics and the University of Chicago, who has been the research director for the project. It deals with the general economic and politico-strategic considerations relating to the free trade treaty proposal. The second volume, *Trade Strategy and the Asian-Pacific Region*, which I edited, appeared early in 1971. It, too, is concerned with general economic and politico-strategic issues, but more particularly with those relating to East Asia and the Western Pacific. The third volume, *Trade Strategy for Rich and Poor Nations*, edited by Professor Johnson, discusses the issues of particular concern to the less developed countries, on the one hand, and the more developed countries, on the other.

Two further Atlantic Trade Study Papers have been consolidated in the present volume. The first paper in the volume, by Barbara Epstein, an American industrial economist who has taken a special interest in the heavy electrical engineering industry, was first published under the title, *Politics of Trade in Power Plant.*

If the liberalisation of world trade is to be carried forward in the 1970s, the attention of governments must focus—now that tariffs have been reduced to a low level—on non-tariff distortions of international competition. These last, more commonly referred to as non-tariff barriers to trade, have been the subject of several recent surveys and analyses. One has been the study by Robert E. Baldwin, *Nontariff Distortions of International Trade*, for the Brookings Institution in Washington[1]; another, the Thames Essay by Gerard and Victoria Curzon, *Hidden Barriers to International Trade*, was published by the Trade Policy Research Centre. It is generally agreed, in these and other studies, that one of the most difficult categories of non-tariff distortion to overcome will be the procurement policies of governments and other public authorities. Yet means will have to be found—whatever negotiating strategy is adopted, whether it be the free trade treaty option, the sector-by-sector approach or any other—for reaching an understanding on how they are to be harmonised.

Heavy electrical engineering is one of the most conspicuous examples of an industry where, in almost every country, public procurement is a vital factor. The politics of international trade in the products of the industry is thus extremely complex. Considerable clarification and discussion will be required before an international *entente* can be achieved between the manufacturers and purchasers of electrical equipment.

[1]London: Allen & Unwin, 1971.

Dr Epstein's study has been a contribution to that end. She was helped by manufacturers of heavy electrical power plant and executives of electricity supply authorities to assemble and use the data and information upon which the study is based. Her paper arose out of a thesis prepared for presentation at the New School of Social Research, New York, and, as a result, benefited from the guidance and criticism of David Schwartzman and the suggestions of Stephen Hymer and Thomas Victorisz. Dr Epstein was also advised by Horace De Podwin, Dean of the Graduate School of Business Administration at Rutgers State University, New Jersey. Finally, comments on an earlier draft of the paper were offered by Professor Johnson, as the research director of the Atlantic Trade Study Programme, and by Duncan Burn, who carried out the second study contained in the present volume.

On the subject of non-tariff barriers to trade, the trade in chemical products is a controversial talking point, if only because of the American Selling Price system of customs valuation which applies to certain chemicals and other items. ASP only affects 1 per cent of United States imports, but it has become something of a *bête noire* with West European governments. In a free trade arrangement, however, such para-tariff barriers would be eliminated along with tariffs. Mr Burn's study is not so much concerned, then, with non-tariff barriers as with the non-tariff forces, relating to comparative advantages, that might be expected to influence more and more the course of trade flows as tariffs are reduced and eliminated.

Mr Burn was greatly helped in the initial analysis of the trade statistics and of the complex European tariff structure by Richard M. Jones, of the University of Manchester, and gained much at the outset from discussions with Don Gibbons, of Arthur D. Little Inc. Numerous officials of chemical companies, trade associations, government departments, international organisations, firms of consultants and banks helped with information and advice, and Professor Johnson commented on an early draft.

While the Atlantic Trade Study Programme has provided the opportunity and the encouragement for their work, the two contributors to this volume are solely responsible for the views expressed in their respective papers.

HUGH CORBET
Director
Trade Policy Research Centre

London *Winter*, 1972

INTRODUCTION
by
Harry G. Johnson

While most studies under the Atlantic Trade Study Programme on the proposal for a free trade treaty among the advanced countries have been concerned with broad overall political and economic questions, it was felt by the "practical" members of the group which initiated the research project—the industrialists and the City men—and also by the research directorate that some studies should be concerned with the probable impact of changes in international trading arrangements on specific industries.

Unfortunately this type of economic research is both expensive and extremely time-consuming, demanding as it does both the familiarity of the researcher with the detailed character of an industry and the amassing of a vast amount of material, some statistical and some concerned with the institutional and business practices of the trade. The original intention of the project was to provide an extensive coverage of the international trading interests of British industry, with special reference to how the various industries might fare under a world-wide free trade association. The available resources, however, permitted the sponsorship of intensive study of only the two industries dealt with in this volume, the chemical industry and the heavy electrical engineering industry.

These industries may not accord with everyone's mental image of what modern industrial competition is about. Some people remain fixated by the traditional industrial base of Britain's economic leadership in the nineteenth century—textiles, steel and shipbuilding (coal no longer has any devotees). Others are fascinated by what they conceive of as the industries of the future—supersonic aircraft and computers. But chemicals and heavy electrical engineering products do represent current industrial realities. Moreover, the international trade problems of these industries are characteristic of the problems that are emerging in international commercial policy discussions.

The Atlantic Trade Study Programme was extremely fortunate to be able to enlist the services of two acknowledged industry experts to survey the international trade problems of these industries and the possible impact on them of free trade arrangements. Duncan Burn can fairly be described as the dean of British industrial economists, a man with vast experience in the intensive study of the organisation and problems of British industry. Barbara Epstein, while considerably more junior, has become expert on an extremely complex industry and especially on its international competitive aspects.

Value of Industrial Economic Studies

Research on industrial organisation and specific industrial trade problems is not only difficult and time-consuming. It suffers from a particular disadvantage not encountered, or encountered only to a far lesser extent, in other kinds of economic research. The disadvantage, briefly put, is that industrialists are accustomed to think of research on industrial organisation—if they think of it at all—as a way of helping them to make money, not as a way of enabling the rest of society to understand them and their problems. In the context of policy research, this means that they are happy with and pleased by research that finds the mote in the neighbour's eye, but distressed and even angry with research that finds the beam in their own. More concretely, they are pleased with disclosure of discriminatory trade practices pursued by foreign firms and governments, but upset by disclosure of similar practices on their own parts which they would like to have regarded as entirely warranted defensive measures against foreign unfairness. This attitude makes it extremely difficult for self-styled "practical men" to accept the results of practical research that regards them, not as heroes fighting a war against insuperable odds, and deserving only of praise for their valour, but as specimens of the genus *homo sapiens* reacting in economically predictable ways to the economic environment that nature and their fellow men have established for them.

Research on industrial problems in the United Kingdom is likely to be a poor relation of economic research in general, so long as "practical men" insist on judging it by the question "what does it do for me?" instead of by the question "what does it do for the country?" The question that industrial research into monopolistic and other practices should raise in the mind of the practical businessman is not: "Am I really a bad man?" To that question the answer cannot be "yes", because he knows that he is loyal to his company and good to his wife and children. Rather the question should be: "If other people in my society consider me to be a bad man, why is it that I am constrained to behave that way in order to survive?" The answer frequently is that his fellow men, through the political process, have constrained him to behave in one way but insist on judging him as if he were free to behave, and should behave, in another.

Thus British industry is criticised for being inefficiently managed. But it is hemmed in by a maze of economic and social restrictions. These require it to provide employment in high-cost-labour areas, buy high-cost British-made components and conform to a system of labour relations that accords labour the right to a job and an income with little or no responsibility for helping management to make it possible to earn that right. In addition, British industry must be ever heedful to the notion that "Whitehall knows best"—especially when it comes to exporting goods like Rolls-Royce engines at a commercial loss in the name of the national interest and for the sake of a possible knighthood to be acquired at a vast sacrifice of the shareholders' profits.

It is no wonder, under these circumstances, that British industry is inefficient, at least as judged by the industrially incompetent politicians and journalists who would like an industrial elephant instead of an ass to ride on into political glory. The proper response, though, is not to pretend that British industry is really efficient, and to try to suppress or dismiss all evidence to the contrary, but to use the results of economic research as a basis for protesting, loudly and clearly, that the fault lies in the environment within which British business is constrained to work. To that end, "practical men" should welcome and encourage independent economic research on industrial problems—and be prepared to devote some of their own thought to what the results really mean.

Limited Importance of Tariffs

The two studies presented in this volume (the fourth volume to be published under the Atlantic Trade Study Programme[1]) deal with industries with quite different economic characteristics. That is part of their value as a combined presentation, since economic discussion, particularly of policy problems, is inclined to be far too aggregative in its approach and to treat both industrial and international trade problems as if production and competition were homogeneous activities undifferentiated by the facts of technology and the practices of governments. What they have in common, from the point of view

[1]The three companion volumes are Harry G. Johnson (ed.), *New Trade Strategy for the World Economy* (1969); Hugh Corbet (ed.), *Trade Strategy and the Asian-Pacific Region* (1970); and Johnson (ed.), *Trade Strategy for Rich and Poor Nations* (1971); all published by Allen & Unwin, London, and University of Toronto Press, Toronto.

of the problem of achieving a better system of international trading relationships, with which the research programme has been concerned, is that they both deal with industries in which tariffs are of relatively little importance as compared with other factors influencing competitive advantage. As such they are extremely instructive in the context of current discussion on international trade policy, which since the conclusion of the Kennedy Round of negotiations under the General Agreement on Tariffs and Trade (GATT) has come to be concerned with the influence on trade of non-tariff barriers, especially those erected by governments.

Where the two industries differ is in respect of the other factors that dominate tariffs in the determination of competitive position in international trade. In chemicals, technological superiority, research and development expenditure, and economies of scale dominate differences in labour costs. This is in accordance with emerging theories of the nature of comparative advantage in the contemporary industrial world, which have come to stress what is usually referred to as "the technology factor". In heavy electrical engineering equipment, on the other hand, international competition is dominated by two factors, both the consequence of governmental policy rather than of economic forces. These are public procurement policies, dictated in Dr Epstein's words by "national pride" (though why any nation should take pride in the fact that its industry cannot compete for orders without a substantial hidden subsidy is something of a psychological mystery), and national technical standards.

Between them, the two studies suggest a paradox in the present concern about non-tariff barriers. On the one hand, the Europeans have made much about the American Selling Price principle of valuation of United States chemical imports as a non-tariff barrier to trade. Yet this principle applies to only a tiny fraction of American imports and, as Mr Burn points out, would disappear automatically with the establishment of free trade. On the other hand, as the Epstein study suggests, public procurement practices and technical standards are of high importance in restricting trade in heavy power plant, and elimination of their influence in distorting trade could not be handled by the conventional type of international trade negotiation. In the light of this paradox, there may well be something in the developing feeling of American public opinion that traditional trade negotiations produce results biased against United States trading interests, and in favour of West European trading interests.

Both studies also raise, though to quite different extents, a problem which has come to excite a great deal of concern in various countries in the past few years—that of the multinational corporation and its operations. For Mr Burn, whose industry has for long been characterised by multinational operations, this is a peripheral question concerned with the direction that new investment might take under different kinds of international trading arrangements; for Dr Epstein, on the other hand, it seems clear that the path towards efficiency in the heavy electrical engineering industry lies in the concentration of production in a few multinational firms, free to operate competitively in an international market from which the restrictions currently imposed by public procurement policies and national differences in technical standards have been removed.

In both case studies, the authors lend little or no support to the euphoric belief that membership of the European Economic Community (EEC) offers Britain a road to economic and industrial salvation. Mr Burn adduces various reasons why the British chemical industry is likely to be at a competitive disadvantage in relation to its major European rival, the West German industry. Dr Epstein provides evidence that the British heavy electrical industry is not currently thinking in the terms of the multinational integrated operations that she believes are indicated by the economic realities of competition in the industry, while some at least of their foreign rivals are. When Britain joins the EEC their analysis will be put to the ultimate practical test.

When the Atlantic Trade Study Programme was initiated in 1966, there was some prospect that the Kennedy Round negotiations would fail. There were also serious reasons for doubting whether Britain would be successful in any third attempt to come to terms with the Common Market.[2] At the time of writing (late winter, 1972), Britain seems set at last to join the EEC, although on terms prospectively unpleasantly reminiscent of Dunkirk. On the other hand, public opinion in the United States has fast been retreating into protectionism.

[2]Britain's second application to join the EEC, foreshadowed in 1966 and formally submitted in 1967, was her third attempt to come to terms with the Common Market, bearing in mind the British-led attempt within the Organisation for European Economic Co-operation to negotiate a European free trade area between the Six and the other countries of Western Europe. For a brief discussion of that attempt see Haruko Fukuda, "First Decade of EFTA's Realisation", in Hugh Corbet and David Robertson (eds), *Europe's Free Trade Area Experiment: EFTA and Economic Integration* (Oxford and New York: Pergamon Press, 1970).

More than that, American protectionism has been taking on new characteristics—characteristics ominous for both the future of world trading relationships and the future of relationships between Western Europe and the United States. American opinion has been moving away from the use of tariffs—which at least offer the foreign producer some scope for competition—towards the use of quotas—which restrict the access of the foreign producer to the United States market, regardless of his competitive advantage. Furthermore, American labour has become strongly critical of the alleged "export of jobs" implicit in foreign direct investment by American corporations. United Kingdom entry to the EEC might, if that were all that happened, prove a Pyrrhic victory in the extreme, in the sense of committing Britain to a purely European role under conditions which might well prove economically disadvantageous, while at the same time providing the United States with the final excuse for a retreat into protectionism and non-commitment to Western Europe—a retreat that would restrict both the flow of trade between Western Europe and the United States and the transmission of American technology to Western Europe through direct investment.

In these circumstances, and in view of the mercantilist aspects of the EEC, especially where agriculture is concerned, there is an even more pressing need than was evident in 1966 for a new strategy sufficiently bold to counter such negative trends and carry forward the movement towards freer world trade that by-and-large characterised the 1950s and 1960s. Freer trade is vital to the building of an integrated and prosperous world economy, not just for the benefit of the already-rich advanced countries of North America and Western Europe, but even more pressingly for the benefit of the developing countries of the Third World.

Traditional negotiations on GATT lines will no longer suffice. They cannot encompass problems of non-tariff barriers to industrial trade, nor can they deal readily with problems of agricultural trade.[3] What is needed is a new approach, free of enmeshment in the legalities and precedents of established commercial policy bargaining procedures; one that is capable of pursuing and establishing the economic realities and not merely the political and legal appearances of an

[3]Negotiating options for a major trade initiative have been analysed in Gerard and Victoria Curzon, "Options After the Kennedy Round", in Johnson (ed.), *New Trade Strategy for the World Economy*, *op. cit.*, and Johnson and Corbet, "Pacific Trade in an Open World", *Pacific Community*, Tokyo, April, 1970.

integrated free trade world. Those who recognise the critical nature of the present conjuncture of world political and economic relationships and potential trends are becoming increasingly interested in the possibilities of negotiating a free trade association among the advanced nations of the world. This association would be capable of dealing with the problems of industrial and agricultural trade as they now appear after a quarter century of international negotiations for the reduction of tariff barriers, and would at the same time provide fair terms of access to the advanced sector of the world economy to countries that are still in the process of economic development.[4]

Those who instituted the Atlantic Trade Study Programme take some pride in the work they have done to put the idea of a free trade treaty among developed countries on the agenda of public discussion of possible future international trading arrangements. Obviously we can take no credit for the basic idea, that free trade is a beneficial arrangement for mankind, since that idea has been around (and by-and-large accepted) for some two hundred years of modern industrial history; at most we can claim to have revived the proposition that free trade is potentially beneficial to the poor as well as to the rich, and that it offers the most promise of the poor being enabled to become rich through their own efforts.

What we have tried to do, through the Atlantic Trade Study Programme, is to apply contemporary concepts concerning the function of serious scientific research in the rational solution of problems of policy choice to a particular problem of policy choice for Britain, and for other major developed countries, in the field of international trade policy that was judged to be of major importance to the citizens of Britain, not only in their capacity as British citizens, but in their capacity as human beings resident for better or worse in a country that has both an influence on and a responsibility for the future evolution of civilisation on this planet. The studies presented in this volume may seem to some to represent a rather mundane approach to a grand objective; but one has to learn to walk before one can run, and empirical studies of the trade problems and prospects of particular industries have their place in building the foundations of a better world system.

[4]For an exposition on the proposal for a world-wide free trade association, in the light of the EEC's prospective enlargement, see Lawrence Krause, "The Spirit of International Economic Co-operation in a World of Peace", an Address to a symposium on international economic co-operation sponsored by *The Yomiuri Shimbun*, Tokyo, April 28, 1971.

Part I

POWER PLANT AND FREE TRADE

by

Barbara Epstein

1 HEAVY ELECTRICAL ENGINEERING INDUSTRY

The importance of electricity for industrialised economies has led to government regulation of electricity systems and, as a frequent by-product, to government protection of electrical equipment manufacturers. In Japan and in many West European countries that have domestic equipment industries this protection is manifested as a virtual exclusion of foreign equipment to generate and transmit electricity. In the United States it is a "Buy American" bias that leads several power agencies to favour domestic producers. In addition to these purchasing restrictions, the most significant distortions to trade are the availability of credit and, also, the multiplicity and variety of technical standards for equipment.

Purpose and Summary of Findings

The purpose of this study, as of all those conducted under the Atlantic Trade Study Programme, is to assess the effects of a free trade treaty approach to the liberalisation of world trade on particular aspects of economic activity or on selected industries. Part of such an assessment is an enumeration of barriers to trade that now exist in each country and an attempt to quantify the advantages these barriers give manufacturers in each country. When the results are combined with the manufacturing advantages enjoyed, an economic evaluation of competitive advantage may be inferred.

This analysis is valid only within the political limitations on trade. The effects of liberalised trade on the manufacturers of heavy electrical equipment will depend largely on the degree to which the attitudes that have led to politically motivated barriers—restrictive procurement policies and technical standards—are liberalised.

In its political aspects, the experiences with trade in heavy electrical equipment may be representative of those in other large and technically-complex engineering products. The manufacture of aircraft, for example, is prestigious, can be vital for defence and the product is bought by publicly-controlled industries. Electronics have a much wider market, but their production is also considered by governments to be necessary for an industrialised economy. Both aircraft and computer manufacture tend to be heavily protected domestic industries, almost irrespective of efficiency.

Politics have affected the sale of large complex equipment as well as its purchase. Where trade occurs, particularly with developing countries, it has been necessary for governments or international agencies to subsidise financing, because the apparatus tends to be expensive and, in the case of heavy electrical equipment, its use shows no immediate return on investment.

If the experiences of the European Economic Community (EEC)[1] and the European Free Trade Association (EFTA) are used as guides, then the probability of free trade in heavy electrical equipment among industrialised nations is very low. Certainly the EEC countries have done almost nothing to foster trade in power equipment. EFTA has made some moves to enforce explicit open purchase regulations, but, at the time of writing, with no appreciable impact.[2]

In the light of these experiences the conclusions presented here are hedged with alternatives based on the degree of trade that is politically acceptable. Completely free trade could result in four to five large multi-product manufacturers operating world-wide. Materials could be bought where prices are lowest and partial or complete manufacturing facilities might be established in locations where manufacturing costs plus transportation charges would be minimal. Continuation of national trade preferences and a host of related barriers to investment and trade could lead, at the extreme, to government-regulated monopolies or duopolies within each industrialised country. Between the two extremes, the number of companies, and of manufacturing facilities, can vary with the number and stringency of barriers. The current economic conditions of manufacturing would dictate a small number of firms. If the present tendency towards restricting trade persists, there are likely to be five to six companies operating world-wide, with complete

[1]The European Economic Community (EEC), the European Coal and Steel Community (ECSC) and the European Atomic Energy Commission (Euratom) have been merged to form the European Communities, but in this study the more familiar initials EEC will continue to be used when referring collectively to the six countries which form the Common Market, often referred to as the Six or simply the Community.

[2]For a discussion of EFTA's rules of competition covering public procurement, see Bengt Rabaeus, "Second Phase in EFTA's Development", and Gerard and Victoria Curzon, "EFTA Experience with Non-Tariff Barriers", in Hugh Corbet and David Robertson (eds.), *Europe's Free Trade Area Experiment: EFTA and Economic Integration* (Oxford and New York: Pergamon Press, 1970).

manufacturing facilities in each of the major trading blocs—that is, in the EEC, EFTA, Japan and North America.

The Industry's Products

Heavy electrical equipment is defined to comprise large steam turbines, generators, power transformers and power circuit breakers (see Figure 1). Steam turbines are used to drive generators which produce electricity. Turbines and generators are often ordered together as a steam turbine-generator set. Power transformers receive electric supply from the generator and raise the voltage to a higher one, more suitable for transmitting large blocks of power over long distances. At each sub-station, another power transformer reduces the voltage for use on distribution systems which make electricity available to final consumers. Power circuit breakers, the third major type of heavy electrical equipment, are protective devices which isolate unsafe circuits, as well as permit control of the system at key points, such as generating stations and network sub-stations. The three types of equipment have several common characteristics.

(a) All three are physically large. For example, the average size turbine-generator ordered by United States utilities in 1968 weighed close to 2,000 tons; the average transformer, 96 tons; and the average circuit breaker, eight tons.

(b) Each piece of equipment is built to customer specifications. Construction takes from one to three years between the date of the order and the date of delivery. In this characteristic, heavy electrical equipment differs from the smaller size electric power equipment, such as distribution transformers and small turbines and generators. These can be produced in assembly line fashion.

(c) The equipment is technically complex. It is often designed jointly by customer and manufacturer. Both the design and production are highly specialised, requiring a high degree of engineering and labour skills. These skills and the long periods of production are reflected in the relatively high unit prices: $4.5m for the average turbine-generator ordered; $130,000 for the average power transformer; and $30,000 for the average power circuit breaker.

(d) The organisation of manufacturing and technical management within the companies that produce a diverse line of electrical and/or mechanical equipment provides a basis for the selected limitation on the size range of each type of heavy electrical equip-

FIGURE 1
PRINCIPAL TYPES OF POWER EQUIPMENT[a]

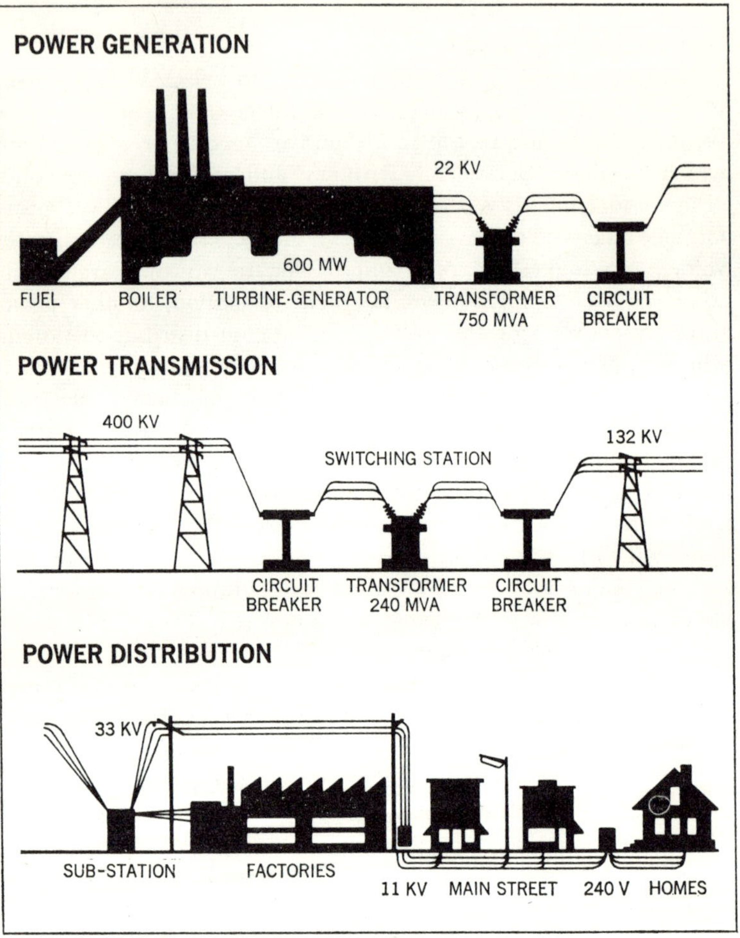

[a]For an explanation of initials used in this figure, and in the tables and other figures, see the list of Abbreviations on Page vi.

ment. In almost all of these companies, steam turbines of 100 megawatts (MW) and larger, power transformers of 10 megavolt-amperes (MVA) and larger, and power circuit breakers of 30 kilovolts (KV) and higher are each produced in separate plants and represent separate profit centres within the company. Most companies, for example, have at least two transformer plants, one for power transformers of 501 kilovolt-amperes (KVA) and larger, and one for distribution transformers of 500 kilovolt-amperes and smaller. As the ratings of transformers have increased, a medium voltage division has been hived off. This was first 501 to 5,000, then to 10,000 and now firms use 501 to 25,000 kilovolt-amperes. Similarly, the lower size limit of large steam turbines has increased and now ranges from 100,000 to 300,000 kilowatts. The voltage classes for circuit breakers have also risen. In the late 1950s high voltage breakers were 230 kilovolts; then extra high voltages of 345 to 500 kilovolts were introduced; and now ultra-high voltages of 735 kilovolts and above are being ordered.

(e) The classification and division of purchasers reflects the same product differentiation as does manufacturing management. Within an electric utility there are generating and transmission and distribution divisions. The work of the divisions is shown schematically in Figure 1. The products included in this study are purchased by the generating and transmission division(s). Generating and transmission equipment used for distribution networks and by large industrial users, such as aluminium factories, are excluded for the reasons cited in (a) to (d) above.

2 CURRENT PATTERN OF TRADE

The industry that produces heavy electric equipment comprises a relatively small number of firms in Canada, Japan, the United States and countries in Western Europe. The combined capacity of the West European and Japanese manufacturers is about equal to that of the Canadian and American firms—about 40m kilowatts of large steam turbines and 155m kilovolt-amperes of large power transformers can be produced each year during the 1970s. (Comparable data are not available for power circuit breakers.)

Despite their roughly equivalent sizes, the direction and importance of trade in these areas differ significantly. Canada and the United States each have had deficits in its respective trade in heavy electrical equipment whereas each of the other major producing countries has maintained a favourable balance. (See Table 1.) The Japanese and West European industries have production capacities from 25 to 50 per cent greater than their domestic markets, where, unlike North America, imports are insignificant. The data for power transformers and turbines are shown in Table 2. (Consistent data on turbine trade are not available.)

The economic rationale for the production capacity of these industries being much larger than home market demand is discussed in Chapters 5 to 7. Here, the effects on trade are covered.

The pattern of trade that has evolved reflects political forces. In industrialised nations, and in those striving to industrialise, these forces are the prestige and importance attached to the retention of a domestic power equipment industry. This has led to the creation of trade barriers to prohibit or to limit imports of power equipment into countries that have their own industries. Individual purchasing policies are examined in Chapter 3.

Facing limitations on exports into most major producing countries, manufacturers have concentrated their overseas sales efforts in countries that do not have power equipment industries. During the second half of the 1960s, over 80 per cent of all transformer exports went to non-producer countries (see Table 2). The destinations of each seller's overseas shipments show definite political patterns. These patterns are summarised here and discussed more fully in Chapter 4.

TABLE I

POWER EQUIPMENT SHIPMENTS, ANNUAL AVERAGES, 1965-68, AND PRODUCTION CAPACITY, 1968

	Power Transformers			*Steam Turbines*	
	Production Capacity (MVA)	*Domestic Shipments (MVA)*	*Trade Balance ($m)*	*Production Capacity (MW)*	*Domestic Shipments (MW)*
Austria	6,000	1,440	+ 1.8	—	—
Belgium-Luxembourg	4,000	1,950	+ 4.3	—	—
France	14,600	8,160	+ 13.0	6,000	1,800
Italy	12,000	6,550	+ 6.5	3,000	1,120
Sweden	12,000	2,690	+ 2.1	1,500	220
Switzerland	5,500	1,390	na	5,000	240
United Kingdom	44,000	35,450	+ 6.3	12,000	6,225
West Germany	20,000	12,790	+ 17.5	10,500	2,340
Japan	35,000	20,110	+ 11.8	6,500	2,360
Canada	20,000	11,000	— 3.2	—	—
United States	125,000	99,770	— 4.3	21,000	15,900

SOURCES:

Survey of Power Equipment, OECD Secretariat, Paris (annual).

West Germany: Aussenhandel, Fachserieg, Statistisches Bundesamt, Wiesbaden (annual).

France: 1965–66: Airgram A-102, American Embassy, Paris, July, 1967.
1967–68: SGCE, January 30, 1969.

Japan: *Electric Power Survey*, Tokyo (half yearly).

United States: *FT410* and *FT125*, Department of Commerce, Washington D.C. (annuals).

Italy: *Statistica Mensile del Commercio Con L'Estero*, Series V, No. 12 (annual).

United Kingdom: *Territorial Analysis of UK Exports & Imports of Electrical & Allied Machinery & Apparatus*, British Electrical and Allied Manufacturers' Association.

na = not available.

First, sales are made according to traditional ties. Thus, France sells to Belgium and Spain. West Germany has large markets in the Netherlands, Belgium, Ireland and Denmark. Britain has sold very little in Western Europe; her traditional markets have been countries in the Commonwealth preference area—Australia, Hong Kong, South Africa and so on.

The second politically-directed group of sales is in areas where direct political ties have weakened. The determinants of export success here are the export credit and economic aid offered by the governments of the sellers' countries. A good illustration of this

TABLE 2
TRADE IN POWER TRANSFORMERS
ANNUAL AVERAGES, 1965–68

Importer / *Exporter*	*Canada and USA*	*Japan*	*Exporting Countries in Europe*[a]	*Other European*	*Other Countries*	*Total Annual Exports*[b] *MVA*
Austria	20.2%	0	12.4%	27.1%	40.3%	3,470
Belgium-Luxembourg	0	0	17.0	23.2	59.8	1,320
France	5.6	0	10.0	19.3	65.1	3,850
Italy	5.1	0	2.0	8.0	84.9	4,790
Sweden	29.9	1.5%	2.2	17.0	49.4	4,850
Switzerland	9.3	.9	32.2	23.5	34.1	1,590
United Kingdom	13.1	0	.3	.7	85.9	4,680
West Germany	1.7	.1	11.9	37.5	48.8	4,450
Japan	12.5	—	0	.3	87.2	8,680
Canada	22.3	0	1.3	1.0	75.4	2,500
United States	1.7	.6	2.3	6.0	89.4	3,460
Importer's Market						
Total Imports: MVA	5,150	112	2,408	5,530	30,440	43,640
Total Size: MVA	115,920	20,222	72,955	16,417[c]	—[d]	—
Imports Share of Total Market: %	4.4%	.6%	3.3%	33.7%	—	—

SOURCE: "Statistics of the Heavy Electrical Equipment Market: an Interim Assessment", unpublished draft of study in progress at the Science Policy Research Unit, University of Sussex; and national trade accounts.

[a]As listed under Exporter in first column of table.

[b]Represents 100 per cent of exports of each exporter.

[c]Excludes domestic shipments in Eastern Europe.

[d]Volume of local production of transformers in Asia and Latin America unavailable.

is the concentration of United States exports to countries that receive United States aid—Greece and India, for example.

A third aspect of export patterns to non-producing countries is the requirement by many of these areas that local production facilities be used for some of the work. This is becoming more important as developing countries strive to establish their own industries.

Since competition is affected by political conditions in virtually all trade situations, little or no inference regarding the competitive strengths of various manufacturers can be drawn from the description of trade patterns. The purpose of the two chapters that follow is to describe the origins and impact of the trade barriers that have evolved.

3 PURCHASING POLICIES IN INDUSTRIAL NATIONS

Heavy electrical equipment is sold primarily to electricity supply companies.[3] Since electric power is considered an essential input to any economy, every country has instituted some degree of government control over its electricity supply system. In England and Wales, France and Italy a central government agency plans and controls the national electricity network of each, although numerous local boards may supervise the distribution of electricity in local areas. In other countries, such as Switzerland and Sweden, there is more than one supply company, each government-controlled. Finally, in West Germany and the United States there is a mixture of private and public utilities, all of which are government-regulated.

TABLE 3
NATIONAL ELECTRICITY SUPPLY SYSTEMS

Country	*Number of Systems*	*Extent of Government Regulation*	*Purchases of Foreign Equipment*
Austria	6	Government runs under one holding company	If domestic unavailable
Belgium	1	Nationalised system	If domestic unavailable
Canada	21	75% public ownership	Extensive
England and Wales	1	Nationalised system	None
France	1	Nationalised system	None
Italy	1	Nationalised system	None
Japan	10	One government owned	Prototypes only
Sweden	2	Over 50% of each, public ownership	Limited
Switzerland	28	Municipal control	None
United States	1,078	40% federal or municipal ownership	50% of market open
West Germany	12	70% government ownership (9 companies supply 75% power)	None

[3]Other purchasers are electric railways and large industrial users, such as aluminium companies. Less than one per cent of equipment shipped in the United States is for non-utility use; in the United Kingdom, 10 to 15 per cent is so destined.

In each country, individual electricity supply companies have been granted regional monopolies over the sale of electricity to the public. In return for these grants, the companies are expected to purchase and install sufficient heavy electrical equipment to meet the maximum demand for electricity in their areas with reasonable margins of safety.

Given the importance of electric power to an economy, every industrialised country has reached the conclusion that it is in the national interest to maintain its own heavy electrical engineering industry to meet its equipment needs; and where feasible there should be at least two companies capable of producing each type of equipment. The means used to secure this position vary from country to country. In several countries, particularly where there is a nationalised supply industry, the utilities try to work with the manufacturers to satisfy the needs of both. This may include agreements on research work, prices, allocation of orders, production quotas and export assistance. According to Sir Ronald Edwards, when chairman of the British Electricity Council: "Anything we can do to help structural changes that make for efficiency we should want to do in our own interest as well as those of export business".[4] In each country, co-operation includes some restriction on imports of equipment.

Overt restrictions on imports are the traditional import duties. By the end of 1971, these had been reduced to 50 per cent of the 1968 levels. (See Table 4.) At that time Canada continued to impose the highest duties, except that Britain continued to have a significant advantage in the sale of steam turbines in Canada due to the preferential Commonwealth rate. Next was Japan with the highest turbine and transformer tariffs and the United States with the highest circuit breaker duty.

The restrictive effect of tariffs on trade are *de minimus* compared with the restrictive effect of utilities' purchasing policies. These policies may include outright embargoes, purchases of prototypes only or strong domestic preferences. Where pressures to liberalise trade arise, utilities can rely on unusual technical requirements to discourage foreign companies from bidding. Equipment standards for safety and reliability and specifications for particular use and location can vary greatly because of differences in electric systems

[4]Sir Ronald Edwards, "Electricity and Economic Policy", presidential address to the British Electrical Power Convention, Brighton, June, 1965.

TABLE 4
TARIFFS ON HEAVY ELECTRICAL EQUIPMENT

	Canada	*EEC*	*Japan*	*Sweden*	*United Kingdom*	*United States*
	%	%	%	%	%	%
Steam turbines						
Pre-Kennedy Round	20.6	10.0	15.5	10.0	17.5	15.0
1972: General	15.0	5.0	9.5	5.0	9.0	7.5
Commonwealth	2.5				0.0	
Power transformers						
Pre-Kennedy Round	22.5	11.0	20.0	10.0	14.0	12.5
1972: General	15.0	5.5	10.0	5.0	7.5	6.0
Commonwealth	15.0				0.0	
Power circuit breakers						
Pre-Kennedy Round	22.5	13.0	15.0	10.0	16.0	17.5
1972: General	17.5	6.5	7.5	7.0	8.0	8.5
Commonwealth	15.0				0.0	

and their loads. They can also differ due to pressures from domestic manufacturers to institute particular requirements.

In the sections that follow, the purchasing policies are set forth for the major producing countries. In each section, the purpose is to indicate barriers to trade that are now the most restrictive and will be the most difficult to dismantle. Following five individual country sections are descriptions of the purchasing policies within present-day trading blocs—the EEC and EFTA.

French Co-operation with Manufacturers

The electricity supply industry in France was nationalised in 1946 by Law No. 46–628. Under this law, the generation and distribution of electricity in France became the responsibility of a public enterprise, the Electricité de France (EdF).

As France's monopolist seller of electricity and the preponderant purchaser of heavy electrical equipment, the EdF has taken on a two-pronged responsibility: (a) to meet the electric power needs of France at the lowest possible cost and (b) to help support an efficient, technically competent French equipment industry. To fulfil these aims, the EdF has used its purchasing power, first, to restructure the French industry and, then, to keep it healthy and efficient.

In its efforts, it has had the full co-operation and encouragement of the French Government. In the early 1960s, three cartels—for large turbines, power transformers and heavy electrical apparatus—were formed by the State among ten of the EdF's suppliers.[5] The EdF then began to encourage mergers among these firms through its purchasing policy. For example, when the first 600-megawatt turbines were ordered in 1963, the EdF stated it wanted only two turbine-generator manufacturers since not more than one set would be ordered each year. Rateau-Schneider and Alsthom appeared to be selected to make the turbine. Compagnie Electro-Mécanique (CEM) insisted on remaining active in the industry. An agreement was reached under which CEM would manufacture the low-pressure turbine end of a 600-megawatt turbine; Rateau-Schneider the high and intermediate pressure sections; and Jeumont-Schneider, the generator. Similar pressures were exerted with respect to power transformers.

By 1965, the French heavy electrical equipment industry had been consolidated into four main groups with these firms producing power equipment: (1) CEM, a Brown Boveri subsidiary; (2) companies owned jointly by Alsthom and Compagnie Général d'Electricité (CGE); (3) Jeumont-Schneider; and (4) Rateau-Schneider. More recent actions have given Alsthom full control of the joint CGE-Alsthom heavy electrical equipment companies, including Delle-Alsthom and Alsthom-Savoisienne and a majority interest in Rateau. Of greater significance is the refusal in 1969 of the French Government to allow the Westinghouse Electric Corporation to purchase a controlling interest in the Jeumont-Schneider group. France is insistent that the latter company should remain French even if this requires that it be merged with the Alsthom companies.[6]

Having encouraged the reorganisation of the French industry, the EdF has continued to use its purchasing powers to help strengthen and preserve the competitive abilities of French firms. First, virtually all equipment is purchased from domestic sources. Only in exceptional cases where agreement cannot be reached to lower

[5] John H. McArthur and Bruce R. Scott, *Industrial Planning in France* (Boston: Graduate School of Business Administration, Harvard University, 1969), p. 386.

[6] *The Economist*, London, December 13, 1969, p. 75.

prices, or, more likely, when French firms have not yet developed a particular technology, are purchases of foreign equipment authorised. Second, the EdF believes that if it were to buy British or Italian equipment, the prices paid would be lower than in the country of export. The EdF, in effect, would be allowing the utilities in those countries to subsidise equipment used in France. The EdF rejects this subsidy in the same way that it balks at subsidising the purchase of French equipment by utilities in other industrialised nations.

During the period of reorganisation, the EdF's prices for power equipment were high compared to those of other countries. Two independent, unpublished, studies showed French prices for transformers to be from 20 to 60 per cent higher than those in other countries in 1968. The EdF conducted a world-wide study of prices and costs and compared them with those in France. The West German situation seemed to be most comparable, so the EdF decided that the prices it pays French manufacturers should be equivalent to West German prices. Devaluation of the franc and revaluation of the Deutschemark helped to narrow the differential. The rest of the transformer price differential was eliminated in talks with the French manufacturers in 1969 when the EdF placed its order for equipment to be delivered in 1970, 1971 and 1972. The prices of circuit breakers in 1972 (net of escalation for rising costs) should be about the same as that in 1966. Domestic French turbine-generator prices (net of escalation) are intended to be fully competitive with those paid by utilities in major producing countries, including the United States.

Within the constraints of limiting imports, the EdF has sought to meet its responsibilities to France and to its power equipment industry. As long as it can continue to pay prices comparable to those in other West European countries and still maintain a healthy domestic industry, it is not likely the EdF's purchasing policies will be changed to include imported equipment.

British Pressure for Industrial Reorganisation

The electricity supply industry in Britain was nationalised approximately at the same time as that in France, in 1948, but it still has not attained the degree of orderly control and efficient organisation achieved by the French.

In 1958 the industry was completely reorganised (under the Electricity Act, 1957). The Central Electricity Authority was formally dissolved and two new administrative bodies were created: the Central Electricity Generating Board (CEGB) and the Electricity Council. Together, they are responsible for the supply of electricity in England and Wales. Scotland had been given its own authority, the South of Scotland Electricity Board, in 1955. The autonomous authority in Northern Ireland is the Electricity Board of Northern Ireland.

Although the CEGB, like the EdF, has encouraged mergers among domestic heavy electrical equipment manufacturers, reorganisation has been more difficult in Britain. There are possibly two reasons: (a) the greater number of firms in the United Kingdom and (b) the large unanticipated fluctuations in CEGB orders for power equipment during the time it was attempting to use its purchasing policy to influence the industry.

In about 1960 the CEGB decided the equipment needs of the British electricity system required fewer than five manufacturers of turbine-generators. On the board's urging, agreements were made between Richardsons Westgarth and the General Electric Company (GEC) and between Associated Electrical Industries (AEI) and C. A. Parsons and Company to share available work for nuclear stations.[7] These arrangements proved to be neither satisfactory in allocating work nor agreeable to the CEGB whose objective was standardisation.

The pressure to merge was reduced when, in 1962, the CEGB undertook an accelerated ordering programme to overcome a shortage in generating capacity. By 1964, when the CEGB accelerated ordering programme was in full gear, growth in electricity demand again began to slow down and the CEGB stretched out its investment programmes. In early 1965, the CEGB wrote to the chairmen of AEI, English Electric, GEC and Parsons, suggesting that fewer firms could best provide the British turbine-generator needs: "the interests of electricity customers would best be served by a reduction in the number of separate designs for the parts they [the CEGB] will purchase".[8]

Within a few months of receipt of the CEGB letter and its appeal, the turbine-generator interests of GEC and Parsons were merged. Parsons took over the GEC turbine factory at Erith and the rotating plant factory at Witton. No existing GEC orders were transferred

[7] *Electrical Times*, London, April 7, 1966, p. 531.
[8] *Electrical Review*, London, May 21, 1965.

to Parsons' Newcastle plant. All subsequent orders are being produced to designs developed by combined technical staffs.

With the GEC-Parsons agreement, Richardsons Westgarth was left out of the industry completely. The firm's work-sharing arrangement with GEC had never materialised and plans for sharing work with English Electric on the Wylfa nuclear station were not sufficient to support the entire plant and organisation. Without orders for a number of years, Richardsons Westgarth was forced formally to cease turbine-generator production, and three turbine-generator manufacturers remained—AEI, English Electric, and Parsons.

British power transformer manufacturers were more reluctant to combine interests. As orders fell off in the second half of the 1960s, the CEGB did not aid transformer makers by holding prices at highly profitable levels. Faced with substantial unused capacity and reduced prices, British firms shaved prices for 1966 orders. The CEGB said it recognised the "thorny problems" faced by the industry and offered to consider proposals for a trading agreement with the manufacturers if they would combine into fewer production units.[9] The CEGB was using its purchasing powers to force mergers.

The CEGB's insistence, combined with poor returns realised by many of the manufacturers, led to a reduction in the number of British producers of heavy electrical equipment from the fourteen firms operating in 1966 (see Table 5). The British turbine-generator and power circuit breakers sectors were cut to two firms—GEC and the Reyrolle-Parsons Group—and the power transformer sector was reduced to six firms.

The proposed agreements between the CEGB and the British manufacturers do not explicitly exclude purchases of foreign power equipment. The option to import gives the CEGB some degree of flexibility and, also, honours its international obligations as a member of EFTA and the GATT. The CEGB can point to one order given to a Canadian manufacturer for two 90-megavolt-ampere transformers in 1962. The reason proffered was that a British manufacturers' cartel was still operating although it had been instructed to dissolve by the British Restrictive Practices Court.[10] The one order was a warning to the British firms to moderate price

[9]Sir Stanley Brown, chairman of the CEGB, as reported in Keith Richardson, "Price Ring Offer on Big Transformers", *The Sunday Times*, London, October 15 1967.

[10]In re Associated Transformer Manufacturers' Agreement, heard before Restrictive Practices Court, London, 1961, LR 2 RP 295.

TABLE 5
MERGERS IN THE BRITISH HEAVY ELECTRICAL INDUSTRY, 1967–69

Company Subsidiary (as of)	*Year Organised*	*Products*
1. Aberdare Holdings Ltd.		
Yorkshire Electric Transformer Co. Ltd. (1968)	1898	Transformers
2. Jute Industries		
Bonar Long and Co. Ltd.[a]	1912	Transformers
3. Ferranti Ltd.	1905	Transformers, testing equipment, electronic equipment
4. General Electric Co. Ltd.	1900	Transformers; nuclear power stations; power generation, transmission, and distribution equipment; domestic appliances; electronic and telecommunications equipment
English Electric Co. Ltd. (1968)	1918	
Associated Electrical Industries Ltd. (1967)	1899	Steam and gas turbine-generators, transformers, circuit breakers, appliances, telecommunications
Hackbridge & Hewittic Electric Co. Ltd. (1967)	1922	Transformers, rectifiers, battery chargers
5. Hawker-Siddeley Group Ltd.		Aircraft, motors
Brush Electrical Engineering Co. Ltd. (1951)	1890s	Transformers, switchgear
Crompton-Parkinson Ltd. (1967)	1913	Transformers
Fuller Electric Ltd.	1898	Transformers, tap changers
6. Reyrolle-Parsons Group (1968 merger)	1886 (R) 1889 (P)	Switchgear, circuit breakers Transformers, steam turbines, electric motors
Bruce Peebles Industries Ltd. (1969)	1906	Transformers, converters, condensers, electronic equipment

[a]Bonar Long has been unsuccessful in its search for a purchaser.

advances. But it was not an indication of a change in CEGB purchasing policy.

Subsequent requests from Canadian firms to submit bids to the CEGB have been denied, despite lower prices and successful operation of the Canadian transformers purchased in 1962. A letter from Sir Stanley Brown, chairman of the CEGB, to the Canadian General Electric Company in January, 1968, cited the following reason for denial:

> "You ask . . . for 'advice as to our policy'. You are no doubt aware of the current situation in which the very low rate of growth of demand in this country coinciding with approaching completion of the main 400-kilovolt grid is resulting in a very abrupt reduction in our requirements for large transformers. Under these circumstances, I think it unlikely that we should need to seek tenders from a wider circle than our home manufacturers."

The CEGB has indicated that continued domestic unemployment and balance-of-payments problems have reduced or eliminated the possibility that foreign manufacturers will be able to enter the British market in the foreseeable future. One representative of the British Government has stated that the British market is not likely to be opened until reorganisation of the domestic industry is complete and the firms are fully competitive.

When and if the British market is open to imports, foreign companies will have another barrier to overcome since CEGB bidding requirements are unusually stringent. Particularly restrictive are the requirements (a) that manufacturers submit design and manufacturing drawings which often are considered proprietary and (b) that firms meet detailed manufacturing specifications, rather than the more usual performance specifications. An example of the latter is the requirement for mechanical couplings of single-phase oil breakers. Continental European manufacturers have discarded this method. To reintroduce it just for the British market would entail a costly design change. This, then, is a technical barrier to trade found in CEGB purchasing policy. Its importance is minor at present, but it could increase if bidding is opened to firms outside Britain.

The British industry is now in a position similar to that of the French. At the insistence of nationalised electricity supply authorities, both industries have been reduced to three or four important manufacturers of heavy electrical equipment. Those manufacturers are likely to work with their respective monopsonist customers to the advantage of both parties.[11] By long-term forecasting and attempts at regular ordering schedules, the CEGB and the EdF can aid the manufacturers to plan investment in expanded facilities and in new techniques and enable them to maintain healthy factory loads with minimum fluctuations. In return, the manufacturers are expected to take measures to increase efficiency and reduce costs in order that administered prices might be at a minimum and comparable with levels in other countries, such as West Germany and Sweden.

The EdF and the CEGB, most likely, will not find it necessary for reasons of equipment shortages or price to import equipment. The industries in France and Britain both are still larger than required to fill the equipment needs of their respective countries. It is extremely doubtful that either market will be opened to international competition in the foreseeable future.

Italian Competition and Subsidies

Purchasing policies and industry reorganisation in Italy have evolved along the same lines as in France and Britain ever since the private Italian electric power companies were purchased by the State under Law No. 1643 of December 6, 1962, and their operations consolidated under one government authority, Ente Nazionale per l'Energia Elettrica (ENEL). The one purchasing rule imposed (Law No. 717 of June 26, 1965) was the requirement to purchase 30 per cent of plant and equipment needs from companies in Southern Italy, a relatively under-developed area of high unemployment.

In the first years of its operation, ENEL did not limit its purchases to domestic equipment. Since it was not fully funded with public money, as are the CEGB and the EdF, ENEL was far more price conscious and attempted to drive down electrical equipment prices. One means of pressure was to import equipment—French and West German circuit breakers, for example. These attempts were successful and by the mid-1960s Italian prices were the lowest in Western Europe.

This severe competition also worked to reduce the size of the

[11]Strong co-operation is advocated by G. B. Richardson, *The Future of the Heavy Electrical Plant Industry* (London: British Electrical and Allied Manufacturers' Association, 1969).

Italian industry. ENEL encouraged a restructuring of the electrical equipment industry into larger and more efficient units. Moreover, ENEL indicated that it preferred these companies to be controlled and operated by Italians. In one instance, ENEL informed a manufacturer of turbo-compressors operating under an American licence that the firm should concentrate its production on another product, that ENEL was buying compressors from a wholly Italian firm. Similarly in 1962, the General Electric Company, the American firm,[12] felt obliged to merge its Italian subsidiary, Compagnia Generale de Elettricita, with Ansaldo San Giorgio to form ASGEN, in order to avoid being labelled a foreign company.

Italian imports of power equipment have declined sharply since 1966. Italian manufacturers are still heavily dependent on foreign technology so that nuclear reactors and equipment parts will continue to be imported.[13] Also, turbines will continue to be imported when Italian manufacturing technology or capacity is inadequate. Otherwise, according to its purchasing director, ENEL will support its domestic industry.

The prices ENEL pays have been rising since 1967 and ENEL indicates that it pays all Italian manufacturers the same price for equipment made to the same specifications. The staff at the Associazione Nazionale Industrie Elettrotechniche ed Electtroniche (ANIE), the Italian trade association for electrical equipment manufacturers, keeps records of changes in the costs of materials and labour. When the prices of either rise, the manufacturers meet and decide how the increases affect total costs. They then agree on the size of increases in prices of equipment. One circuit breaker manufacturer stated that ENEL once did threaten to import circuit breakers again if prices continued to rise, but no one in Italy believed ENEL really would do so after insisting on a reorganisation of the industry to best meet its needs.

In addition to limiting imports, Italy is one of the few countries that still directly subsidise electrical equipment exports. The Italian State Railway charges Italian manufacturers lower freight rates for export shipments than for domestic shipments. For distances up

[12]The American corporation will be cited hereafter as General Electric, whereas the British company of the same name will be cited as GEC.

[13]Paul M. Popple, United States Department of State Airgram, No. A-188, from American Consulate in Milan, August 23, 1968, p. 2.

to 200 km, rates are reduced 10 per cent. Over 200 km, the rate reduction is increased to 15 per cent.[14]

The Italian Government, through its Law 639 of July 5, 1964, grants direct subsidies for exports of metal-mechanical products, including heavy electrical equipment. The amounts rebated for power equipment represent from one to four per cent of the f.o.b. (free on board) value of the equipment.

TABLE 6
ITALIAN EXPORT REBATES, LAW 639

	Lire per Kg	*Per cent of f.o.b. value*[a]
Steam turbines	40	1.4
Electric generators	35	1.3
Power transformers	45	4.3
Circuit breakers	20	1.1

[a]Based on a 75-megavolt-ampere transformer weighing 198,000 lb; a 250-megawatt turbine weighing 615 tons; a 250-megawatt generator weighing 340 tons; and a 220-kilovolt, 12 gigavolt-ampere circuit breaker weighing 18,900 lb.

Italy's partners in the EEC have protested against these export rebates since 1961; and in 1965 (Court Decision No. 45/64) the Court of Justice of the Community decided the rebates must not be granted on Italian products shipped to other members of the EEC. In a subsequent complaint, the other members insisted that Italian rebates on products exported to third countries "can falsify competition": (a) by giving Italian industry an unfair advantage in these markets and (b) by causing customers to demand lower prices from other Common Market members.[15] Britain and the United States have also protested by levying countervailing duties on a number of products covered by Law 639.

Japanese Cartels

The Japanese maintain the most overt restrictions against imports of foreign heavy electrical equipment. The barriers include quota systems, import deposit schemes and licensing of domestic manufacturers as a prerequisite for selling in Japan.

[14]Information obtained by Counsellor for Commercial Affairs, United States Embassy in Rome, letter dated June 18, 1969, and cable dated August 27, 1969.

[15]*Agence Europe*, Brussels, April 24, 1969, p. 5.

Since World War II, imports of heavy electrical equipment into Japan have been subject either to "import quota" or to "automatic import quota" procedures, both of which are administered by the Ministry of International Trade and Industry (MITI). These regulations require importers to obtain import licences before ordering equipment from overseas firms. The application affords the Japanese Government an opportunity to refuse to grant a licence. Cabinet Order No. 336 in September, 1963, urges the government agencies to show preference for domestic products and asks private industry to do the same. The Ministry of Finance, in Notification 382, listed 14 product categories for which domestic preference should be shown. One category was thermal generating equipment. As recently as 1968, the Japanese Government re-confirmed this restrictive position when it stated that "steam turbines (including steam condensers)" would continue on the list of 121 products Japan would not import except as prototypes. The Japanese stated that turbine-generators "still need time to develop international competitiveness".[16]

When Japan does import equipment, it is only of a size never before used in Japan. Imports of these prototypes include an agreement that the seller will license a Japanese firm to manufacture future units.[17] This means that virtually all foreign sales are limited to the three largest power companies in Japan—Tokyo Electric Power, Kansai Electric Power and Chuku Electric Power. The other Japanese utilities, including government-owned utilities, use equipment with lower ratings.

Imports of prototypes, as well as all other products, are subject to import deposit schemes and standard methods of payment, both of which add to the cost of the goods imported into Japan.[18] MITI sets import deposit requirements at one to five per cent payable in cash, eligible securities, or a bank guarantee. Standard methods of payments do not include advance payments or progress payments, both of which are common in the purchase of heavy electrical equipment and both of which are available to domestic Japanese

[16]"Industrial Technologies in Japan", *The Japan Economic Journal*, Tokyo, June 17, 1969, p. 20.

[17]Unpublished report, "Japanese Non-Tariff Barriers", United States Embassy, Tokyo, Fall, 1969, section 12.

[18]Article 13, Import Trade Control Order, Cabinet Order No. 414. December 29, 1949, as amended, and Ministry of Finance Ordinance No. 62, October 31, 1962.

producers. By refusing to grant non-standard methods of payment for imports, MITI has the power to discriminate against imports. These deposit and payment schemes could be important barriers if ever Japan lifts import embargoes.

This lack of foreign competition in Japan facilitates the ability of Japanese firms to operate comprehensive cartels. All aspects of their business are covered, from investment in plant and equipment, to prices and market shares, to co-ordination of export efforts. In all their endeavours, the manufacturers have the full co-operation of their government. MITI supervises and co-ordinates activities.

United States "Buy American"

The United States, unlike the four countries discussed in the preceding sections, has a very large number of utilities which do not have a common purchasing policy. The individual policies with respect to steam turbine-generators can be divided into four classes: (a) those that have imported equipment, (b) those that will consider imports, (c) those that will not consider imports, and (d) the remainder for which no information is available. Utilities which have accepted or will consider accepting foreign bids comprise the largest group. Together they account for 59 per cent of the generating capacity in the United States.

Comparable data for transmission equipment are not available,

TABLE 7
UNITED STATES ELECTRIC UTILITY PROCUREMENT POLICIES

	Installed Steam Generating Capacity, 1968[a]	
	MW	*% of USA*
Have imported equipment	51,690	24
Will consider imports[b]	76,216	35
Will not consider imports[b]	33,649	16
Policy unknown	54,037	25
Total[c]	215,592	100

[a]Federal Power Commission and Rural Electrification Administration; excludes steam turbines of 10 megawatts and less.
[b]Unpublished report, "The United States Electric Utility Market", Board of Trade, London, 1969.
[c]One utility, representing 2,961 megawatts, equal to 1.3 per cent of total United States thermal capacity, is subject to Buy American Act differential of 6 per cent.

but it is recognised that the proportion of utilities which have imported or are willing to import power transformers and circuit breakers is larger than for steam turbines. Several utilities indicated that while they hesitate to import a turbine, they would import transmission apparatus.

The only utilities which are restricted in their imports of transmission equipment are the federally-owned utilities, principally, the Corps of Engineers, Bonneville Power Administration, Bureau of Reclamation, and Tennessee Valley Authority. These federal utilities accounted for about 6.5 per cent of power transformers ordered in the United States from 1965 to 1968. Their procurement of heavy electrical equipment falls within the provisions of the Buy American Act.[19] Under this Act, American suppliers are given specific advantages in bidding on contracts for federal authorities:[20]

1. The lowest foreign bid, including import duty and costs of entry, must be at least 6 per cent below the lowest domestic bid.
2. The differential is 12 per cent if the domestic product is to be produced in an area of substantial unemployment.
3. Utilities may accept a domestic bid exceeding the differential (a) for reasons of national interest, (b) to assist small business firms, (c) to protect national security.

The degree of protection offered by the differentials has been minimal. For example, from 1965 to 1968, foreign bidders lost 13 contracts, representing 7.1 per cent of awards for power transformers of 10 megavolt-amperes and larger by Bonneville Power Administration, the Bureau of Reclamation, and Tennessee Valley Authority, and 4.4 per cent of total United States awards. These three federal agencies apply foreign differentials of 6 per cent and 12 per cent, which serve more to antagonise foreign bidders than to impede imports.

Restriction of imports in the interests of national security has been much more effective. The Department of Defence, including the Corps of Engineers, virtually precludes purchases of foreign equipment by a 50 per cent differential (including duty).[21] Since the

[19]47 Stat. 1520 (1933), 41 U.S.C. 10a-c (1958), and Executive Order No. 10582, 19 Fed. Reg. 8723 (1954).

[20]Laurence A. Knapp, "The Buy American Act: Review and Assessment", *Columbia Law Review*, Columbia University, New York, March, 1969, p. 439.

[21]"The Buy-American Policy of the United States Government: its Balance of Payments and Welfare Effects", *New England Economic Review*, Federal Reserve Bank of Boston, Boston, July-August, 1969, p. 6.

Corps of Engineers has ordered no thermal generating equipment and less than one per cent of United States transmission equipment in recent years, this effective embargo has worked primarily with regard to hydroelectric equipment. As recently as 1968, the United States Secretary of the Interior, then Mr. Stewart Udall, invoked the Buy American Act to exclude foreign bids for three 600-megawatt hydroelectric turbine-generators for Grand Coulee Dam. Mr. Udall gave as the reason that American manufacturers needed the opportunity "to demonstrate their inventive capability in the design and manufacture of these turbines and generators . . ."[22]

The Buy American Act applies only to federal procurement. "Buy American" as a purchasing policy has been adopted by many municipal and private utilities. The reasons vary from national security to better service to the desire or need to support domestic industry.

Although a number of American utilities, committed to supporting American industry, are not apt to import at all in the foreseeable future, more and more utilities appear willing to consider importing heavy electrical equipment. In a survey conducted in 1969 of United States investor-owned utilities, of those which have not imported heavy electrical equipment, utilities representing 51 per cent of the generating capacity in the United States said they are willing to consider importing. Their condition is that overseas firms undertake the same sales effort and assure the same service as American firms. A large United States utility stated the objection this way: "Taking us to lunch once a year is not sufficient".

With a liberalising of purchasing policies in the United States, technical barriers may become more important. One example of this is the American requirement that circuit breakers be designed for two-cycle operation. Most West European countries allow three-cycle operation, so that any West European circuit-breaker manufacturer who wished to sell in the United States would have to re-design its breaker. A second example is the United States standard for on-load tap-change gear for power transformers. Differences in voltage and current philosophy require West European transformer producers to use booster transformers with tap changers on transformers for the United States. Firms such as Legnano of Italy bid in the United States only on contracts where this type of tap changer is not required.

[22]Reported in *Business Week*, New York, July 27, 1968, p. 52.

Extent of Trade Among EEC Members

Three members of the EEC—France, West Germany and Italy—have large internationally significant heavy electrical equipment industries. Two others—Belgium and the Netherlands—produce some transformers and generators.

Article 33(7) of the Treaty of Rome, under which the Community was created, provides for the elimination of restrictive procurement policies. On November 5, 1969, the EEC Commission issued a directive to the members asking that they take measures

> ". . . to eliminate laws or regulations which reserve procurement of products intended to meet the needs of the State, the regional and local authorities and other public agencies partly or entirely to producers of the same State; the directive also covers the regulations which partly or completely exclude imports as a way of fulfilling such procurement contracts or make the supply of imported products more difficult or more expensive than the supply of national products."

Apparently, the directive was necessary because of restrictive public purchasing policies, including those of the buyers of power equipment. The highly protective policies of the French and Italians have been described in preceding sections. These policies apply to EEC members as well as other countries.

The West German situation differs because there is no nationalised electrical industry as customer. Instead twelve to fifteen utilities purchase 85 per cent of the heavy electrical equipment sold in West Germany. Their purchasing policies, in many ways, appear to be similar to those of the private sector of the United States utility market during the first half of the 1960s.

No agreements or formal co-operation exist between the utilities and the major West German manufacturers—AEG, Brown Boveri-Mannheim, Maschinfabrik Augsburg-Nürnberg (M·A·N) and Siemens—concerning prices, market shares, or assistance of any type. In effect, however, the purchasing policies have worked to maintain fairly stable market positions among the four firms. The larger utilities, particularly Rheinisch-Westfälisches Elektrizitätswerk (RWE), check West German prices by inviting bids from manufacturers in other countries—Sweden and Britain, for example. Rarely has any equipment been imported. If foreign bids are lower, it has been the practice to give West German manufacturers an opportunity to meet the lower bids. For this reason, imports of heavy electrical equipment by West German utilities have been insignificant.

The fact that there is a great number of utilities in West Germany and that these utilities are not government-owned should mean that there is scope for increased trade with West Germany. There is little reason to believe this trade necessarily will be realised. West German utilities, as those in most other countries, prefer to buy domestic. The larger utilities appear inclined to consider outside manufacturers if they are from countries whose markets are open to West German manufacturers. Thus, the only West German heavy electrical equipment imports have been from Sweden, an EFTA country. The West German manufacturers believe this was a reciprocal purchase, since the Swedish Power Board had ordered West German equipment. Similarly, imports from France would be highly unlikely, given the closed French market and the fact that two West German firms—Brown Boveri and M·A·N—have French affiliates.

One indication that this situation is likely to remain static over the next decade is the French insistence on a "French solution" to the problem of its weak electrical equipment companies. Not only was France unwilling to allow Westinghouse to acquire a controlling interest in Jeumont-Schneider (Page 12 above), but the refusal extended to the West German companies as well. A second indication of the lack of free trade in the Community is the fact that Brown Boveri maintains complete manufacturing facilities in France and West Germany and partial facilities in Italy and the Netherlands. It will be indicated later (see Page 125) that this is not the most economic arrangement of plant and would not be continued except for the restrictive national purchasing policies.

Opening EFTA Country Markets

Procurement policies of EFTA countries are set forth in Article 14 of the Stockholm Convention of 1959. Austria, Denmark, Norway, Portugal, Sweden, Switzerland and the United Kingdom agreed that public undertakings in their respective countries would not, in their procurement policies, protect domestic manufacturers or discriminate against suppliers in other member states. The EFTA Ministers, meeting in Lisbon in October, 1966, emphasised the obligations of members regarding non-discriminatory public purchasing. A published list of public agencies in each country included these purchasers of heavy electrical equipment: the Austrian Federal Ministry of Transportation and Public Enterprises, the Norwegian Water-Resources and Electricity Board, the Swedish State Power Board, the British CEGB, the Electricity Board of Northern Ireland, the South of Scotland Electricity Board and the North of Scotland Hydro-Electric Board.

Of the three countries with important heavy electrical equipment industries—Sweden, Switzerland and the United Kingdom—Sweden has gone the farthest towards opening its power equipment markets. At first the opening was nominal only. As in West Germany, Swedish power companies once accepted foreign bids, but then gave Swedish manufacturers an opportunity to meet the lowest foreign bid. Since the mid-1960s, there have been indications that the State Power Board, the predominant Swedish customer, has ended this practice. In a July 5, 1968, statement, the president of the Swedish State Power Board asserted:

"The Swedish State Power Board is firmly committed to a policy of open competition and free trade where qualified bidders throughout the world are welcome to compete and are assured a fair evaluation.

. . . .

We would like firmly to state and make clear:

(1) It is our practice to purchase equipment from any qualified supplier with the lowest evaluated bid, who fulfils the requirement of our specifications.

(2) The order is placed with the lowest evaluated bidder without preference for domestic suppliers.

(3) The Swedish Government has no tax rebates or artificial supports that allow domestic suppliers to compete at an advantage.

(4) The Swedish customs tariffs are low (generally similar to the United States) and will go down considerably the next four years according to the Kennedy Round, and we have no 'Buy Swedish Act'."

The sincerity of these statements was shown in 1968 when English Electric won an order for two 375-megawatt turbines for Ringhals power station in Sweden. In 1969, Kraftwerk Union, of West Germany, was awarded a contract for a 250-megawatt turbine. Brown Boveri, of Switzerland, has won several awards.

The United Kingdom is the only other EFTA member with a

significant domestic demand for heavy electrical equipment. The prospects for the CEGB's opening the British market to competition from outside manufacturers were discussed above. There is good reason to believe that the CEGB position reflects the attitudes of both the British Government and the British manufacturers.

The British Government's position, as conveyed in statements by spokesmen of the Department of Trade and Industry, is this: (a) The British industry is going through a period of reorganisation. Until this is complete and the effects worked out, the manufacturers cannot be fully competitive. Until these firms are competitive the government would not care to see the British market opened. (b) There is definitely a need for freer trade, but the British are not about to take the lead, especially when barriers such as "Buy American" still exist.

The British manufacturers have taken the position that power equipment is so heavy that there is no logic to two-way trade in which the United States ships transformers to Britain and Britain ships transformers to the United States. Since Britain is smaller than the United States, the direction of trade in this equipment can only go from Britain to the United States. These arguments exclude entirely the economics of trade and international competition. The desire of British manufacturers to forgo the free market route as a test of their efficiency was explicitly stated in a recent paper published by them wherein it is advocated that provision be made for a minimum profit level to be earned on sales in the British market:

> "Whatever the commercial arrangements adopted in these [heavy electrical equipment] markets, they should be such as allow home prices to be maintained at profitable levels despite temporary excess capacity. For this result to be achieved, either there must be collaboration in the determination of prices or firms must each be independently able and willing to refrain from quoting prices that will destroy the industry's profitability. . . ."[23]

Although the CEGB may feel pressured to buy British, considering the very severe financial strain caused by the treacherous fluctuations in its orders during the 1960s, it has not precluded imports. In the first arrangement the CEGB concluded, with the circuit-breaker manufacturers, "the CEGB [did] not undertake to order grid switchgear exclusively from the GSM [grid switchgear manu-

[23] G. B. Richardson, *op. cit.*, p. 320.

facturers]" (Section 13 of the Agreement). If, however, the CEGB did decide to invite foreign tenders, as did the North of Scotland Hydro-Electric Board in 1968, it is likely that public and government criticism would be intense. In the near future, it is unlikely that any non-British manufacturer, in or outside of EFTA, will receive a CEGB order of a heavy electrical equipment similar to that produced in Britain.

Summary

The purchasing policies in countries that have nationalised electricity-supply companies—France, Italy, Japan and the United Kingdom—are domestically oriented and tend to be highly protective. The continuation and growth of duplicative manufacturing facilities to overcome national purchasing preferences is one indication that these preferences are expected to continue. Another is the statements by purchasing officials as referenced in the sections above.

In other countries in which there are substantial domestic industries producing heavy electrical equipment, procurement is less restrictive. The propensity in these latter areas, particularly Sweden and a large part of the United States, definitely is towards open competition. West German utilities show indications of opening bidding, but the progress is slower.

Where trade is opening, it is international. There appears to be no conscious preference among members of trading blocs for products of other members of the same bloc, either in the EEC or in EFTA. There is some tariff advantage in exporting to another member, but this advantage will be reduced as the full Kennedy Round tariff cuts are made by 1972. There is little reason to believe that national purchasing policies would be affected by the entrance of the United Kingdom, with or without other EFTA members, into the EEC.

4 SALES TO DEVELOPING COUNTRIES

By far the largest proportion—over two-thirds—of heavy electrical equipment which enters into world trade goes to countries that do not have adequate manufacturing facilities of their own. Since most of these countries have had little experience in operating or evaluating equipment, they have tended, in the past, to rely on manufacturing nations to which they have been politically tied. Thus, when France installed electricity networks in its associated African countries, the systems resembled those in France and the technical advisers were apt to recommend the use of French equipment. The same was true of Britain and her "associates" such as India, Hong Kong and Australia.

Although many of these ties have persisted, especially where power networks have grown too slowly to enable local skills to develop, the major concern now is the development aid that sellers can offer. The availability of aid appears to be highly important in deciding who sells power equipment and where. Two aspects of this competition—export credit and use of local facilities—are discussed in this chapter. The conclusions that evolve are these: (a) the nationalistic preferences that pervade government domestic purchasing policies carry over in aid to exports; and (b) the desire of developing countries to build their own heavy electrical industries is working simultaneously to increase world capacity to manufacture the equipment and to close markets.

Export Credit

Heavy electrical equipment has a very high initial cost, while its use shows a very low initial return. Developing countries generally have very small capital resources and many needs, so their purchasing policy appears to be to seek, first, the most liberal credit terms and, second, the lowest price. This is traditional of all new utilities and has affected competition.

Financing Power Systems

Utilities have had difficulties in financing purchases of power equipment since the onset of its use in the late nineteenth century.

At that time, electricity supply companies were an industry of uncertain potential. They had no capital and no credit standing. Manufacturers of heavy electrical equipment had to finance sales by extending credit, by accepting part ownership of the purchaser in payment, or by actually building and financing power stations themselves. Brown Boveri, for example, financed the formation of Motor Columbus in Baden, a firm which arranged the financing, construction and then the sale of power plants to private concerns.[24] A prominent example in the United States was General Electric's creation of the Electric Bond and Share Company in 1905, to hold the securities of power companies.[25]

One impact of these arrangements was to tie the utility to a particular manufacturer. Inherent in the financing plans was an understanding that the electricity-generating company would buy all or most of its equipment from the equipment manufacturer that granted it loans or held its stock. Utilities were not only financially indebted to a particular manufacturer, but also technically dependent on the equipment installed by a particular firm. This tended to limit entry into the manufacturing industry in its early years; only companies that could afford similar credit and technical assistance could compete.

The financial position of utilities improved rapidly as they gained status as growth companies or were put on more stable footing through government control. The problems of adequate financing and technical expertise still exist, however, in developing countries. Competition among heavy electrical equipment manufacturers for orders in these areas hinges in great part upon the credit terms a firm can offer.

Development Aid

Soon after World War II, countries that previously had been tied to Western Europe found that the electrical equipment manufacturers in Britain, France and West Germany were fully occupied in rebuilding their own electricity networks. They could supply neither equipment nor engineering advice for new systems nor funds with which to build power stations.

[24] *75 Years Brown Boveri* (Baden: Brown Boveri, 1966), p. 23.

[25] *Study of Electrical Equipment and Competitive Conditions* (Washington, D.C.: US Government Printing Office, for the Federal Trade Commission, 1928), pp. 128–130.

The United States was in the best position to provide equipment and financing. It did so in the form of development grants and loans. The most relevant of these, now, are the development loans granted by the Agency for International Development (AID). These are long-term loans on highly favourable credit terms, such as 30-year loans at very low interest rates, made with the proviso that all equipment purchases (including power equipment) made with the loans be made in the United States. In effect, the AID buys American-made power equipment and sells it to developing countries on highly favourable credit terms.[26] Half of American export sales of heavy electrical equipment in the 1960s have been made with AID loans.[27] The largest proportion of these loans has been to Latin American countries, although a significant number went to India and Greece. The political motivation for this aid has always been explicit.

In the late 1950s, when West European countries again were actively seeking export orders, developing countries demanded credit terms similar to those of the United States loans. The standard terms were those established at the Berne Convention—a maximum term of five years. No country had export credit facilities set up for handling long-term loans at very low rates. Moreover, West European countries had only limited funds for development aid.

Combined Aid-Credit

In order to compete for power projects in developing countries, the Europeans developed programmes that combined aid with commercial credit. These involved combining government development loans with commercial credit offered at low rates subsidised by the government.

Britain's economic assistance loans are administered by the Overseas Development Administration—part of the Foreign and Commonwealth Office. They are made primarily to other Commonwealth countries and are tied to British goods. The money is provided by the British Government and is extended for long terms

[26] In Chapter 10, it is indicated that when the market rate of interest is very high in industrialised countries, favourable credit terms become an important form of non-price competition.

[27] United States industry data for the period 1962–67; AID loans were responsible for 44 per cent of American turbine-generator exports, 91 per cent of power transformers exports and 60 per cent of power circuit breaker exports. Data collected by the National Electrical Manufacturers' Association.

at low rates of interest.[28] To supplement direct aid, export credit can be obtained through commercial banks. For credits extended for two years or more, the banks have agreed to provide financing at a fixed rate of 7.0 per cent.[29] The Bank of England refinances either 30 per cent of the loan outstanding or repayments due to be made by the buyer in the subsequent 18 months, whichever is greater.[30] Under a separate scheme the Bank of England will finance the entire outstanding balance of insured export credit after the first five years.

West Germany, in 1961, designated the Kreditänstalt für Wiederaufbau (KfW), created in 1948 to finance post-war reconstruction, as the official agency for administering the country's foreign aid for development projects.[31] KfW transactions for the West German Government are carried out with public funds whereas long-term export credit (over ten years) is granted out of the KfW's own funds. For a large project, such as a power plant, the two can be made complementary; that is, when West German heavy electrical equipment manufacturers are bidding for a project, their offer can be backed by a government development loan on very liberal terms.

The operation of this combined aid and trade is seen in a 1969 contest for a Pakistan contract. A. Reyrolle and Company, a British firm, and Brown Boveri, of Mannheim, in West Germany, were both bidding for a $6m order for the supply of switchgear for 36 power sub-stations in Pakistan. Reyrolle submitted the lowest bid. Credit terms offered were 12 years at 5.5 per cent on the condition that the Pakistan Government would also use $19.2m in tied British aid to pay for capital costs of the sub-stations. Reyrolle lost the order to Brown Boveri. The latter asked a higher price, but offered better credit—a loan at 3 per cent for 25 years.[32]

Austria, France, Italy and Japan also have instituted government programmes for facilitating low-cost export credit. The governments in these countries provide funds for financing the difference

[28] *Export Credits and Development Financing: National Export Credit Systems* (New York: United Nations, 1969), p. 86.

[29] *The Financial Times*, London, October 1, 1970. (The rate was 5.5 per cent until mid-1970.)

[30] *Export Credits and Development Financing: National Export Credit Systems*, *op. cit.*, p. 88.

[31] *Ibid.*, p. 32.

[32] *Electrical Times*, London, February 13, 1969, p. 6.

between the market rate of interest and low rates for long-term export credit.[33]

The United States industry, although favoured with substantial tied-aid sales, has been hindered in bidding by lack of discretionary credit facilities. American manufacturers have no source of low-cost credit to use when they obtain export orders not tied to AID or Export-Import Bank loans. In 1970 and 1971 steps were taken to provide long-term credit facilities comparable to those offered by West European countries.[34]

Standardised Terms

With the institution of long-term credit facilities in the United States the credit war could intensify. International organisations concerned with the economics of developing countries are encouraging the negotiation of an agreement among industrialised countries to establish minimum terms of loans that would separate aid from credit and limit competition on credit terms. This would allow utilities to select the most appropriate equipment at the lowest price without undue emphasis on credit availability. One possible agreement might provide for development loans to be for terms of 25 years and longer and for credit to be for 15 years or less. Another scheme frequently suggested is that all development aid be channelled through an international organisation such as the World Bank. This would eliminate the political aspects of aid. Credit terms could then be standardised.

Local Production Facilities

The second determinant of trade with developing countries is the willingness to use their newly established facilities for manufacturing heavy electrical equipment. Important examples include Spain, Brazil, Argentina, Mexico, India and Pakistan. The capabilities for manufacturing power generators and transformers in each country are given in the table below. Except for Pakistan, the countries have the capacity to supply most of their own power transformer needs.

[33]*Export Credits and Development Financing* (New York: United Nations, 1967), Part I, p. xvii.

[34]Richard Lawrence, "Exporters Offered New Loan Service", *The Journal of Commerce*, New York, March 8, 1971.

TABLE 8
MAXIMUM SIZE OF POWER EQUIPMENT BUILT BY DOMESTIC MANUFACTURERS

	Power Transformers[a] *Size in MVA*	*Generators Size in MVA*	
		Hydro	*Thermal*
Spain	170	225	81
Brazil	70	70	—
Argentina	60	8	—
Mexico	100	—	—
India	250[b]	37	—
Pakistan	2	—	—

Source: Ayhan Çilingirōglu, *Manufacture of Heavy Electrical Equipment in Developing Countries* (Washington: International Bank for Reconstruction and Development, 1969) p. 32.
[a]Three-phase units.
[b]Completed in 1970.

Brazil and Spain can produce transformers up to 400 kilovolts.[35] Only Spain has facilities for producing thermal generating equipment.

Spain and India started their industries prior to World War II; the others were begun in the post-war period. All six achieved respectable proportions only during the 1960s. These countries were encouraged to produce their own power equipment (a) to substitute for imports and (b) because it is considered a prestige item necessary for the industrialisation of any country.

Joint Ventures

To acquire the technology necessary to build heavy electric equipment, established firms were invited to construct manufacturing facilities in developing countries. The usual arrangement is one of joint participation of foreign and local concerns.

All of the major international manufacturers have participated in joint ventures with local companies. In Brazil, for example, Brown Boveri and General Electric started full-scale manufacturing operations in 1960–62. ASEA, Siemens and AEG built plants

[35]Ayhan Çilingirōglu, *Manufacture of Heavy Electrical Equipment in Developing Countries* (Washington, D.C.: International Bank for Reconstruction and Development, 1969), p. 32.

primarily for power transformers.[36] Their motivation seems to be two-fold. First, there is the desire to maintain shares of developing markets. If these countries insisted on local production, the only way to obtain sales was to produce in those countries. Second, the situation appeared to offer opportunities for establishing low-cost manufacturing centres from which to export either complete apparatus or components. This is especially attractive when "obsolete" capital equipment from home factories can be used.[37]

So far, the manufacture of heavy electrical equipment in developing countries generally has been inefficient. One reason is that too many plants were established in each country so that none could attain adequate size. Another cause is the lack of labour skills of all types, from the factory worker to the technician to management. In some cases, such as that of India, firms attempted to institute transformer manufacturing techniques similar to those used in the home country. The Indian worker was not able to adapt to the methods or hours expected of him. Where trained labour has been available, as in Brazil, it has been competed for by several industries, all expanding simultaneously, creating bottlenecks in every industry.

A third problem resulting in high production costs has been the need to import many materials. Although often they can be brought in duty-free, the costs of imported copper, electrical steel, rotors, castings, insulation and bushings are relatively high. In some cases, raw material allocation by the government delays production. In other cases, the government is promoting local production of materials. The quality of these products is apt to be inferior. The availability of materials can influence significantly the timing and feasibility of introducing improved products and production techniques.

Trade Barriers

To encourage foreign manufacturers to establish manufacturing facilities and to keep them operating, developing countries have had to offer substantial protection from imports. The measures invoked range from import controls to very high tariffs on items which can be made locally.

Another form of protection offered to infant industries is the

[36] *Ibid.*, p. 25.

[37] Nathaniel H. Leff, *The Brazilian Capital Goods Industry, 1929-1964* (Cambridge, Mass.: Harvard University Press, 1968), p. 26.

requirement that foreign bidders for contracts for power stations agree to use local production facilities wherever possible. In many cases, the contract will stipulate what equipment is to be procured locally. Foreign bidders must be able to comply with this stipulation and, in addition, must have access to credit for financing local costs. (The latter is another aspect of competition in export credit terms.)

As these local industries learn to produce technically acceptable products, there are indications that they will be offered export incentives to sell to other countries. Mexico has already won one power transformer order in the United States—two 50-megavolt-ampere, 230-kilovolt transformers for a Swindell-Dressler company project, awarded in September, 1968. And Pakistan won orders for switchgear in Kuwait and Australia. Since Pakistan's domestic prices are reported to be at least 25 to 35 per cent above competitive levels, export incentives must be in the form of subsidies at least this large.[38]

The impact of local production on trade in heavy electrical equipment most likely will be most severe in power transformers for which there is already excess manufacturing capacity in the world. Local production will close a number of markets in developing countries and particularly in those where the market growth is greatest. Furthermore, the capacity of these local plants appears to be greater than necessary to fill local demands so that these new industries will seek to export with sales heavily subsidised.[39] Both situations should tend to increase competition among established industries in markets that are open. Assuming that governments in developing countries continue to subsidise their infant industries, it is the established firms that will find it more and more difficult to obtain sufficient sales at prices that yield an acceptable return on investment. Those that survive will do so because their governments are willing to support them or because their technology and manufacturing techniques are so superior that they achieve substantial cost advantages.

[38]Çilingirōglu, *op. cit.*, p. 31.

[39]Brazilian capacity for producing transformers is 21 times the estimated demand. *Basic Equipment in Brazil*, Vol. 1 of *The Manufacture of Industrial Machinery and Equipment in Latin America* (New York: United Nations, for the Economic Commission for Latin America, 1963) pp. 18–19 and 31–33, reported in Leff, *op. cit.*, p. 30.

5 IMPORTANCE OF TECHNOLOGICAL COMPETENCE

The present-day attitudes toward trade in heavy electrical equipment, as set forth in Chapters 2 to 4, have led each industrialised country to support two or more producers of each type of heavy electrical equipment (see Table 9). Developing countries are imitating this pattern; each is establishing and protecting its own domestic manufacturing facilities. The question now is this: "If purchasing policies were less restrictive, would the international industry structure be any different?" The answer is, "Yes". The economics of developing, manufacturing and using power equipment indicate that the optimum size firm is larger than many of the existing firms. With open trade, therefore, the structure of the industry world-wide very likely would be different.

If world markets were open, it would be found that industry structure would be dictated largely by the onerous and very expensive task of building power equipment to meet the changing requirements of electricity networks. The technological and manufacturing competence necessitated by these changes is outlined in the next few pages. Its impact, in terms of industry structure, is discussed in Chapters 6 and 7.

Changes in Electricity Networks

The firms that have survived in the heavy electrical equipment industry are those that have maintained their ability to design and manufacture equipment to meet the changing needs of electricity networks. Over the history of the widespread use of electricity in industrialised countries, these electricity systems have expanded at a rate adequate to meet a 7 per cent per year increase in the demand for power. To satisfy the continuous growth in electricity generated without having streets and country-sides swamped with massive generating stations and strangled by networks of low voltage transmission lines, manufacturers have been required to undertake continuous research to increase the output capacity of equipment.

In the first decade of the century, power stations were small with turbine-generator sets no larger than 10 megawatts. The stations

TABLE 9 MANUFACTURERS OF HEAVY ELECTRICAL EQUIPMENT[a]

	Turbine-Generators	*Power Transformers*	*Power Circuit Breakers*
EEC			
Belgium		ACEC (Westinghouse)	
France	Rateau-Schneider	Jeumont Schneider	Merlin & Gerin
	Alsthom	Alsthom-Savoisienne	Delle-Alsthom
	CEM (Brown Boveri)	CEM (Brown Boveri)	CEM (Brown Boveri)
Italy	Franco Tosi	Legnano	Galileo
	Ercole Marelli	Ercole Marelli	Magrini
	Ansaldo	Italtrafo	ADDA
	TIBB (Brown Boveri)	TIBB (Brown Boveri)	
	Breda	Savigliano	
West Germany	Brown Boveri	Brown Boveri	Brown Boveri
	Kraftwerk Union	Transformatoren Union	Siemens
	M·A·N		AEG
EFTA			
Austria		Elin-Union	
Sweden	Stal-Laval (ASEA)	ASEA	ASEA
Switzerland	Brown Boveri	Brown Boveri	Brown Boveri
			Sprecher and Schuh
United Kingdom	Reyrolle-Parsons	Reyrolle-Parsons	Reyrolle-Parsons
	GEC	GEC	GEC
		Ferranti	
		Hawker Siddeley	
Japan	Hitachi	Hitachi	Hitachi
	Toshiba	Toshiba	Sumitomo
	Mitsubishi	Mitsui	Mitsubishi
		Fuji	
United States	General Electric	General Electric	General Electric
	Westinghouse	Westinghouse	Westinghouse
		McGraw Edison	Allis-Chalmers
		Allis-Chalmers	

[a]Full names listed in the note on Abbreviations on Page vi above.

were built so that they could be extended and sets added as demand increased. These stations usually were located in or near towns where the electricity use was greatest (called load centres).

Since the early 1900s, demand for electricity in most countries has doubled every ten years, and the pattern of power-station construction has changed (see Table 10). Larger turbine-generators (measured in megawatts of electrical output) have been used in these stations as utilities found that it is less expensive to build and operate a few large power stations rather than many small ones. For example, the findings of a recent study are that a 10 per cent increase in the size of turbine-generators can yield a 1.56 per cent decrease in the cost of electricity per kilowatt-hour.[40] The larger

TABLE 10
TYPICAL PATTERN OF POWER STATION CHANGE

Year	*Station Capacity, Installed MW*	*Turbine-Generators*		*Steam Conditions*		*Station Thermal Efficiency %*	*Transmission Voltage KV*
		No.	*MW*	*psi*	*°F*		
1910	·20	2 1	5 10	200	500	7·7	11
1920	60	2 2	10 20	300	750	10.5	22
1930	120	4	30	400	850	16.0	33
1940	240	6	40	600	900	24.0	66
1950	500	5	100	1,500	1,000	32.0	132
1960	1,000	4	250	2,300	1,000	35·0	275
1970	2,000	4	500	2,300	1,000	36.0	400

turbine-generators were operated at higher steam conditions and the efficiency of stations rose. The stations themselves were sited on the outskirts of towns and feeder lines were used to take the electricity supply to the load centres. Modern stations are constructed in the best place for operation, not use, and high voltage transmission systems carry power to local areas.

The most important consideration in the development of higher capacity generating and transmission equipment has been its unquestionable reliability and safe and consistent performance. A poorly designed or constructed piece of equipment is a lethal weapon

[40]Charles E. Olson, *Cost Considerations for Efficient Electricity Supply* (East Lansing: MSU Public Utility Papers, Michigan State University, 1970), p. 37.

that not only can destroy itself and the power station, but also can have catastrophic effects on the whole electricity system.

Since no electric utility purchaser can afford to take a chance on the quality of equipment it uses, no manufacturer has been able to survive without the technical knowledge and skill to incorporate safely the most advanced techniques into its equipment. A firm's design and manufacturing competence determines its viability, yet few firms have been able to afford the very large expenditure required to maintain adequate research and development programmes since the expenditure is not divisible. A firm producing a few units per year must incorporate into its equipment technology equivalent to that used by a firm with a large annual output. Moreover, the effort is continuous. It cannot be cut back significantly for any length of time because the firm's research and engineering staff would be lost and its product would lag behind its competitors' in terms of technical sophistication.

It is proposed that the significance of investment in research and development sets a minimum limit on the size of firm that can survive. The evolution of this requirement and its implications for present-day firms are discussed in Chapter 6.

Production Characteristics

Technical competence is the key to survival in the heavy electrical equipment industry because no manufacturer can sell technically inferior apparatus. Technical capability is also vital for producing equipment at competitive costs. To minimise the cost of production, firms rely on their engineering staffs to design equipment (a) that requires the least amount of material and (b) that can be produced over a long period with the smallest number of design changes.

In addition to the multitude of technical standards and specifications that govern the design of power equipment have been the problems of transporting large turbine-generators and power transformers. As the size of units has increased, it has surpassed railway capabilities. Un-strengthened roads and older bridges cannot stand the weight of very large and heavy pieces. In some cases, special transport equipment has been designed. In Britain, the CEGB developed air-cushion equipment—operating on the hovercraft principle—for use on road transporters to carry transformers and generator stators from manufacturers' plants to the CEGB power stations. The purpose was to eliminate the need to strengthen bridges and roads. Similarly, in the United States, General Electric has designed and had built its own railway cars to accommodate larger equipment. In West Germany very large transformers are transported on 20-axle Schnabel rail-cars. In Sweden, ASEA is using air cushions to move transformers in its factories.

These measures provide partial solutions for weight problems, but not for the problems of dimensions of large turbine and generator casings and transformer tanks. Narrow roads and bridges and low tunnels restrict the size and shape of these outer housings. Each change in dimension to accommodate transportation limitations requires corresponding changes in the internal components and design. For example, restrictions on height make a completely different core necessary, such as a five-limbed core rather than a three-limbed one. This, in turn, affects all other components of the transformer used to arrive at the desired machine efficiency.

Some of the changes are relatively minor and require little re-designing. Others, particularly on large units, demand extensive special development. On the latter, a manufacturer may spend months working out the design details. Use of computers has been a great help in reducing the time and man-hours required for this work.

The number of combinations possible, as well as rapid technological advance, precludes mass production or producing for stock. The increase in average size of generating equipment is one example of this evolution. Another example is the adoption of extra high voltage transmission—that is, 345 kilovolts and higher. For example, since 1965, extra high voltage has accounted for approximately 75 per cent of additions to transmission capability in the United States. Many of the transformers and circuit breakers produced for stock during the decline in ordering that occurred in the United States in 1961–62 would have gone unsold in the subsequent upturn. The change continues to be rapid. The first 500-kilovolt line was installed in 1964, but, at the start of the 1970s, 500-kilovolt lines were expected to have by the mid-1970s the greatest transmission capability of any single voltage class.[41]

These specifications are all external, given by the purchaser. Within each factory, the design staff has a multitude of alternative

[41]National Industrial Conference Board, *Survey of Power Equipment Requirements of the US Electric Utility Industry*, 1969–1978 (New York: National Electrical Manufacturers' Association, 1970), p. 9.

designs from which they may select to arrive at a design that will meet specifications at the lowest possible cost. Each year new steels, improved insulation procedures, more efficient drying methods, and the like, are discovered. Each may represent only a small contribution to lowering costs, but stocking parts in advance may eliminate the possibility of using advanced techniques. Thus, manufacturers who produce for a large number of different customers indicate that no two turbine-generator sets are exactly alike, even two produced for the same power station. Similarly, over a year's output of power transformers, it is rare to produce two identical transformers, except those made under one contract.

Even if duplication were doubled, the degree of standardisation achieved would not be sufficient to warrant establishing an assembly-line production flow for heavy electrical equipment. Following World War I, a standard preferred turbine unit was introduced in the United States. Subsequently, these units represented over 25 per cent of total production, but the volume was not sufficient to warrant installation of a standardised production line. Similar results occurred when General Electric introduced a standard transformer design in the mid-1950s—its "black box" design.

The general conclusion is that turbines and transformers have not been standardised and are unlikely to be in the foreseeable future. Manufacturers will continue to custom-build each machine to suit the electricity system on which it will be used and the means of transportation necessary to get it to its site.

Building to individual requirements with the secondary aim of reducing equipment weight increases the demands made on design and engineering teams. This, again, accentuates the importance of expenditure on research and development for the successful firm, particularly in open markets where firms must compete in terms of price as well as technical ability. The significance for the size of firm producing each type of equipment—turbines, transformers, and circuit breakers—is discussed in Chapter 7.

6 TECHNOLOGICAL FOUNDATIONS OF THE INDUSTRY

Technology is the keystone of the heavy electrical engineering industry. The stringency of technological requirements is shown by the fact that the firms that now comprise the industry are those that founded the industry and then went on to build and maintain superior technical and manufacturing facilities. Those few that entered the industry in later years or whose technological progress was interrupted by war were forced to rely on licences from others in order to build acceptable equipment. The prime examples are Italy and Japan, whose heavy electrical industries, 25 years after World War II, are still dependent on technology licences from manufacturers in West Germany, the United States and the United Kingdom. Similarly the formation of electrical industries in developing countries has been determined by the willingness of established firms in the field to provide technical know-how. It is suggested here that some firms could not now afford the required research and development expenditure if they were forced to forgo all outside technical and financial aid. Open trade could very well provide the force that reduces the size of the industry.

Electrical Industry's Founders

In order to understand why the industry is structured as it is at the turn of the decade, and how free trade might alter the structure, it is necessary to look at its evolution. Several men in the United States and Western Europe—George Westinghouse, Elihu Thomson, Charles Parsons, Sebastian de Ferranti, Werner Siemens, Charles Brown and Walter Boveri—were the founding fathers of the industry. Each began by selling electrical equipment they themselves produced.

Beginnings in the United States

George Westinghouse was the founder of the Westinghouse Electric and Manufacturing Company in America. He began with a scheme to transmit electrical power. In 1885 he obtained, for $50,000, the patent rights to an alternating-current (a.c.) transformer invented by Lucien Gaulard and John Dixon Gibbs, of Britain. William Stanley, a Westinghouse consultant, improved the a.c. transformer so that current from hydro-electric or steam generating plants could be transmitted cheaply at high voltages for many miles. Westinghouse's system won favour in 1896 when his electric generators tapped the power of Niagara Falls and transmitted it 20 miles to Buffalo. This development was the basis for the subsequent growth of the Westinghouse Electric Corporation, now the world's second largest electrical apparatus manufacturer.

Elihu Thomson and Edwin J. Houston, two professors of physical science in Pennsylvania, established the Thomson-Houston Company in the 1880s to produce and sell electric lighting systems. They produced an imitation of the Edison incandescent-lighting system and later developed a.c. generators based on Thomson's designs, which were based, partly, on a dynamo built by Charles Brush in the 1870s. The company sold power systems in competition with the Westinghouse a.c. systems and the Edison General Electric Company direct-current (d.c.) systems.

In 1891, Thomson-Houston was indicted for infringing on the Edison electric lamp patents. The Edison company, at that time, was short of capital since its assets were over-burdened with the debt of electric utilities. The solution to both problems was a merger, and the companies merged, creating the General Electric Company in 1892, which later became the world's largest producer of power equipment.

General Electric and its forerunners were responsible for helping to establish a number of European electrical companies, including the British Thompson-Houston Company, Deutsche Edison-Gesellschaft (whose name was changed in 1887 to Allgemeine Elektricitäts Gesellschaft), and companies in France and Italy.

Establishment of German Firms

In Germany, Werner Siemens, in partnership with his brother Karl and a mechanical engineer named Halske, established the Siemens and Halske Company in 1847, primarily to make telegraphic equipment. In 1866, Siemens introduced his invention of a self-excited dynamo which was a major turning point in the evolution of the generator used today.[42] Halske later sold his shares in the firm and in 1903 the Siemens company merged its heavy engineering divisions with Schuckert and Company in Nürnberg.

This created the forerunner of the present-day firm of Siemens Aktiengesellschaft.

The second electrical giant, Allgemeine Elektricitäts Gesellschaft (AEG), started as an Edison company and began producing turbine-generators in 1904, first with its own design created by Riedler and Stumpp, then using a de Laval type of construction and, finally, with a Curtis system (see Page 49 below).

Widespread Facilities of Brown Boveri

Two electrical engineers, Walter Boveri (a German) and Charles E. L. Brown (an Englishman), left the Oerlikon Engineering Works in 1891 and founded Brown Boveri and Company. They built a factory in Baden, Switzerland, when they were promised a contract for the first electric power station to be built there.[43]

From the beginning, Brown Boveri recognised the need both to sell in other countries and to establish foreign manufacturing subsidiaries. The existing and potential Swiss market was too small to sustain a manufacturer of power equipment. Also, prohibitive import tariffs in other countries, high cost of transport and traditional preferences for domestic products limited the scope for Swiss export sales. And finally, purchasers of power equipment insisted that adequate repair facilities be readily accessible to power plants. Thus, within a few years of its founding, Brown Boveri had established manufacturing subsidiaries in Germany, France, Italy, Norway and Austria, all of which had access to the parent company's technical and manufacturing know-how. These five subsidiaries and the Swiss parent are still the most important members of the Brown Boveri group in terms of size and contribution to company profits (see Table 11).

British Firms Established

The British Westinghouse and Thomson-Houston companies were established, by respectively, the American Westinghouse and Thomson-Houston companies in the late 1890s. At first, the British affiliates simply acted as agents and handled installation work, but in about 1900 they undertook some manufacturing. Both factories

[42] *Werner Siemens and His Work* (Frankfurt: Siemens and Halske, 1936), p. 11. Two British engineers, Charles Wheatstone and S. A. Varley, introduced similar equipment simultaneously and independently.

[43] *75 Years Brown Boveri*, *op. cit.*, p. 20.

TABLE 11
BROWN BOVERI AND COMPANY AND MAIN SUBSIDIARIES[a]

	Country	*Founded*	*Ownership*	*1969 Employees*	*1969 Turnover*
Brown Boveri and Co. Ltd.	Switzerland	1891	parent	20,820	1,046m SF[b]
Brown Boveri and Co. AG.	Germany	1898	56%	39,600	1,798m DM
Cie. Electro-Mécanique	France	1894	about 40%	10,908	833m FF
Tecnomasio Italiano Brown Boveri SpA	Italy	1903	over 50%	3,617	13,477m Lire
Osterreichische Brown Boveri-Werke AG.	Austria	1910	about 80%	2,184	662m Sch
Aktieselskapet Norsk Elektrisk and Brown Boveri	Norway	1901	about 60%	2,847	286m nKr
Total for Company[c]				91,900	4,580m SF[b]

[a]In 1925 Brown Boveri established a United States subsidiary called American Brown Boveri Electric Corporation. A number of existing companies were acquired for their manufacturing and marketing facilities: Moloney Electric Company for power transformers, New York Shipbuilding Corporation for large turbines and generators, and Condit Electric for bulk oil circuit breakers. The onset of the depression in 1930 temporarily destroyed the market for power equipment. Brown Boveri now intends to enter the United States power equipment market through imports and by providing United States based service facilities.
[b]Year ended March 31, 1970.
[c]Includes subsidiaries not listed in table.

were planned in the United States. The machine tools were American. Factory managers were sent from Britain to the United States to work in the General Electric and Westinghouse factories until the British factories were completed. When the plants were ready, complete staffs of American executives went to Britain to start the organisations operating.

In 1919, Westinghouse sold its interest in British Westinghouse and its name was changed to Metropolitan Vickers. In 1927, this company was bought by General Electric and merged with British Thomson-Houston, Ferguson Pailin, a switchgear firm, and Edison Swan, a light bulb and cable producer.[44] The successor firm was Associated Electrical Industries (AEI), which is now part of GEC.

William Siemens came to Britain in the 1850s as an agent for his brothers' firm in Germany and established Siemens-Halske and Company, of London, to produce cables and telegraph equipment. (The name and organisation were changed to Siemens Brothers and Company in 1880.) In 1901, the company entered the heavy electrical equipment field. Siemens Brothers Dynamo Works was built at Stafford, Britain, and leased to Siemens-Schuckertwerke in Germany for ten years. Profits were poor and after World War I the dynamo works were sold to English Electric.[45] Other divisions of Siemens Brothers were acquired by AEI in the 1950s.

An Englishman who started out in the experimental department of Siemens Brothers and then went on to form his own company at the age of 18 was Sebastian de Ferranti.[46] In 1885, de Ferranti took out a patent on a complete parallel distribution system. When he first introduced the transformers into the British power station, he replaced the Siemens dynamos with his own generators wound with copper tape rather than round wire.[47] About 1889, de Ferranti conceived the idea of generating electricity in bulk and transmitting it to sub-stations. He designed a slow-speed generator that generated at the highest voltage that any power station in any country had attempted.[48]

[44]Sir Joseph Latham, *Take-Over: the Facts and the Myths of the GEC-AEI Battle* (London: Iliffe Books, 1969), pp. 11 and 14.

[45]J. D. Scott, *Siemens Brothers, 1858-1958: An Essay in the History of Industry* (London: Weidenfeld and Nicolson, 1958), p. 87.

[46]W. L. Randall, *S. Z. de Ferranti* (London: Longmans Green, 1944), p. 20.

[47]R. H. Parsons, *The Early Days of the Power Station Industry* (Cambridge: Cambridge University Press, 1940), p. 22.

[48]*Ibid.*, p. 28.

During World War I, the Ferranti works were devoted to production of shell cases. Afterwards, the factory was rebuilt and the decision made to concentrate production on meters, transformers and instruments.[49] Manufacture of generators has been limited to impulse generators for testing high-voltage transformers and cables.

The formation of the C. A. Parsons Company was different from that of other electrical companies. Unlike most of his contemporaries, Charles A. Parsons' first contribution was in the mechanical field. In 1884, he introduced a turbine that operated faster than any contemporary generator, so Parsons constructed his own generator based on the design introduced by Varley in 1866.[50] Both the turbine and the generator were forerunners of modern-day turbine-generator sets.[51] Parsons licensed American Westinghouse, Brown Boveri, Siemens, English Electric, Allis-Chalmers and Ansaldo to produce his reaction type turbines.

Sweden's Industry

At the same time that Parsons was working on his reaction turbine, engineers in Sweden developed different type turbines. One was the Ljungström type, still used for the smallest size turbines, but unsuitable for larger sets. The second type was an impulse turbine invented by Gustav de Laval in 1882. Its use, also, was believed to be limited to lower powers, but the basic idea was adopted by other engineers and incorporated into designs that have persisted to present times.

A General Electric engineer, C. G. Curtis, modified the de Laval design by pressure compounding on the Parsons principle.[52] British Thompson-Houston and AEG, of Germany, manufactured the Curtis velocity-compounded turbine.[53] A Frenchman, A. Rateau, and a Swiss, Henry Zoelly, also worked on more efficient variations of the de Laval turbine. British Westinghouse adopted the Rateau version.[54] English Electric, in 1914, replaced its Parsons licence with one to produce the Zoelly-type impulse turbine marketed by

[49]Randall, *op. cit.*, p. 15.

[50]Rollo Appleyard, *Charles Parsons: His Life and Work* (London: Constable, 1933), p. 41.

[51]Parsons, *The Steam Turbine and Other Inventions of Sir Charles Parsons* (London: Longmans Green, 1942), p. 7.

[52]Parsons, *The Early Days of the Power Station Industry*, *op. cit.*, p. 4.

[53]Appleyard, *op. cit.*, p. 54.

[54]*Ibid.*

Escher Wyss.[55] Escher Wyss also licensed M·A·N of Germany, Mitsubishi in Japan, and Schneider and Company, of France.

Swedish engineers were also at the forefront of electrical engineering. In 1890, Jonas Wenström took out Swedish and British patents for a complete three-phase alternating current system with a generator, transformer and inductor motor. This laid the technical foundations for Allmänna Svenska Elecktriska Atiebolaget (ASEA), the Swedish electrical giant.

Technological Evolution of the Industry

As larger and larger power stations were constructed and greater efficiency was demanded, the heavy electrical equipment produced had to meet the rapidly advancing specifications or it would not be purchased. A very large proportion of the notable technical achievements in turbine-generator design were made by the same few firms that were originally successful in designing and selling this equipment. Several respected established companies failed to keep up with technology. By the early 1960s, those firms were either out of business or building only the smaller sets.

Brush Electrical Engineering, a British company, was producing a Ljungström-type turbine in the 1950s. This type was highly efficient up to about 20 megawatts, but less satisfactory for larger sizes. A few unfortunate accidents, such as that at the York Cooper Power Station, discouraged later orders of the Ljungström turbine. Brush finally ceased production of large steam turbines. The company was acquired by the Hawker Siddeley Electrical Company in 1959.

A second example is the poor operating experience that the Tennessee Valley Authority (TVA) had with a 500-megawatt turbine-generator set Parsons delivered in 1962 to TVA's Colbert-5 power station. When the set was tested in August, 1965, it did not meet the efficiency rate guaranteed by Parsons. The deficit, less than one per cent, cost Parsons about $600,000 in penalties to TVA and, more important, the respect and confidence of a major United States electrical equipment purchaser. Other prospective purchasers in the United States also appeared to become wary, with the result that Parsons, as of mid-1971, had not received a single turbine-generator contract in the United States since the TVA order in 1959.

[55]*Early Histories of Some Companies of the English Electric Group* (Stafford: English Electric), p. 21.

A more recent example concerns Allis-Chalmers Manufacturing Company in the United States. Consolidated Edison of New York City was running short of generating capacity in the summers of 1969 and 1970 due to poor planning and delayed deliveries of nuclear sets. During periods of peak use in July and August of both years, the company's largest unit, a 1,000-megawatt Allis-Chalmers turbine-generator at Ravenswood, Queens, went out of service. In 1969, this was caused by a piece of insulation material which had lodged against the generator conductors and bent them out of shape. Repairs consumed over a month. The 1970 repairs were not completed until May, 1971, and cost $4·5m. During both outages, Con Edison was forced to curtail service and the public was inconvenienced and angered. The utility has had to justify its poor planning and has had a much more difficult time obtaining a rate increase. Allis-Chalmers, manufacturer of the 1,000-megawatt unit, ceased production of turbine-generators in 1963, primarily because it could not afford the development work required and, therefore, serious problems arose with its equipment. The company had been trying to cover research and development expenses on 10 per cent of the American market, whereas the other two firms, General Electric and Westinghouse, had 55 and 35 per cent shares, respectively.[56] In 1970 Allis re-entered the industry by acquiring technology from Kraftwerk-Union in West Germany.

Development of Transmission Equipment

Circuit-breaker development has followed the growth in electricity use, but in a different pattern. While breakers are used to control the normal power flow, they also must be capable of isolating faulty equipment from a healthy circuit and so avoiding widespread disruptions of service. The possibility of a massive power failure, such as the one in New York City in November, 1965, causes purchasers to accept only breakers of the highest quality and reliability. The entire system can be at the mercy of the circuit breakers' performance.

Until about 1925 there was no definite proof that the breakers used would prevent a crisis. The manufacturers of breakers were those who produced other electrical equipment, particularly

[56]Unpublished report on turbine-generator manufacture in the United States and the United Kingdom, 1964, p. 19.

generators. Since these firms were concerned about the operation of the overall electrical network, they were determined to make circuit breakers more reliable. The large multi-product firms built testing stations which could simulate fault conditions. They also developed systems analyses that enabled utilities to know what might happen, in terms of fault conditions, at various places on their systems.

The first result of short-circuit testing, as it was called, was that virtually all circuit breakers had to be re-designed, although oil was still retained as the interrupting medium. During World War II, oil in breakers fuelled fires started by bombing, so considerable sentiment developed for eliminating oil. This led to the development of alternatives, such as circuit-breakers using air or SF6 gas rather than oil.

The smaller companies that manufactured breakers could not afford to install adequate testing equipment, so the large firms made facilities available to them. An exception was the Electricité de France, which constructed its own test facilities and made them available to the French firms, Merlin and Gerin and Delle-Alsthom. This was an important aspect in helping these two firms to become major factors in the circuit breaker industry.

Although transformers are the least difficult type of heavy electric equipment to produce, there are complexities in testing large units. Some of the problems firms run into as they extend their product line are impulse testing techniques, surge protection (shielding), and provision of drying-out facilities.

Since utility engineers rely on the manufacturing industry for practical and theoretical help in system development, it follows that some firms keep a definite lead in the industry. Others that lack the necessary technical and financial resources concentrate on more standard equipment for which design parameters are well established. Thus, in the United Kingdom, Ferranti, GEC and Parsons have diverse capabilities whereas Bonar Long, Brush Electrical Engineering and Yorkshire Electric Transformer tend to stick to conventional sizes and designs. Similarly, in the United States, Moloney Transformer, Central Transformer and Federal Pacific Transformer produce more standard equipment.

Technological Requirements

To maintain their technological competence, the major companies have established themselves as leaders in two areas: training of engineers and quality and quantity of research. The two are interdependent and both require a continuous flow of financial resources.

The largest companies will undertake research and development programmes on several levels: (a) non-product-oriented research over a broad spectrum; (b) product development to find more efficient, more economical equipment to produce and distribute electricity; (c) development efforts to improve existing manufacturing and equipment methods; and (d) contract-by-contract engineering work to design the best equipment to fit each particular use. The first of these research areas is undertaken only by the large, and usually diversified, firms and is financed on the corporate level. Each product division is assessed at a given rate to support research. In periods of low profits, work in this area can be most easily curtailed.

The other types of research and development are less postponable. Projects in these areas are undertaken and financed by each product division. Since all manufacturers of each type of heavy electrical equipment are competing primarily on the basis of their designs and manufacturing competence, all of their research and development efforts must achieve comparable results. Although it cannot be asserted that results are directly proportional to money spent, the association is approximate. A manufacturer who tries to carry all his turbine research and development on sales of 4,000 megawatts per year is less likely to achieve the same technological competence as the firm with a 10,000 megawatt per year output, without help. It is likely that the smaller firm will build equipment that is one to three technological generations behind.

On the basis of estimates by industry officials and from observations of successful firms, it may be concluded that a firm is required to produce minimum annual outputs to cover the necessary research and development expenditures (see Table 12). The figures, of course, can only indicate ranges, with the actual figures determined by productivity of research and development efforts and salaries of engineering staffs.

With outputs in these ranges, allocations for product development will be about 5 to 8 per cent of sales. Drawing and engineering can add another 5 per cent to the cost of each unit. For a turbine-generator division, this might mean \$6m to \$10m a year, spread over 8,000 to 10,000 megawatts annual output—20 turbine-generator

TABLE 12
ANNUAL SALES REQUIREMENTS FOR ADEQUATE RESEARCH AND DEVELOPMENT[a]

Turbine-generators	8,000 MW = \$80m
Power transformers	10,000 MVA = \$10m
Power circuit breakers	200 units for 220 KV duty = \$15m

[a]Output can be from one or more plants using same design.

sets. This does not include the corporate assessment for company-wide research facilities. For circuit breakers, the cost of drawing and engineering is lower, but the cost of development is relatively higher because of the relatively short—that is, ten-year—life of breaker designs. Westinghouse, for example, announced it spent \$5m over a 5-year period to re-design its SF6 breakers.[57]

These figures are, of course, approximations. The productivity of research effort and cost are two factors that cause the amount to vary. A third factor is the amount and type of research done on a company-wide level, and a fourth is the total value and cost of royalties received from selling technology to others.

Acquisition of Technology

Companies that cannot afford extensive and comprehensive research and development programmes have acted as follows: (a) they have been satisfied to lag the industry by one or more technological generations; (b) they have purchased technology from major firms in the industry and/or received government assistance for research and development.

Firms in the first group are likely to be the first to encounter difficulties with any increase in international competition. The number has already diminished because firms lacked the technical experience to compete effectively with larger, full-range producers. Some, such as Escher Wyss, are absorbed into larger firms and assume production of the smaller sizes of equipment for the whole company. Those firms that persist do so, in large part, because they can serve protected markets. Examples are Franco Tosi and Breda in Italy and smaller transformer manufacturers in the United States. These

[57]*Electrical World*, New York, February 23, 1970, p. 61.

firms are being squeezed out as demand for equipment changes. An increase in international competition would be likely to eliminate these firms first.

A second group of producers comprises those heavily dependent on purchased technical and manufacturing know-how and on government support. Probably not all of these firms are viable enterprises. With a reduction in barriers to trade and investment, many of these firms would be unable to continue producing technically advanced equipment at competitive prices. The pressure would be particularly acute for the Italian firms that have relied on licensing agreements for virtually all of their technology.

Technical Agreements

Immediately following World War II, American manufacturers were among the few firms in the world that still had adequate engineering staffs and know-how. The majority of experienced European engineers and factory workers had been lost or dispersed.

In accord with the overall United States policy to aid West European recovery, American manufacturers, with strong encouragement from the United States Administration, either licensed the use of proprietary technology to or concluded technical exchange agreements with overseas manufacturers of heavy electrical equipment to help them re-establish themselves. West European and Japanese firms dependent on American technology after World War II are listed in Table 13.

The state of agreements, now, varies with the companies involved and the assistance granted by their home market customers. Larger firms, such as English Electric in Britain, Alsthom in France, and Siemens and AEG in West Germany have tended to end their technical exchange agreements. While the French and British manufacturers now rely primarily on their own facilities, product development is aided substantially by their respective nationalised electricity supply industries (see Pages 62-65). In those cases where technical exchange agreements still persist, they provide obvious benefits to both parties.

Smaller firms are almost totally dependent on technology purchased through licensing agreements. Italian firms are representative of those whose sales are so small they can afford no research and very little product development. Instead, they acquire technical and manufacturing know-how through licences at a cost of 4 to 8

TABLE 13
POWER EQUIPMENT TECHNICAL AGREEMENTS
IN THE POST-WORLD WAR II PERIOD

General Electric		*Westinghouse Electric*	
Company	*Product*	*Company*	*Product*
Alsthom-Savoisienne	Transformers	Jeumont-Schneider	Transformers
		Merlin and Gerin	Circuit breakers
AEG	Circuit breakers, turbines, transformers	Siemens	Turbines, circuit breakers, transformers
AEI	Turbines, transformers	English Electric	Transformers
ASGEN	Turbines, transformers	Franco Tosi	Turbines
		Ercole Marelli	Generators, transformers
Hitachi	Turbines		
Toshiba	Turbines	Mitsubishi	Turbines, transformers
		ACEC	Transformers

per cent of sales and even as high as 10 per cent on turbines.[58] Some Italian firms are actually subsidiaries of non-Italian companies. Others are just licensees. For example, Tecnomasio Italiano Brown Boveri is a wholly-owned Brown Boveri subsidiary, producing generators, transformers, and circuit breakers to its parent's design. Similarly, Adda is the Italian circuit breaker licensee of Delle-Alsthom, a French company. Legnano and Savigliano produce transformers under licences from Ferranti of Britain and ASEA of Sweden, respectively. General Electric has a 10 per cent stake in Ansaldo San Giorgio and Compagnia Generale de Elettricita (ASGEN), a diversified electrical equipment producer. Westinghouse has a small interest in Franco Tosi, a turbine maker, and in Ercole Marelli, a producer of generators and transformers.

Franco Tosi is a good example of the technological reliance of the Italian electrical equipment industry on foreign sources of advanced research and development. The two main Franco Tosi products are turbines and boilers. The only product of original design is compressors used primarily by the chemical industry. The rest are all built under licences, as enumerated in Table 14.

[58] Çilingirōglu, *op. cit.*, p. 24.

TABLE 14
FRANCO TOSI LICENCES

Turbines	Westinghouse Electric
Boilers	Combustion Engineering
Gas Turbines	Associated Electrical Industries
Hydraulic Turbines	Joint R and D Office with ASGEN
Pumps and Heat Exchangers	Westinghouse Electric
Compressors under 150 Kg	Own design
Desalinisation Plants	Baldwin Lima
Welding	Lloyd's

The firm's engineering staff is very small, only sufficient to adapt drawings to fit Italian conditions. For example, Westinghouse drawings must be converted from feet and inches to metres. With no original work assigned, outstanding engineers are not apt to be drawn to Franco Tosi.

Manufacturing Techniques

The overall cost to Franco Tosi of foreign-based technology is greater than the licence fees alone. There are also expenses involved in time lags and adaptation and in market restrictions. From the licensee's viewpoint, the fundamental drawback to buying know-how is the difficulty in improving manufacturing techniques to produce the more advanced equipment. Indeed, a United States commission on technological innovation found the cost of manufacturing engineering for a new product to be two-and-a-half times the research and design expenses (see Table 15).[59]

When a new design is needed, reliance on the foreign source intensifies. For example, when Franco Tosi received an order from ENEL in 1963 for a 600-megawatt turbine, five Tosi engineers went to Pennsylvania to work on the design with Westinghouse engineers. At the same time, they observed manufacturing techniques.

Acquisition of techniques does not assure that the licensee will be able to use them efficiently. All the details and adaptation to local materials and preferences must be made.[60] Frequently, problems

[59] *Technological Innovation: its Environment and Management* (Washington D.C.: United States Department of Commerce, for the Panel on Invention and Innovation, 1967). Original data included a percentage for marketing start-up, not considered relevant here.

[60] Leff, *op. cit.*, p. 91.

arise in the machining of a component or in a manufacturing process itself. If it is a major new technique, more of the firm's engineers must fully understand its intricacies.

TABLE 15
TYPICAL COST OF PRODUCT INNOVATION

	%
Research—advanced development	10
Engineering and designing the product	18
Tooling and manufacturing engineering	60
Manufacturing start-up expenses	12
	100

SOURCE: Philip Sporn, *Technology, Engineering and Economics* (Cambridge, Mass.: MIT Press, 1969), p. 12.

Where one company does all the work from design to production, extensive co-operation is required to prepare the factory to produce a new design. An excellent description of the co-ordination has been given in an ASEA publication:

> "No sooner does the design office turn out a new design which, in collaboration with the laboratories, is turned into a better, cheaper, and more effectively applied new construction, than the difficult problem arises of applying the new idea to workshop construction. This generally implies the building of new apparatus and plants on a more extensive scale. It is here a question not only of attaining reliable working results and of taking advantage of the experience gained in the laboratory, but also of ensuring maximum efficiency in respect of production from a technical point of view. This demands a most intimate co-operation between the laboratories and the shop.[61]

Where such co-ordination is not possible or practical, such as with a licensor and foreign licensee, delays and errors can be time consuming and costly. Richardsons Westgarth stands as an example of a first-class engineering firm that bought good turbine designs, but had difficulty with manufacturing techniques.

[61]Eric Wennerlund, "Co-operation between Shops and Process and Materials Laboratory at the Ludvika Works", in *Technical Achievements of ASEA Reesearch* (Stockholm: Allmänna Svenska Elektriska Atiebolaget, 1946), p. 325.

Richardsons Westgarth made small turbines in the first decades of the twentieth century, but were not serious contenders against the other five firms. Brown Boveri tried to break into the British market, but, except for one or two orders in the late 1920s, was not successful. Both Brown Boveri and Richardsons Westgarth, therefore, found it advantageous for the latter to try to increase its share of the British market by building well-designed turbines in Britain under licence from Brown Boveri. It was difficult for Richardsons Westgarth to convince buyers it was producing a British machine. The company's engineers had to follow, almost blindly, the advice of Brown Boveri without really having enough experience to question any points which normally arise in the manufacture of complicated large machines. Utility engineers had to be content with looking upon a licensee as an "entrepreneur", a situation they disliked intensely. It is, therefore, not surprising that this agreement was not a success, and Richardsons Westgarth ceased to manufacture large turbines.

It appears that the only successful licensee arrangements in the turbine industry are those in which the licensee is capable of doing his own development and designing, but finds it expedient to take out a licence to save development time. An example of this is the General Electric arrangement with ASEA for high-voltage direct-current transmission. No one would doubt the ability of General Electric to do this itself, but it apparently paid it to use ASEA developments to enter the market.

The problems in adapting technology are less severe in the manufacture of transformers and circuit breakers than in turbine-generators. There are significant instances of licensees starting with purchased technology and then moving on to develop their own designs. One example is low oil volume breakers developed by Adda, the Italian subsidiary of Delle-Alsthom. The Adda breaker, an adaptation of an original Delle design, could be extended to higher capacities and was less expensive than Delle's. For about two years, until Delle improved its own design, it imported from Adda. In a second example, Canadian General Electric designed a more compact and less costly series of air blast breakers than those of the parent company. The General Electric design was later modified. General Electric's Italian licensee, ASGEN, also has bested the parent's design, this time in power transformers. The Italian designs, especially in the lower ratings, are 10 to 15 per cent lighter.

If trade were to be opened up, it is likely that some of these licensees would be dropped while others would become overseas manufacturers or assembly plants for the licensor.

Freer Trade and Licensees

Established companies are much more inclined to grant licences to firms which serve markets barred to the licensor. The best example of this is the extension of manufacturing licences to the Japanese after World War II. American firms would have much preferred to export to Japan, since it was clear from the type of agreements formulated that the Japanese were interested in acquiring technology only as a catalyst. They now provide stiff competition in many parts of the world.

Other licensees are so dependent on the licensor that they are, in effect, overseas manufacturing affiliates. Freer trade might result in the closing of some licensees altogether. Delle-Alsthom, for example, has indicated it could serve the Italian market from its French facilities more economically than can its Italian licensee, Adda. Similarly, it is doubtful that Brown Boveri would find it economical to produce a full line of turbines at CEM in France.

With freer investment opportunities, it would appear that some of these licensees would be acquired completely and used as overseas assembly or manufacturing facilities perhaps for production of components or of units for export. ASGEN is a large world exporter of transformers. It would seem likely that General Electric would want to rely on ASGEN for a large portion of the total company transformer exports, as long as the costs could be kept below those of the United States.

A third possibility is the merger of a number of small firms. Witness the Westinghouse attempt to acquire and combine the Jeumont-Schneider facilities in France, Ateliers de Constructions Electriques de Charleroi (ACEC) in Belgium, Franco Tosi and Ercole Marelli in Italy, and Cenemesa in Spain. It is likely that these facilities would be reorganised to eliminate duplication and modernised to form a competitive West European complex for manufacturing heavy electrical equipment. These decisions and others would be made on economic, rather than political, grounds. It does appear, however, that with freer trade and investment, dependent licensees would be the most likely to succumb first. One can look to Italy for the most likely candidates.

Shared Research

Producers with outputs between the limited production of small Italian firms and the large outputs of American companies undertake their own product development and do much less pure research. For both, they depend on inter-company co-operation and government subsidies.

The problem is stated simply by reference to British turbine development. Between 1959 and 1966, unit size was increased nine times, better than one design change per year. At this rapid pace, almost none of the research and development expenditures could be recovered by large repeat orders at reasonable prices. The British market is not large enough for this. In a recent lecture entitled "Research, Education and the Heavy Electrical Industry", by Professor G. H. Rawcliff, of the University of Bristol, it was advocated that Britain establish an Industrial Research Act to spread the cost of research throughout the industry.[62]

None of the other national West European markets or the Japanese markets is, by itself, large enough either. A study by the Organisation for Economic Co-operation and Development (OECD) of the problem concludes that only the creation of a single, free West European market will offset the American advantage. The report says: "the structure of their markets represents for European and Japanese manufacturers a serious handicap for successful competition with American counterparts and for realising the full economic benefit of their great research and development efforts . . . A single, really free market comprising all European Member countries can bring a basic remedy to this situation". The report continues by suggesting technical co-operation as a temporary remedy: "some relief can be found through much closer technical co-operation amongst equipment manufacturers and between them and the electric power supply companies".[63]

The British and French manufacturers have recognised the advantages of co-operation and have been working with their respective governments and electric supply companies to cut the size of research and development expenditure. Examples of their co-operative efforts follow.

[62]Reported in the *Electrical Times*, January 15, 1970, p. 50.

[63]*Twenty-first Survey of Electrical Equipment* (Paris: OECD Secretariat, 1968), p. 98.

French R and D Grants

French manufacturers receive loans for development of particular projects. These loans are granted by the Délégation Générale à la Recherche Scientifique et Technique (DGRST), a department under authority of the French Prime Minister. Few grants were awarded by DGRST and almost none to private industry until 1965. The Fifth French Plan for industry development initiated in that year included provision for strengthening DGRST and emphasising particular industries. The first areas chosen were mechanical, electrical and electronic equipment because (a) the government wanted to stimulate the production of appliances, such as refrigerators and television sets, and (b) it was believed desirable to maintain France's important world position in the construction of high-voltage apparatus. Special emphasis was placed on transformers, circuit breakers, cables and current rectifiers.[64]

Merlin and Gerin received a loan for research on high-voltage circuit breakers. The company was granted between $250,000 and $300,000 for development of a 765-kilovolt circuit breaker.[65] This product had no application in France where the highest system voltage is 420 kilovolts, and the EdF indicates no immediate intention of installing higher voltage lines. The breakers, therefore, were developed for export to Canada and the United States, the only open markets that use voltages over 500 kilovolts. This was explained by Pierre Aigrain, the director of DGRST:

> "The government funding programme made possible the development of a 765-kilovolt circuit breaker for high-voltage transmission lines by a company in Grenoble. . . . Not a single one has ever been sold in France, and probably none will be sold in France for some time to come. . . . The [Merlin and Gerin] Company in Grenoble had the technology available and there was obvious need for the product outside of France."[66]

Repayment to the government of the development loan must be made only if the project is commercially successful. Repayment is figured as a small per cent on sales after the first two years. The total

[64]"La Politique de L'Etat en Faveur du Développment Industriel des Resultats de la Recherche", *Le Progrès Scientifique*, Paris, June, 1966, p. 59.

[65]Interview with Pierre Aigrain, director of DGRST, Paris, April, 1969.

[66]Pierre Aigrain, "Some Factors Inhibiting Technology Innovation in France", speech delivered at National Academy of Engineering, Washington, D.C., April, 1968.

interest charge is 10 to 20 per cent paid out over five to seven years (2 to 3 per cent per year). The amount repaid each year is greater if the manufacturer receives income from licensing the technology to others.

France also aids its manufacturers through the EdF's facilities and contracts. The availability of the EdF's test facilities was mentioned above (see Page 52). The EdF's research department has within its responsibility the Test and Research Centre of Fontenay-aux-Roses, the medium power station of Renardieres, and the test station for motors at Saint Denis. It also operates test laboratories, such as sub-stations at Chesnoy and Creney, which are linked to the transmission network and used for operating experience. The facilities are equipped for tests according to various different specifications: for example, French, West German and American. Manufacturers have access to all EdF facilities at prices equal to or lower than the actual test costs.

When EdF foresees the need for a new device, EdF's equipment department informs the manufacturers and, with them, arrives at the specifications of prototypes of the new equipment. Recently, this has occurred with respect to 600-megawatt turbine-generators, 660-megavolt-ampere transformers, and 245-kilovolt switchgear in metal-clad sub-stations.

Each French manufacturer receives an order for the prototype so that the EdF is certain to get competitive designs. The prices paid for the prototype units are as much as 50 per cent higher, the increment being intended to cover the cost of development. The EdF assumes that once the equipment is in production, prices do not include factors to cover the development of the product. In this way, the EdF is offsetting the disadvantage of a smaller market. And if it should decide not to re-order, the cost of development has been covered.

In a large competitive market characterised by free trade, it is not certain that all of the French firms could survive. Delle-Alsthom appears to be the most competitive firm at home and abroad. Jeumont-Schneider, Alsthom-Savoisienne, Rateau-Schneider, Alsthom and Merlin and Gerin are much more dependent on the EdF and, frequently, have had low or no profits during the 1960s. It is likely that one or more of these firms would not survive without the EdF's help or without merger into larger West European groups.

British R and D Aid

British heavy electrical equipment manufacturers have benefited from research projects undertaken by the CEGB. Technological research on generation and transmission is conducted at the CEGB's laboratories.[67] This work ranges from projects to improve the reliability and efficiency of fuel in nuclear stations to monitoring the performance of turbine blades. The findings are available to all the manufacturers.

Since 1967, the CEGB has collaborated with the manufacturers on research work. In that year, a Power Engineering Research Steering Committee was formed by GEC, Reyrolle-Parsons and British Insulated Callenders Cables (BICC) to co-ordinate and exchange information and, thereby, try to avoid the expense of duplicative efforts.[68]

When CEGB demand declined over 50 per cent in 1968 and very few orders were planned for the next few years, British manufacturers indicated that they would not be able to afford research and development expenses.[69] The CEGB, therefore, set up a pilot programme for awarding development contracts to British manufacturers so that they would be able "to maintain their research and development efforts and hence their competitiveness".[70] While these new contracts are similar to the arrangements for collaborative research, they also cover proprietary work undertaken by individual manufacturers.[71] The Department of Trade and Industry also is offering financial incentives. In 1970, Parsons was given a small grant "to investigate metal working systems relating to the machining of the static parts of turbines".[72] Prior to these formal research and development contracts, the CEGB offered development aid through its purchases of prototype equipment,[73] a procedure similar to that undertaken by the EdF.

The British manufacturers have not been able to rely on the normal flow of orders to pay for their research and development, but have required additional aid. If there were fewer but larger firms in

[67] *The Electricity Council Annual Report and Accounts, 1968–69* (London: HM Stationery Office, 1969), p. 33.

[68] *Electrical Review*, June 27, 1969, p. 925.

[69] *Electrical Review*, March 15, 1968, p. 385.

[70] *Electrical Review*, June 27, 1969, p. 925.

[71] *Electrical Times*, June 26, 1969, P.S.

[72] *Electrical Times*, January 29, 1970, p. 7.

[73] *Electrical Review*, June 27, 1969, p. 925.

Britain, there probably would be a better opportunity for each to succeed on its own. The 1968 merger of the turbine-generator facilities of AEI and English Electric was a beginning towards achieving the required size. Duplicative research facilities were eliminated and equipment designs reconciled. Whether or not the reorganisation will be successful must await a longer market test. The planned annual turbine-generator output of the company, 6,000 megawatts, is smaller than the announced capacities of other major turbine manufacturers.

Summary

The volume of basic product development and engineering that must be done or acquired by a major force in the heavy electrical equipment industry is fixed. To do this work requires a professional staff with skills in many different areas. Manufacturers with large annual outputs can spread the research and development expenses over many units and reduce the per unit expense. Moreover, large firms can afford to use the full capacity of their staffs and facilities because the development expense will be covered over a much shorter time. It is proposed that firms with annual outputs of less than 8,000 megawatts of turbines, 10,000 megavolt-amperes of power transformers, or 200 circuit breakers suitable for duty at 220 kilovolts would be at a disadvantage if subjected to world competition. Such firms will require government assistance to maintain their technical competence.

7 LARGE FIRMS: LOW COSTS

In Chapter 6 the importance of research and development expenditure in maintaining technical competence was explored. Here it is proposed that such expenditure is also vital for minimising cost of production. Approaches to manufacturing heavy electrical equipment are remarkably similar in established firms in Western Europe and the United States. Any basic differences in costs of production for these firms derive from product design, scale of production and efficiency. This conclusion has been reached after visits to the world's major factories and is confirmed by analyses which are presented in this chapter.

While no two producers have the same factory layout or duplicate all of one another's machine tools, almost all factories are using, or are in the process of adopting, similar manufacturing techniques. The main reason is that all manufacturers of heavy electrical equipment face the same manufacturing problems. A second reason is that innovations in individual machining techniques rarely remain undetected beyond a few years because (a) mobility is high among engineers and technical people, (b) licences give manufacturers across the world ready access to the most advanced production techniques and (c) sales efforts by manufacturers of machine tools make the most sophisticated equipment available to all.

Despite similarities in factories, there are differences in costs of production. The purpose of this chapter is to point out that the economics of manufacturing and transporting heavy electrical equipment dictate an industry comprised of fairly large firms. First, large volume permits continuous investigation into product design. New advanced designs have resulted in continually declining size and weight of equipment per unit of electrical output. The lower weights are achieved through the use of new materials or, more generally, less material, which can mean lower total material cost per unit of output. Second, development of advanced manufacturing methods, tailored to meet the needs of a particular plant, can reduce costs. Technical economies of scale may be achieved in plants which produce a relatively large volume of goods, and thus these plants can use machines and manufacturing techniques which would be too costly to expend over smaller outputs.

When the cost advantages of large-scale production are combined with the substantial economies in research and development, it would appear that fewer, but larger, firms would constitute a more efficient industry structure. This proposition is discussed separately for each type of equipment—turbine-generators, power transformers and power circuit breakers.

Economical Turbine-Generator Production

A steam turbine-generator set consists of a turbine and a generator. The basic principles of operation are illustrated in Figure 2. The teapot is equivalent to a boiler or nuclear reactor that generates

FIGURE 2
TURBINE-GENERATOR PRINCIPLE

Source: Y. S. Hargett, *Large Steam Turbine-Driven Generators* (New York: General Electric Company, 1967), p. 3.

steam. The fan represents a turbine. The steam strikes the turbine blades which are attached to a shaft (a rotor) that runs the length of the turbine. The shaft rotates and turns a corresponding shaft running through a generator. The magnet (generator rotor) rotates within the wire cylinder (the generator stator) and produces a voltage at the end of the cylinder.

For each tandem turbine-generator set there is one generator and one turbine. The turbine is made up of from two to five turbine cylinders—one high-pressure cylinder, one to three low-pressure cylinders, and possibly one intermediate-pressure cylinder. As the electrical output capacity (measured in megawatts) of the turbine-generator increases, the size of the high-pressure cylinder grows slowly; the intermediate-pressure cylinder is added and its size increases gradually; and the low-pressure cylinders increase in number and size (see Figure 3). Furthermore, the physical size of a low-pressure cylinder for a nuclear station is often almost twice that for a coal- or oil-burning power station.

Factory Loading and Scale of Plant

The increase in number and size of low-pressure cylinders as size of turbine increases means that a factory's ability to produce turbines efficiently can be gauged, in large part, by the facilities for low-pressure cylinders. As the average size of set produced rises, an imbalance occurs in factory loading. When balance is restored, the output capacity of the plant inevitably is increased. Look at an example to understand the elements of this evolution.

The typical set ordered in the 1960s was less than 400 megawatts. As shown in Figure 3, a 300-megawatt set has two low-pressure cylinders. When 500- and 600-megawatt turbines became common in the mid-1960s, three low-pressure cylinders had to be produced for each turbine, rather than two. This led to bottlenecks in production. Factories had to be reorganised, often with the addition of new machinery, to provide for a better flow of work; that is, so that all five cylinders for each turbine could be completed simultaneously.

Reorganisation of plants to enable production of more low-pressure turbine cylinders automatically leads to an increase in output capacity of the plant, measured in megawatts. Continuing the example above, four 300-megawatt turbines comprise 16 cylinders—four high-pressure, four intermediate-pressure, eight low-pressure—and have a total combined electrical output capacity of 1200 megawatts. Each 600-megawatt turbine has five cylinders, each slightly larger than those of the 300-megawatt unit. These larger components may take up to 25 per cent more time to machine and assemble, so perhaps only three 600-megawatt turbines can be turned out with the reorganised facilities during the time that it took

FIGURE 3
TYPICAL TURBINE-GENERATOR LAYOUTS
Tandem Compound Sets

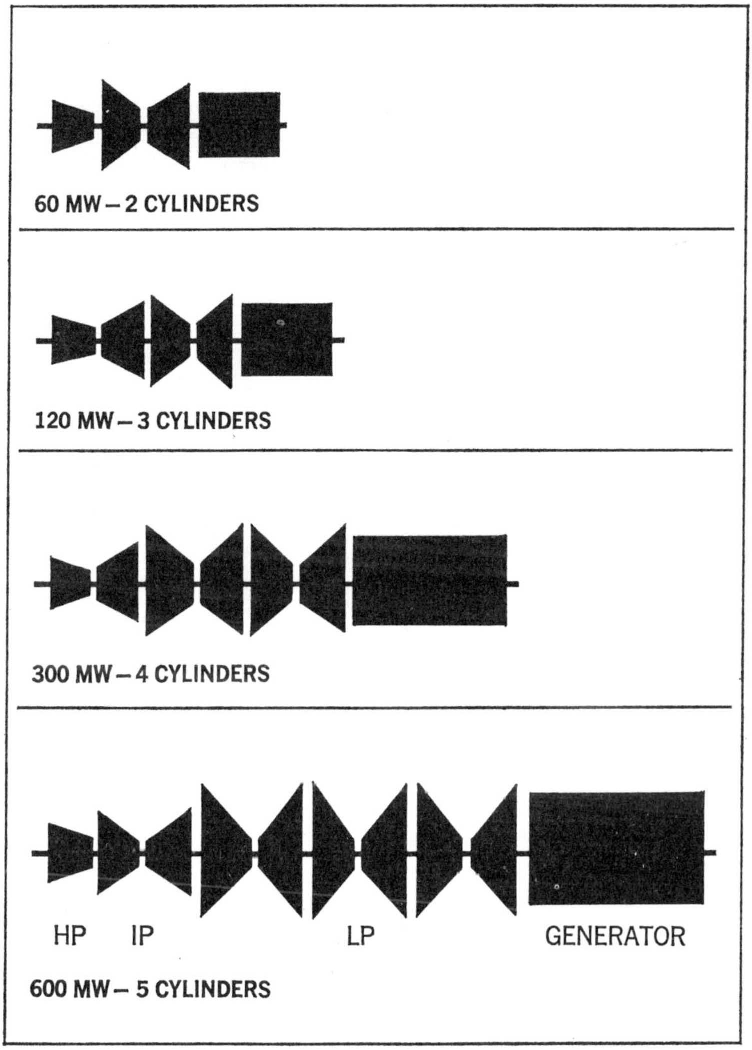

SOURCE: Manufacturers' Product Literature.

to finish four 300-megawatt units. The total megawatt output, however, will have increased 50 per cent—from 1,200 to 1,800 megawatts. In practice, there would be a mixture of the smaller and larger sizes, so the increase in output would be less than 50 per cent. The greater the average size of turbine produced, the larger the total output capacity of the plant.

The conclusion drawn is that there is not one scale of plant that is optimum at any one time. The optimum scale for factories is determined, first, by the projected volume of orders and, second, by the estimated mix of turbine sizes in the factory. For factories already in operation, a third consideration is the equipment already installed.

In the first half of the 1970s, the largest sets installed will be in the 1,000-megawatt range, compared with 600 to 800 megawatts in the late 1960s. Manufacturers that wish to maintain positions at the forefront of technology have been required, again, to expand and reorganise their plants. This latest reorganisation of facilities could not be accomplished by routine expansion of existing facilities in most factories. Factories constructed 25 or more years ago can no longer simply be reorganised.[74] In some cases, the structures are not strong enough to support overhead cranes with lifting capacities of up to 200 tons for turbines and 600 tons for generators. A building that was designed for crane capacities of 150 to 200 tons often cannot be strengthened to support more than 400 tons. A second reason why more thorough reorganisation is required is the physical size of components under manufacture. The total length of a low-pressure section of a 60-megawatt set, the most common size when most plants of the 1960s were constructed, was about 25 feet long. The overall length of a low-pressure section for a 1,100-megawatt set can be 100 to 120 feet and, moreover, the 1,100-megawatt set requires three low-pressure cylinders compared with the one for a 60-megawatt set.[75] The increase is reflected in the space required for fabricating and machine cylinders, machining rotors and assembling and testing each turbine.

In the mid-1960s, most West European turbine factories had annual production capacities of 3,500 to 4,500 megawatts. By 1972,

[74]I. C. Bell, "The Heavy Machine Shop", in *Developments in Large Steam Turbine Generating Plant* (London: English Electric, 1965), p. 57.

[75]F. N. Thomas and D. G. Virgin, *Influence of Design and Manufacture on Erection* (London: Institution of Electrical Engineers, 1969), p. 89.

manufacturers will have reorganised and expanded their facilities. It is argued in the following paragraphs that efficient West European plants in the mid-1970s should have output capacities in the range of 8,000 to 10,000 megawatts per year. Plants in the United States will have to be larger because of the larger average size of set produced and in order to achieve the same unit costs as their West European counterparts.

Extent of Economies of Scale

The reorganisations in 1968-71 presented manufacturers with an unusual opportunity to evaluate the advantages of a limited range of plant scales and of a small number of alternative production techniques. Each firm looked at the market and selected a scale of plant most efficient for its anticipated volume of orders. Observation of the conclusions reached gives some indication of possible sources of economies of scale. The most likely operations appear to be in blading and in machining cylinders.

Blading is considered the most important area of design and manufacture of a turbine. It is in blading designs where the greatest variety of manufacturing methods occurs. At the present time, at least four manufacturing techniques are used: machine forgings, precision machining of entire blade, extrusion and electro-chemical machining. No manufacturer produces all its blades the same way as any other manufacturer. Furthermore, within any one factory the methods used are continually under revision in search for means to improve the technical properties of blades. To say that one method or set of processes is superior in terms of cost and quality of product would most likely draw disagreement from every manufacturer. Comments here, therefore, will be limited to observed economies of scale in individual plants.

The first observation is that blades are usually made in a self-contained shop which may or may not be part of or even near the main turbine factory. Of all turbine parts, blades have the highest value/weight ratio and, therefore, are the least costly to transport. In the reorganisation of production facilities to enable manufacture of larger turbines, blading may be moved to a new location, but there remains only one blading shop for all large steam turbine production. It appears to be economical to have all blading done in one location in order fully to utilise machine capacity and manufacturing skills.

The second observation is that there are several different sizes and shapes of blades that go into each turbine. The labour used and the delays incurred in setting up for each blade size if only one machine line were used would be more costly than installing multiple machines. Moreover, a failure or problem with a single machine could cause expensive delays in the production schedule for the entire factory. Costs are reduced when a number of blade machining processes are operated simultaneously, each one on different size blades. The greater the total volume of production, the longer each run can be. The key to efficient blade production is combining the number of machine lines and factory production to minimise set-up time while avoiding bottlenecks.

The third observation concerns the volume of output required for efficiency. This varies with the methods chosen. The newer processes, such as electro-chemical machining and extrusion, so far, have just been used for small blades. One manufacturer indicated that the output of his electro-chemical machine is sufficient to supply his plant's annual requirements for these blades. The more traditional blading processes—either machining of forgings, precision forgings, or precision machining the entire blade—can be handled efficiently by smaller volume shops. The biggest problem is obtaining sufficiently long production runs. To reduce the high labour use in transferring blades from one machine to another and in setting up each machine, a machine transfer line has been developed. At the new Westinghouse plant in Winston-Salem, North Carolina, for example, eight fixed machine tools are tied together with a line operated by two men. The elimination of separate machine set-ups results in a 50 per cent saving in direct labour. Westinghouse indicates that if its output were one-half of the planned output of 20,000 megawatts—that is 10,000 megawatts—automated transfer lines would still be used, but the design would be different.

So far, most West European firms have not been forced by high labour rates to turn to high volume, highly automated processes. (See international comparison of wage levels on Page 81 below.) They can absorb more man-hours of labour on each component without realising a competitive disadvantage *vis-à-vis* larger American firms. If the small-scale plant were to operate in the United States, however, it would incur higher average factory costs relative to Westinghouse or General Electric. Similarly, if a larger-scale plant were to be constructed in Western Europe, it might achieve a factory cost advantage.

A parallel trend towards reducing labour content is seen in the machining of inner casings for low-pressure cylinders. Since the number of low-pressure cylinders increases as the output capacity of turbines rises, this component quickly becomes a production bottleneck in factories laid out for smaller sets. In the latest reorganisation of plants, manufacture of low-pressure cylinders has been removed from the main factory. Companies segregating production are these: General Electric and Westinghouse Electric have built plants in Charleston, South Carolina, and Charlotte, North Carolina, respectively, to produce low-pressure cylinders. Brown Boveri (Switzerland) is producing complete low-pressure cylinders in its new Birrfeld facilities while high-pressure and intermediate-pressure cylinders remain in Baden. The merged facilities of English Electric and AEI were replanned so that generators could be made in Stafford; blades, high-pressure, and smaller intermediate-pressure cylinders, in Rugby; and larger intermediate-pressure and low-pressure sections, in Trafford Park. Similarly, Kraftwerk Union will produce all high-pressure and intermediate-pressure cylinders in the former Siemens plant in Mülheim while a new Mülheim factory is being built for the production of low-pressure cylinders.

Construction of new plant and equipment has permitted installation of new processes for machining high-pressure and low-pressure cylinders. In the past, a manufacturer with a small annual output, say 2,000 to 3,000 megawatts, could use the same machine tools for machining casings and for other products and thus achieve the same cost level as a larger manufacturer. This, in fact, is what Siemens and CEM did by producing gas turbines in the same plant as steam turbines. M·A·N and Rateau-Schneider still produce turbines in multi-product plants. More recently, the very large size of casings has encouraged the development and use of new manufacturing techniques to minimise the man-hours used in moving these large pieces and setting up machine tools. One such technique is the machine line which moves the component from one tool to another mechanically. Another is the machining centre. In the latter process, the component is stationed on a table adjacent to a complex machine comprising several different tools. In the more sophisticated versions, the centre may have a second table where the next component can be set up while the first is being machined. The whole centre is numerically controlled and its output is four times that of a conventional group of separate machines. Similarly, using a horizontal boring machine centre for inner cylinders can cut the time required by two-thirds. Output capacity is three to four times the conventional vertical boring mill. Both machines are economical only in plants with outputs of about 8,000 megawatts per year.

These and similar manufacturing techniques are designed to reduce the man-hours of manufacturing time. Firms in countries, such as the United States, where wage rates are high are apt to be the first to develop such methods. For example, in some operations in new United States turbine plants, one man is performing the job three or four men did in the older plant.

As long as wages differ internationally, high labour cost countries, such as the United States, will be forced to seek methods of reducing man-hours. Since these methods have always been more costly, it is expected that United States manufacturers, to be cost competitive, must operate larger plants. Thus, while an efficient plant in Western Europe may turn out an annual turbine production of about 8,000 to 10,000 megawatts per year, American firms must produce closer to 12,500 megawatts.

Scale of Firm and Salaries

The differences in scale between Western Europe and the United States are accentuated by the higher salaries in the United States. A comparison of salaries for the same job classification in each of six countries made by an international firm shows salaries in the United States to be two times those in the United Kingdom and 10 to 15 per cent above those on the continent (see Table 16).

Salary overhead accounts for 25 to 30 per cent of the total cost of a turbine. If it is assumed that the productivity of salaried workers is the same in each country and that the minimum size of staff is the same, then it follows that American manufacturers are required to operate firms at least 15 per cent larger in order to spread the cost of salaried research and engineering and commercial and administrative staffs over a larger volume of sales. (Higher productivity in the United States would decrease the required increment; lower productivity would increase it.) Since the size of commercial staffs will be expanded as sales expand, the actual percentage difference would be larger. Turbine producers in the United States might

TABLE 16
COMPARISON OF GROSS SALARIES, 1968[a]
Index Numbers; UK Salary = 100

UK Salary	*France*	*West Germany*	*Italy*	*Sweden*	*United States*
£5,000	178	146	153	187	211
£7,500	173	185	186	186	203
£10,000	172	188	175	187	199
£12,500	172	190	167	na	196

[a]Comparison of factory labour rates show similar differentials. See Table 18 below.
na = not available.

require a minimum volume of 15,000 megawatts per year over which to defray the higher fixed costs of salaried employees. This production does not have to come from one plant since these economies are not in manufacturing.

Economies and Turbine Trade

When all manufacturing operations are considered, economies of large-scale production measured in terms of cost appear to level off at about 8,000 to 10,000 megawatts in Western Europe and 15,000 in the United States. Looking at the turbine industry in these terms it becomes apparent that its current structure is not the most efficient. Barriers to trade have led to an uneconomical duplication of manufacturing facilities throughout Western Europe.

As long as the size of turbine-generator sets was below 800 megawatts, a number of smaller firms could survive by purchasing technology or by depending on government aid. When the size of individual sets reached 800 megawatts and larger, the scale of plant required to manufacture such large units became such that with a proliferation of smaller firms all could not operate profitably. The clearest illustration of the pressures is seen in the formation of Kraftwerk Union.

Siemens and AEG-Telefunken are two large, multi-product manufacturers of electrical equipment. Both have well-established reputations for quality production. Both produced large steam turbine-generators in West Germany. Siemens had a technical exchange agreement with Westinghouse, and AEG with General Electric. Each of their plants was capable of 3,000 to 4,000 megawatts per year. When, in the late 1960s, larger sets were demanded, from 600 to 1,200 megawatts, neither manufacturer had adequate production facilities. If both firms were to erect factories with output capacities adequate to cover the development expense and the capital investment, a minimum of 12,000 megawatts of output capacity would have replaced 7,000 megawatts. The total West German market demands only 4,500 megawatts per year. The solution was to form a joint company—Kraftwerk Union—which would build one modern plant capable of turning out 8,000 megawatts per year of turbines of 100 megawatts and larger. Production facilities are capable of the very largest turbines envisioned.

Since demand for such large sizes in West Germany is limited, it was decided that orders for these sets would have to be sought in overseas markets in order to cover the research and development expense. The United States is virtually the only market ordering large turbines. Consequently, Kraftwerk Union concluded an agreement with Allis-Chalmers, a United States firm which wanted to re-enter the industry. The terms of the agreement provide that, initially, Allis' plant will be used for servicing and for machining turbine components, such as casings, for which transportation costs are high. Components for which there are substantial production economies, such as blading and control systems, will be shipped to the United States from West Germany.

By 1973, at least four West European manufacturers, in addition to Kraftwerk Union, will have manufacturing facilities equipped with machine tools to produce sets in the 1,000-megawatt range. To use these tools, such as a slotter for a generator rotor, even up to 50 per cent capacity, two or more orders for sets of this size must be received each year. The demand for 1,000-megawatt sets in Western Europe does not total even one set per year. To obtain experience and to load their factories economically, West European manufacturers are competing in the United States market, where over ten sets in this size range are ordered each year. A similar situation occurred in the mid-1960s when first Canada and then the United States began ordering transmission equipment for system voltages of 735 and 765 kilovolts respectively. Manufacturers the world over sought to gain experience with advanced technology. On a smaller scale, Sweden encountered similar competition in the 1950s when it was the first country to install a 400-kilovolt network. The conclusion is that to maintain a position at the forefront of technology, manufacturers must expand and reorganise their plants and then seek orders wherever the most advanced technology is required. Rarely can a firm rely on its own market to provide it continually with the necessary experience. A corollary is that as size of set increases, rising economies of scale in manufacture could force West European utilities to purchase non-domestic equipment. The alternative would be the subsidisation of inefficient producers.

Power Transformer Cost Reduction

Large transformer manufacture has been a constant quest for ways to decrease overall size and weight in order to economise on materials and to overcome problems in transporting very large units. Unlike a turbine-generator, a power transformer is not readily sub-divided into components for easier transportation and then re-erected on site. Thus, the successful transformer manufacturer continually must seek new ways of increasing electrical output per pound of material used to build a transformer. It is proposed in this section that the importance of product development cost is far more significant than technical economies of large-scale production in determining success in transformer manufacture.

Materials and Transformer Design

Manufacturers must design and build technically acceptable equipment. Beyond this, the successful manufacturer will design units that are the least expensive to produce. When the shop cost of a typical power transformer is broken down into input factors, materials account for more than half the production cost.

TABLE 17
TYPICAL COMMERCIAL COST OF A POWER TRANSFORMER

	Percentage
Materials	56
Direct labour	11
Overhead	33
Shop cost	100
R and D, commercial and administrative charges	35
Commercial cost	135

Since 1910, when the basic design and construction of a transformer was established, development work has been confined to increasing the output of a transformer through better quality and use of materials.[76] According to Mr. John W. Stirling, vice-president and general manager of the Westinghouse transformer division: "Progress in transformer design [can be charted] in terms of first, kilovolt-amperes per pound of total weight, and second . . . effectiveness of insulation materials . . ."[77]

As a measure of the success of the leading transformer manufacturers in designing low-cost transformers, a comparison was made of the bids to Tennessee Valley Authority for contracts for the largest transformers it has ordered during the past ten years—400 megavolt-ampere, 500 kilovolt. The results show a trend towards decreasing weights of transformers offered to TVA (see Figure 4).

Progress made by each manufacturer has varied somewhat. For example, in 1963 and 1964, Elin-Union offered the lowest weight transformers, but its subsequent progress was mediocre. By contrast, ASEA, which began with equipment just slightly heavier than Elin-Union, dropped its transformer weight about 24 per cent. By 1970 ASEA offered the lightest transformers for this specification. English Electric weights showed a steady decrease, totalling about 15 per cent. Since Ferranti did not bid between 1967 and 1970, it is not known whether this firm continued to reduce the weight of its transformers.

Important, also, in this weight comparison is the efficiency of the transformer (that is, heat losses during operation). Here again ASEA generally had the lowest losses. All companies except General Electric and Westinghouse showed decreasing losses.

The comparatively heavy transformers offered by General Electric and Westinghouse are somewhat of an enigma. A possible answer is that these companies may not have been competing aggressively in the public sector of the United States market which is wide open to import competition. The private sector of the United States market is much larger and, in the early 1960s, was less subject to intense foreign competition.

By contrast to United States producers, West European manufacturers have rarely been able to rely on their home markets to

[76]C. A. Abdy, "The Early Years of the Power Transformer", *Electronics and Power*, London, August 1968, p. 338.

[77]Reported in *Electrical World*, April 8, 1968, p. 48.

FIGURE 4
DRY WEIGHT—400 MVA TRANSFORMERS
(*3-Winding, Single Phase, 60 Hz, 500/161/13.2 KV*)

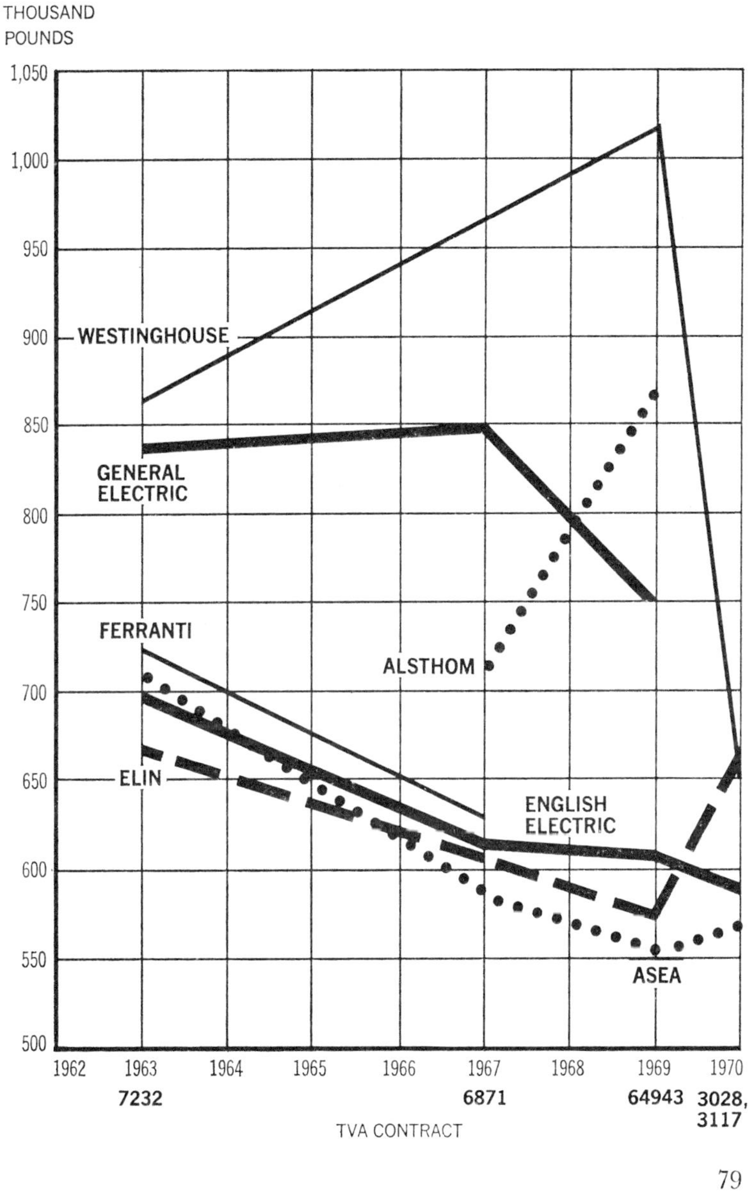

fill plant capacity. Forced into open export markets, West Europeans have had to work continually to develop lower cost designs. The development effort provides a source of virtually unending economies of scale. The greater the volume of sales over which expenditure on research and development can be spread, the lower the cost per unit. The finding of Chapter 6 was that a minimum output capacity of 10,000 megavolt-amperes is required to afford the necessary research and development expenditure. Part of this is necessary to produce technically acceptable equipment; the remainder, to produce cost-competitive designs. Thus, a smaller firm, such as Elin-Union with an annual output of less than 5,000 megavolt-amperes, has not been able to maintain expenditure on reducing transformer weights. This reveals itself in Elin's declining share of world markets which, in turn, reduces its funds for design improvement.

The 10,000-megavolt-ampere volume need not come from one plant, but may include that of subsidiaries and licensees. When considering the increasing difficulties and expense of transporting very large transformers, the possibility of multiple plants becomes quite attractive. The feasibility will depend, in part, on the extent of technical economies of scale in manufacture.

Economies of Scale and Labour Rates

Research has revealed that direct labour costs in the manufacture of power transformers are similar around the world. Some countries, particularly the United States and, to a lesser extent, Sweden, pay higher wages, but firms in these countries reduce the number of employees by seeking more automated techniques. As a result of

TABLE 18
LABOUR COSTS FOR A POWER TRANSFORMER, 1968

	Index of Direct Labour Cost	*Hourly Wages Including Benefits* $
France	105	1.70
Italy	99	1.65
Sweden	107	2.60
United States	110	3.25
United Kingdom	100	1.80
West Germany	105	2.00

their efforts, direct labour costs vary only 5 to 10 per cent among efficient companies in each country, despite differences of 80 to 100 per cent in wage rates.

Manufacturers in high-wage countries are continually seeking ways to substitute capital for labour. It is indicated in the sections to follow that most of the opportunities for substitution probably lie with larger-scale operations. In transformer manufacture, however, smaller-scale production has not necessarily meant significantly higher manufacturing costs.

In the table below are listed the minimum factory outputs required before a factory will undertake in-house production of each of the main transformer sub-assemblies. The data represent a consensus derived from the experiences of major transformer manufacturers in Western Europe and North America. Their statements are based on current manufacturing techniques and product designs. Two manufacturers had recently completed studies to determine the break-even points for each component.

TABLE 19
TYPICAL SHOP COST BREAKDOWN OF TRANSFORMER COMPONENTS

	Proportion of Shop Cost %	*Approximate Minimum Factory Output Required*
Bushings	11.5	30,000 MVA
Radiators, piping	10·0	10,000 MVA, tubes
		20,000 MVA, panels
Tank	5·5	5,000 MVA
Coils	25·5	7,500 MVA, insulating copper
		Negligible, windings
Core	30.0	Must be done in shop
Insulation (solid)	12.5	—
Sundries	5.0	—
	100.0	

Firms with smaller-scale plants do not necessarily have higher cost operations. Almost all of the components of a transformer can be sub-contracted to companies whose production is sufficiently large to take advantage of all possible economies of scale. Radiators and tanks, for example, are relatively simple metal products that can be made by steel fabricators. Porcelain columns for bushings are produced by the several manufacturers of electrical insulators. Offsetting the small-scale transformer producer's savings from sub-contracting are the inconvenience and the reduced reliability of delivery, which require tieing up more money in inventory. Producers who are large enough to make components in-house report that, on balance, there are no significant differences in total cost between in-house and bought-out components.

As the state of technology progresses, the minimum output required for in-house production of some components increases. The effects have been observed primarily in core construction. The transformer core is built up of laminations of cold-rolled grain-oriented silicon steel. The smallest firms could buy laminations from a steel supplier, but this is never as satisfactory as being able to produce them in-house as and when they are required. When an immediate change of programme is required to keep up production, absolute control over production is critical. Since the core is the heart of the transformer, such flexibility is much more important than for radiators or bushings. As a result, almost every transformer manufacturer prepares his own laminations, although it may be more costly to do so. Even if the cost increment were 10 per cent of the core cost, this would mean only 3 per cent on total shop cost and 2 per cent on total cost, a supportable difference. As the size of plant increases, more automated and more integrated core processes are used. A highly automated plant will unwind coils of steel under tension, slit to required widths, punch holes if necessary, shear, anneal, varnish and dry in one continuous operation. More automated equipment usually costs two to three times conventional equipment, has double to triple the output capacity and reduces the manpower requirements. Plants in the United States, faced with rapidly rising wage rates, have taken advantage of all possible economies of scale. Similarly, ASEA of Sweden has increased the size of its plant much faster than other West European firms. The minimum size of an efficient plant in Sweden might be 10,000 megavolt-amperes, while in the United States the output would be around 15,000 megavolt-amperes. Both depend on the mix of sizes in the plant.

The need for larger outputs in the United States is reinforced by the higher costs of salaried employees. The engineering and commercial and administrative staffs of transformer firms can add as much as 35 to 40 per cent to shop cost (see Page 77). This is about 25 per cent of total cost. To offset the higher salaries, United States firms must spread this higher total overhead over more units perhaps 17,500 megavolt-amperes per year. This output may come from more than one plant. Thus, we see American firms operating multiple plants in the United States, each covering a different range of sizes—up to 500 kilovolt-amperes, 501 to 25,000 kilovolt-amperes, and larger than 25,000 kilovolt-amperes.

Minimal Impact of Economies of Scale in Manufacturing

The conclusion drawn from the experiences of power transformer manufacturers is that economies of scale in manufacturing are of minimal significance in cost of production differences. More important are the economies in product development. In order to have sufficient funds to invest in continuous research and development programmes to develop lower cost reliable designs, sales volume must be at least 10,000 megavolt-amperes per year. At lower volumes, firms find that the bulk of research and development expenditure must go towards developing technically acceptable equipment and too little an amount remains for seeking lower cost designs.

Power Circuit Breaker Design

A power circuit breaker acts as a safety valve in an electrical system. When a line is over-loaded, the breaker switches off the current. The operation is similar to turning off a light switch on a wall.

Experience has indicated that an average of five years is required to develop a breaker design, and about every ten years major changes in electricity system requirements necessitate the introduction of entirely new or substantially changed breakers. For example, circuit-breaker manufacturers who relied on air blast breakers in the 1960s have now developed low oil volume breakers for lower duties. This contrasts markedly with turbines and transformers for which the basic technologies have changed imperceptibly. Unlike this other power equipment, however, once a circuit-breaker design is accepted, few, if any, modifications are required for each order. The reason is that breakers are not used directly with other power equipment, so that the number of technical combinations specified for breakers is very much lower.

The differences in the development programme and production of power circuit breakers have enabled manufacturers to realise a degree of standardisation of production not possible for other heavy electrical equipment. In this section it is indicated that the firms best able to exploit the potential advantages of standardised production are those that (a) have designed breakers with modular components and (b) have sufficient volume of production to cover the costs of introducing specialised labour functions.

Proficiency in Air Blast Breaker Manufacture

A circuit breaker, theoretically, can be built to any specifications from some combination of standardised parts. At any particular point in time, the need to re-design a breaker to meet particular system requirements can be greatly reduced and, in most cases, eliminated.

During the 1960s, the most successful high-voltage and extra high-voltage circuit-breaker manufacturers were offering equipment that replaced oil with air as a breaking medium. Most offered two designs—one for heavy duty use, the other for lighter duty. The test ratings for each breaker are presented in Figure 5. Without explaining the technology, it is possible to see the results with respect to international competition.

The French manufacturers, Delle-Alsthom and Merlin and Gerin, covered the greatest span of specifications with their respective breakers. Due to the particular requirements in their home market and the poor performance of their prior oil breakers, the French were forced into developing acceptable air blast breakers before manufacturers in the rest of the world. This head start gave the French more time to improve their equipment and find the best combinations of designs for the time.

Until 1965, Brown Boveri had little call for breakers with very high interrupting capacities. Its oil breakers were competitive in the 132-kilovolt range, and this is what most of its customers required. Indeed, in 1967–68, Brown Boveri was the second largest exporter of circuit breakers in the world. For the few markets requiring higher ratings, Brown Boveri offered a very large, heavy-duty air blast breaker, the DMF. This is very costly to produce and is now, in the words of a company official, "obsolete". In the mid-1960s Brown Boveri recognised the need for a lighter, lower-cost, more competitive air blast breaker and began development of its DLF design. Thus, unlike the French firms, Brown Boveri developed two different designs for heavy and light duties. This double effort had to be more

FIGURE 5
INTERNATIONAL COMPARISON OF CIRCUIT BREAKER PERFORMANCE, 1968

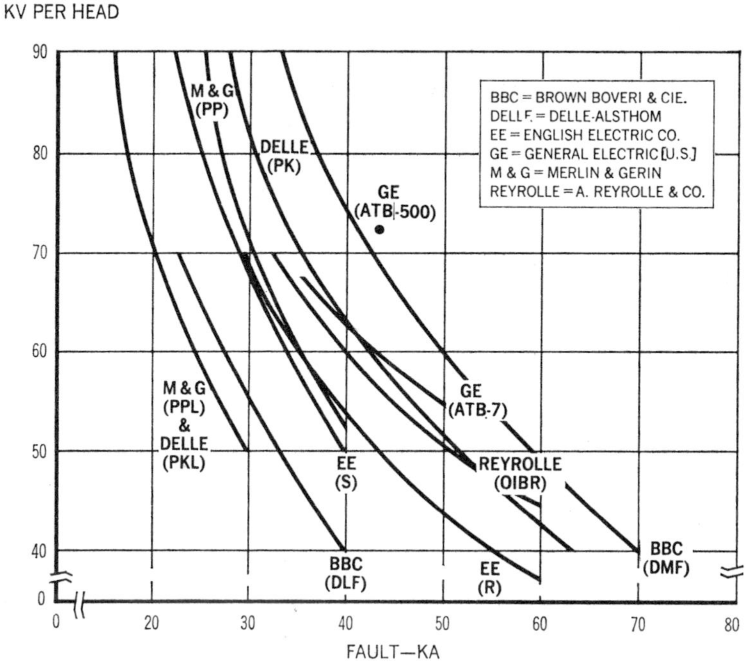

SOURCE: Test data published in technical literature.

costly to develop and, as is indicated below, more costly to produce.

The British manufacturers did not begin to concentrate on high-voltage air blast breakers until 1960. In that year, the CEGB decided to introduce a 400-kilovolt network and gave the British firms five years to design 400-kilovolt breakers. To expedite development, the CEGB worked with the manufacturers to standardise on a design suitable for the especially heavy duty required by the British system. No immediate consideration was given to the needs of export markets.

When English Electric decided it needed a breaker for export, it worked with Scarpa and Magnano, an Italian switchgear manufacturer, to produce a lighter breaker similar to continental standards. Many of the safety and quality features of the home market ("r" frame) design were retained in the new "s" frame. The capacity of the "s" breaker, however, is about the same capacity as the Merlin and Gerin heavy-duty breaker. Rather than spanning a range of breaking capacities, the kilovolt per head possible was increased, so English Electric is still not competitive in low-capacity, low-voltage areas. As of this writing, in July, 1971, there are reports that the GEC Switchgear Company, of which English Electric is now a part, is developing a new breaker design.

Reyrolle's OIBR breaker was also too heavy for most of the world's requirements. In early 1970, Reyrolle introduced a new range of breakers. For heavy duty use, Reyrolle redesigned its air blast breakers although the high breaking capacity and current ratings of the new breaker were still required in few countries outside of England and the United States.

General Electric's ATB–7 series of breaker is similar in design to Reyrolle's OIBR design. General Electric cannot hope to compete favourably in export areas with this breaker. Furthermore, the ATB–7 goes only as high as 345 kilovolts. For very high voltage and breaking capacities in the United States, General Electric has had to develop a new design, the ATB–500 kilovolt. This, as is shown below, is costly.

ASEA of Sweden also offered an air blast breaker in the mid-1960s. As duty requirements increased, the breaker design could not be up-graded inexpensively so ASEA withdrew the breaker from the market.

One aspect in the choice of designs by all these manufacturers is the importance of requirements in their home markets. The French were well situated, because EdF specifications were suitable for a wide range of countries. By contrast the British were saddled with extremely heavy and costly breakers which were not competitive anywhere else in the world. Part of the British problem was the CEGB's establishment of manufacturing specifications rather than performance specifications. The CEGB requires the porcelain columns of circuit breakers to be lined with fibre-glass which can double the cost of porcelains. Continental manufacturers do not use them and so far there have been no adverse effects either on West European systems or service on the more onerous American networks. For trade to be effective, it is necessary that procurement policies be open not only in terms of suppliers, but also be co-ordinated with respect to equipment specifications.

Standardising Circuit Breaker Production

In addition to its suitability for a wide range of market requirements, Delle-Alsthom's air blast breaker was successful due to its low cost. First, it is light in weight. For example, the air blast circuit breaker made by Delle-Alsthom for TVA for duty at 500 kilovolts, 3,000 kilovolt-amperes weighs about 55 tons. An air blast breaker made in the United States by General Electric for the same duty weighs 88 tons. (Both weights include current transformers.) The prices bid by each in 1966—$315,000 by General Electric and $235,000 by Delle-Alsthom—indicate that General Electric was not able to offset the difference in cost of materials used.

Another disadvantage, beyond volume of materials used, can be manufacturing economies of scale due to standardised equipment design. To see the effect, the cost of one company's circuit breakers is compared with the cost of another's for the same specifications.

TABLE 20

COST COMPARISON OF CIRCUIT BREAKER DESIGNS

Cost of 115 KV Air Blast Breaker = 100		
KV	*Company A*	*Company B*
115	100	100
220	209	160
380	325	360
500	435	850

Although the delivered costs of 115-kilovolt breakers are about the same for both breakers, Company B's cost at 500 kilovolts is nearly 50 per cent higher.[78] The difference is that Company A's design covers the voltage range from 115 to 500 kilovolts whereas Company B's design for 500 kilovolts is different from that produced for lower voltages.

Success in the machining and assembly of air blast breakers appears to rest on designing a breaker such that the parts can be mass produced and assembled by semi-skilled labour. The manufacturer who achieved the greatest degree of standardisation in air blast breaker production was Delle-Alsthom. The extent to which

[78]The differences in 220 kilovolts and 380 kilovolts are due primarily to the difference in overhead charges added by Company B: that is, the 380-kilovolt breakers carry a heavier load.

Delle accomplished this is indicated by the fact that a breaker is not designated for a particular customer until four weeks before shipment.

Since a circuit breaker design is produced in very large quantities over a period that averages only ten years, it is generally not economical to invest time and money in developing specialised production machinery that could be used only a short time. Standard tools are used. The addition of new machines or additional machine time occurs in small steps, so there appear to be no significant economies of scale realised through indivisible machine units. The minimum scale, as set by machinery, seems to be no more than 75 twin heads per month, or less than 150 breakers rated 220 kilovolts per year. This is half of Delle's output, and to perform most operations, Delle has two or more machines of each kind.

Economies of scale in the production of circuit breakers are not in the use of machinery, but in overheads. A 40 per cent increase in Delle's production required installation of new, higher output machinery and a 60 per cent increase in direct labour. The increase in the rest of the labour force, however, was negligible. The breakdown is shown in Table 21 below.

TABLE 21

CHANGE IN DELLE'S LABOUR FORCE WITH A 40 PER CENT INCREASE IN PRODUCTION

	Per cent
Direct labour	60
Indirect labour	
Operating labour	0
White collar	5
Engineering	1

Delle believes production could be increased another 50 to 60 per cent—to 200 breakers—with the same indirect labour and engineering staff. With a ten-fold increase in production during the 1960s, there has been a negligible increase in the size of the engineering staff. Commercial and administrative expenses have also risen at a slower rate than output. Again, annual outputs of plants in countries with higher labour costs must be 20 to 30 per cent higher.

Economies and Circuit Breaker Trade

The relevant factor in keeping circuit breaker manufacturing costs low reduces to supplying as many of one type breaker for as many different voltages as possible. Volume must be sufficient to justify a large expenditure on special development to find a method for making assemblies with parts machined to small tolerances by semi-skilled labour.

Delle-Alsthom has licensed subsidiaries in Italy and Spain to produce breakers to the Delle design for their own domestic markets. Delle believes that if the French, Italian and Spanish markets were open it would be less costly to manufacture breakers for all three markets in one plant. It is likely that other manufacturers would face similar motivation to reorganise.

Technology and Large Firms: Summarised

The thesis of this and the previous two chapters is that the technological requirements encountered by manufacturers of heavy electrical equipment can be met only by large firms.

Technological requirements are established by electricity generating and transmission systems. Responsible for these systems are utilities which are either owned or regulated by governments. Utilities are obligated to meet all demands for electricity at the lowest possible cost consistent with safe and reliable electricity networks. As the demand for electricity has doubled every ten years, utilities have found it is less expensive and more efficient to operate a few large power generating stations rather than numerous smaller ones. The economies in operating large power stations place a burden on manufacturers to develop equipment with higher and higher output capacities. In Chapter 6, it was argued that the large and continuous expenditure on research and development this burden necessitates can be made only by large firms with annual sales in the range of 8,000 megavolts of turbine-generators, 10,000 megavolt-amperes of power transformers, and the equivalent of 200 power circuit breakers capable of 220-kilovolt duty. These figures are approximations. The actual volume required will depend on engineers' salaries and productivity.

Firms must invest in research and development not only to produce technically acceptable equipment, but also (a) to develop low-cost designs and (b) to develop efficient manufacturing techniques. In Chapter 7, it was proposed the relative importance of design and factory techniques varies with the type of equipment. The manufacture of turbine-generators is such that economies, particularly in machining blades and casings, can be realised in large-scale plants. In the 1970s, economies appear to level off at outputs of 8,000 to 10,000 megawatts per year in Western Europe and about 15,000 megawatts in the United States. The amount differs with the level of wages paid and the mix of sizes produced. For success in transformer manufacture and sale, economies of scale are far less significant than product design. Components of transformers are such that they can be easily produced by sub-contractors, so small-scale transformer plants, in the range of 7,500 megavolt-amperes per year, have a negligible cost handicap *vis-à-vis* larger producers. The more important determinant in keeping costs low seems to be continual reduction in the weight of transformers—that is, reduction in materials used. This, again, requires investment in engineering which can be made at the level of the firm, rather than the plant. Finally, the low-cost manufacture of power circuit breakers combines low-cost design and economies of scale. Development of a breaker design suitable for use in multiples for all voltages permits manufacture of standardised parts. Costs can be reduced through specialisation of labour. For air blast circuit breakers, it appears that a manufacturer would have to produce at least the equivalent of 200 breakers for 220-kilovolt duty before the benefits from specialisation are optimised.

Until the mid-1960s and the push towards mergers (described in Chapter 3), many firms and plants operated at less than the most efficient scale. Some, particularly several Italian firms, continue to do so. In the remaining chapters the outlook for the 1970s is examined in order to indicate the probable change in structure of the heavy electrical equipment industry.

8 FLUCTUATIONS IN MARKET DEMAND

The major finding of the last three chapters is that the economics of designing and manufacturing heavy electrical equipment dictate that the most efficient production units are parts of firms sufficiently large (a) to afford continuous and extensive research and development, (b) to cover the expense of developing cost competitive designs and (c) to take advantage of economies of scale in technology, particularly in the manufacture of turbine-generators. How close the industry world-wide will come to approaching optimum efficiency in the 1970s depends on the probable world demand for power equipment and the extent to which trade barriers are reduced. These questions are the subject of the remaining discussion. In Chapter 9, the volume of world demand in the 1970s is projected in an attempt to see how many firms might operate profitably. Various alternatives for trade groupings are posed to see their likely impact on industry structure. The commercial behaviour expected from heavy electrical equipment firms in response to demand conditions is discussed in Chapter 10. Then, the findings of the remaining analysis, and of the study as a whole, are marshalled in the final chapter, Chapter 11.

The effects of one aspect of the demand for power equipment—that is, fluctuations in demand—underline the projections and conclusions of these last four chapters. Therefore, a brief discourse on this aspect is given here.

Derived Demand for Power Equipment

In every country individual electricity supply companies have been granted regional monopolies for the sale of electricity to the public. In return for these grants, each utility is expected to purchase and install sufficient heavy electrical equipment to meet safely the maximum demand for electricity in its region.

Utilities' investment in power generating and transmission equipment is based on the relationship between existing and required facilities. In a study of the factors affecting investment in plant and equipment by private electric companies in the United States, Avram Kisselgoff and Franco Modigliani formulated a hypothesis based on these characteristics:[79] Gross investment in plant and equipment is a function of (1) the change in the annual rate of plant utilisation, (2) the current rate of utilisation of plant capacity, (3) electric companies' net income and depreciation, and (4) the optimum rate of plant utilisation, approximated by a function of time.

The authors found that the four variables explained 95 per cent of the annual variation in capital expenditure during the period 1926–41. Their equation was found to be accurate in predicting post-war (1951–55) investment levels when time was not extrapolated. The effects of profits and interest rates were found to be secondary. The most important result of a decline in profits is the postponing of orders of auxiliary pieces of equipment.

Kisselgoff and Modigliani concluded that investment in heavy electrical equipment is based on an acceleration principle—the relationship between existing and required facilities. Given five- and ten-year forecasts of electricity demand, utilities plan annual investment programmes that should yield a desired ratio of reserve capacity, which, in the United States, has been about 17 per cent.

Fluctuations in Demand

When the Kisselgoff and Modigliano analysis is applied to utilities' investment for the years 1956–67, their hypothesis is still valid, but the variables appear to account for less of the variance in investment than in earlier periods. They explain 70 per cent in the recent decade compared to 95 per cent in the years 1941–56. While the demand for electricity has continued to grow at a steady rate, fluctuations in demand for equipment, illustrated by orders for large steam turbine-generators, have become more exaggerated. The two series are compared for the United States as a whole in Figure 6.

Three-year moving averages for order data were used in order to reduce the effects of bunching and block purchasing. Still, the relative variation for the equipment series was at least 15 times the relative variation in the maximum demand for electricity.

The fluctuations in demand for generating equipment are similar to those occurring in derived demands for other capital equipment, such as cranes, machine tools, and industrial motors. The demands

[79] Avram Kisselgoff and Franco Modigliani, "Private Investment in the Electric Power Industry and the Acceleration Principle", *The Review of Economics and Statistics*, Harvard University, Cambridge, Massachusetts, November, 1957, p. 379.

FIGURE 6
UNITED STATES ELECTRIC UTILITY INDUSTRY
ANNUAL PEAK LOAD AND
ORDERS OF TURBINE-GENERATORS

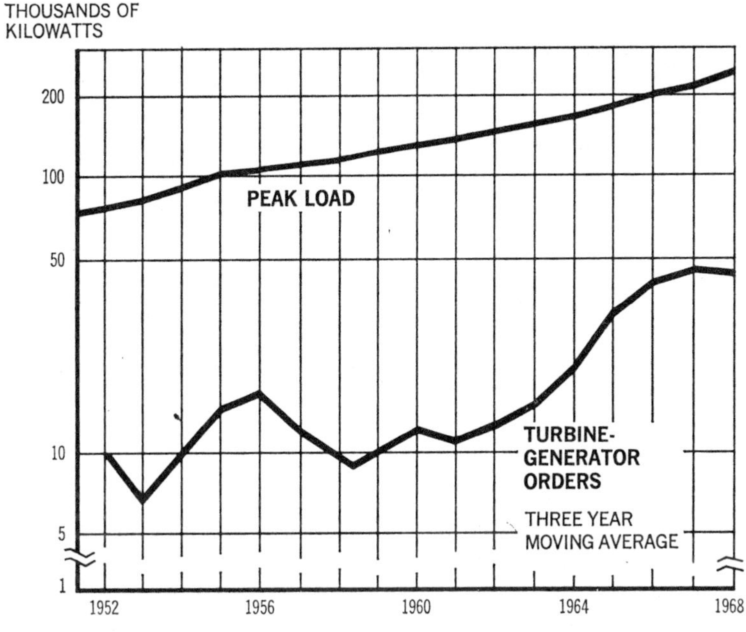

SOURCE: *Year-End Summary of the Electric Power Situation in the United States*, Edison Electric Institute, New York (annual).

NOTE: The non-linear regressions and coefficients of relative variation are

Orders: $\log Y = 3.8188 + 0.0417X$ $V = 0.030$ or 3 per cent.

Maximum demand: $\log Y = 4.828 + 0.02974X$ $V = 0.002$ or 0.2 per cent.

for these products are also subject to an accelerator effect, wherein the fluctuations in demand for productive machinery are far more intense than those in the output of that machinery. The difference between other products and power equipment is that the demand for electricity, from which the demand for power equipment is derived, appears to grow at a relatively stable rate (see Figure 6) whereas the growth in final output of the other products manifests fairly well-defined fluctuations. Several utilities in the United States and Western Europe were asked why they could not ignore fluctuations in electricity demand and plan investment to meet the long-run average growth. Three reasons were given.

First, fluctuations in business activity which affect electricity use also affect capital available for new investment. In business recessions, utilities that rely on government appropriations find that the latter are cut back when government revenues slow down.

The second reason offered is inadequate forecasting techniques. Utilities are committed to meeting peak demand. When unexpected spurts (drops) occur in this demand, such as occurred in 1955 and 1964 (1956 and 1961) in the United States, utilities do not know if these variations are permanent shifts in the average rate of growth or flukes. Since generating equipment must be ordered three to five years in advance, utilities are unwilling to wait and see what happens. They all rush to order (or to postpone new orders for) new equipment. The long lead time between the dates on which power equipment is ordered and those on which it is put in service may very well serve to accentuate fluctuations by causing utilities to respond promptly to slight changes in electricity demand. For example, the rapid upturn in orders in the late 1960s was exaggerated when utilities seemed to panic at the unanticipated lengthening of delivery times for nuclear equipment.

The third reason utilities do not smooth out fluctuations in orders for equipment is that the rapid advances in technology and the high costs of plant construction and maintenance make it uneconomical to build a power station before it is needed. One study of the effect of turbine-generator prices and efficiency on the cost of generating electricity was made by Charles R. Dean and Horace J. De Podwin for the period 1954–59.[80] They start with the proposition that once a utility has forecast electricity demand and decided the number and type of power stations required, it then can attempt to construct and operate these stations so that the cost of generating electricity is minimised.

The finding of their study was that during the 1954–59 period, the portion of generating costs attributable to turbine-generators rose only 2.7 per cent, although the price of the equipment rose over 40 per cent. The increases in turbine efficiency, therefore, were

[80]Charles R. Dean and Horace J. De Podwin, "Product Variation and Price Indexes: a Case Study of Electrical Apparatus", paper given to American Statistical Association, December 29, 1961, p. 40.

almost sufficient to offset increases in turbine prices. Indirect cost savings from more advanced equipment erase the difference completely.[81]

One important inference drawn from this study is that industry demand for power equipment is relatively price inelastic. If prices are cut in an attempt to gain more orders during a down-turn in demand, utilities may take advantage of the low bids and put in advance orders based on partial and preliminary specifications. The final details are not worked out until the utility is ready to construct the power station. The total number of orders over any period, however, is not increased by a price cut; it is just spread out.[82] When this occurs, manufacturers may not gain any benefit. First, final specifications are not established immediately so production cannot begin; factories remain under-utilised. In 1962, for example, equipment was still being delivered that had been ordered in the "White Sale" of 1954 and 1955. Second, the prices paid for the equipment in 1961 and 1962 were substantially below manufacturers' costs, which had risen appreciably since the order date.

From the reasons given for the recurrent fluctuations in demand for power equipment, it is concluded that the fluctuations will continue as long as there are general fluctuations in business activity, lead times remain long, and the efficiency of equipment continues to improve.

Fluctuations and Free Trade

Open and free trade in power equipment could reduce the impact of fluctuations in orders on manufacturers because turning points have not been concurrent in every country. Those firms with excess capacity due to few domestic orders could export to countries where demand is strong (see Table 22). The amount of excess capacity in each firm should tend to decline, also, since firms could install production capacity to meet average demand rather than maximum demand in their own countries.

[81]Two sources of indirect savings are lower construction costs for one big plant and reduced manpower requirements. See, for example, D. K. Anderson, "Thermal Power—What Should it Cost?", *Electric Power*, London, November 1963, p. 47; and Philip Sporn, *Technology, Engineering, and Economics* (Cambridge, Mass.: MIT Press, 1969), p. 82.

[82]See, also, G. B. Richardson, "The Pricing of Heavy Electrical Equipment: Competition or Agreement", *Bulletin of the Oxford University Institute of Economics and Statistics*, Oxford, May, 1966, p. 76.

TABLE 22

TURNING POINTS IN POWER EQUIPMENT ORDERING, 1960s

	United Kingdom	France	West Germany	Italy	United States
Down-turn	1966	1963	1964	1963	1961
Up-turn	1963	1965	1966	1965	1963

SOURCE: *Survey of Power Equipment*, OECD Secretariat, Paris (annual). Data are for power transformer shipments. Two-year lag between order and delivery is assumed.

In projecting world demand for power equipment and suggesting the number of firms required to satisfy it, the existence of fluctuations becomes a critical parameter. It is proposed in Chapter 9 that less manufacturing capacity would be required in the world if markets were open and trade accepted readily. In Chapter 10, the commercial practices and policies common in the sale of heavy electrical equipment are shown to have evolved, in large part, in reaction to the adverse effects of severe and recurrent fluctuations in demand for this equipment.

9 INDUSTRY UNDER ALTERNATIVE TRADE CONDITIONS

The 1970s will see an excess of production capacity for heavy electrical equipment. This conclusion is based on comparisons of expected world production capacity and volume of demand for each type of equipment. It might be expected that the impact of the excess capacity will lead to further concentration of the industry. Whether this will occur during the 1970s depends on the extent to which each of the major industrialised nations permits imports of heavy electrical equipment. In this chapter, the structure of the industry in the 1970s is postulated given the optimum size of firms, as established in Chapters 5 to 7, and alternative world trade situations. The first situation considered is free and open world trade among industrialised nations. Industry structure is discussed separately for turbines and transformers.

Number of Firms and World Turbine Demand

The continuous increase in the average size of set ordered has been important in limiting the number of optimum size steam turbine-generator firms. During the 20-year period from 1951 to 1970, the total megawatts of generating capacity annually ordered by United States utilities, for example, increased three-fold. At the same time, the average megawatt capacity of sets ordered grew nine-fold from 63 megawatts in 1951 to 556 megawatts in 1970. Consequently, the number of sets ordered each year fell from 187 to 54.

The effect of this change in demand on manufacturing facilities was described in Chapters 6 and 7. Economics of scale now peak at 8,000 to 10,000 megawatts per year in Western Europe and Japan. In the United States, outputs must be at least 15,000 megawatts per year in order to achieve the same unit costs as West European firms. When these efficient production levels are viewed in terms of free world demand in the 1970s, it appears that fewer plants could serve the current world need for turbine-generators.

Projections of demand indicate that to produce the required turbines, six or seven producers would be sufficient, rather than the 18 turbine manufacturers now operating. Look at each area separately. In Japan, there are now three manufacturers where one could satisfy home demand. In Western Europe, 13 operate complete manufacturing facilities for turbines of 100 megawatts and larger, where two, or three at the most, could serve efficiently. Three firms could survive in North America. Finally, the total demand in other areas, as projected for the 1970s, could be handled by facilities of existing firms. (See Table 23 below.)

TABLE 23
WORLD DEMAND AND MANUFACTURING CAPACITY FOR STEAM TURBINES
Average annual megawatts, 1970s

	EEC and EFTA	*USA and Canada*	*Japan*	*Other Countries*[a]	*Total*
Home demand	14,650	39,200	6,950	6,500	67,300
Capacity, 1975[b]	44,600	44,000	10,000	[c]	98,600
Available capacity	+29,950	+ 4,800	+ 3,050	(6,500)	+31,300

[a]Excludes countries dependent on Soviet bloc equipment.
[b]From the factory standpoint, capacity is more accurately measured in value of output, or tons of material, or manhours. These data, however, are not available on a consistent basis.
[c]East European nations are in the process of rebuilding their turbine industries. During the 1970s, it is expected that these markets will be closed to Western Europe. Moreover, Eastern Europe will begin exporting to countries now served by Western Europe and Japan.

This industry structure, consisting of six or seven optimum size firms, would be adequate to serve world demand if trade were completely open, unrestricted by domestic purchasing preference or other trade barriers, and if peaks in ordering cycles do not coincide. Turbines would be exported (a) to countries which have no domestic turbine industry and (b) to countries experiencing peak periods in their demand for turbines. Partial manufacturing facilities might be maintained in export areas. The current trend towards West European firms establishing North American service and repair plants stands as a guide to the type of activities that might be expected in the future. Generally, facilities in these partial plants would be capable of machining the heaviest turbine pieces, such as cylinder casings, and of performing any repair work required on turbines sold. As industrialisation progresses in developing countries in Asia, Africa and Latin America, it is anticipated that these countries will begin their turbine industries by producing components, under licence, for turbines supplied by established manufacturers.

One assumption underlying this evolving free trade structure is highly significant and stands reiteration. As long as wages and salaries paid in the United States are higher than those paid in Western Europe and Japan, American-based manufacturers must continue to operate larger firms in order to cover the additional costs.[83] This means that as West European firms merge, establish partial plants, and thereby increase firm output, sales of United States firms will have to be expanded also. There is, too, the possibility that American firms will be obliged to shift some of their operations overseas in an attempt to offset higher salaries in the United States.

Overall Demand for Transmission Equipment

Although the sizes of transformers and circuit breakers have grown rapidly, the number of units ordered has not decreased, as has the number of turbines. Each time a new power station is installed, power transformers and circuit breakers are required for the station, for the extra high voltage transmission lines leading from the station, and at the switching stations and in the substations between the extra high and high voltage lines. (Refer to Figure 1 on Page 4.) In 1959, American transformer manufacturers shipped 591 power transformers with total combined ratings of 32,094 megavolt-amperes. By 1969, the number shipped had risen threefold, to 1,912 units totalling 122,612 megavolt-amperes. As long as the economic savings in generating electricity in large stations is sufficient to offset the cost of transporting electricity to load centres, the number of transformers and circuit breakers ordered will

[83]Labour—factory and salaried—represents approximately 48 per cent of the f.o.b. factory cost of power equipment; materials are about 44 per cent; and capital, about 8 per cent.

continue to grow. What does this mean for the international structure of the industry?[84]

The economies of large-scale power transformer production are limited. A 7,500-megavolt-ampere West European plant would have no discernible disadvantage *vis-à-vis* larger scale producers, as long as it had access to high voltage testing equipment, either the testing facilities of another manufacturer or a utility. The efficient size of a firm is larger, however. Minimum sales of 10,000 megavolt-amperes are necessary to cover expenditure on research and development. In the United States, firms must produce as much as 15,000 to 17,500 megavolt-amperes to be competitive.

TABLE 24
WORLD DEMAND AND PRODUCTION CAPACITY FOR POWER TRANSFORMERS
Annual average megavolt-amperes, 1970s

	EEC and EFTA	*USA and Canada*	*Japan*	*Other Countries*	*Total*
Home demand	82,000	170,000	38,000	40,000[a]	330,000
Capacity, 1975	139,000	200,000	70,000	n.a.	409,000
Available capacity	+57,000	+30,000	+32,000	(40,000)	+79,000

[a]This is import demand only.

Looking at the total demand facing West European, Japanese and North American producers (see Table 24), it appears that 25 to 30 plants could serve the world market in the 1970s. The assumptions underlying this statement are these: (a) Much of the growth in demand in developing countries will be satisfied by local industries, which are protected by their governments from outside competition. (b) The order volumes in Western Europe, Japan and Canada will grow at 8 per cent per year, as in the 1960s. Demand for the United

[84]The lack of data on circuit breaker demand or production capacity precludes a detailed analysis. At present, there are about 16 manufacturers, at least six of which are dependent on others for technology. Not more than three or four of the 16 were profitable in the late 1960s, even with protected home markets. Considering the higher product development costs for circuit breakers (see Pages 54 and 83); it is likely that six to eight firms could serve the market profitably.

States is based on the forecast by the National Electrical Manufacturers' Association in the United States of negligible growth during the 1970s.

At present, there are over 40 power transformer firms, some with more than one plant, in Western Europe, Japan and North America. Their combined capacity will be nearly 20 per cent greater than that required in 1975 by their domestic markets. Twenty-five to 30 plants could fill their home market needs and still have capacity to satisfy the import demand of developing countries.

These 25 to 30 plants are assumed to have capacities of 10,000 megavolt-amperes in Western Europe and Japan and 17,500 megavolt-amperes in the United States. These were the levels established in Chapters 5 to 7. The size range covered by each of these plants may not be the same. Since the need for smaller power transformers—unlike turbines—does not diminish as the size of transformer increases (see Page 99 and Figure 1), plants producing only the lower range of transformers can operate profitably. This has occurred with firms whose products remain one or two technological generations behind the most advanced.

If multiple-plant firms are operated, the number of firms would be less than 25 to 30. There are two main organisation possibilities. In the first case, manufacturers of a full range of power transformers might split production by size of transformer, with the dividing line somewhere between 25 and 50 megavolt-amperes. The trend towards this structure was indicated in Chapter 7 for the United States. West European firms also are heading in this direction as mergers occur. The second possibility for organising multi-plant firms, and this is not mutually exclusive of the first, is for several firms to operate two or more plants in different parts of the world. This would be the counterpart of turbine firms establishing full-scale service and repair facilities in export areas. Since economies of scale for transformer plants were found to be substantially less significant than for turbine plants, complete transformer manufacturing facilities could be constructed in the second location, rather than just partial plants. Again, the minimum size efficient transformer plant would be about 7,500 megavolt-amperes in Western Europe and double this in the United States.

The total number of multi-plant firms would depend on how many plants each firm operated. Since economies in research and development and parts of company overhead are almost limitless, unit costs should fall as a firm adds new plants. At some point, the dis-economies in managing multi-plant firms may increase sufficiently to offset the economies realised in research and development. Experience is currently insufficient to establish the optimum number of plants per firm when trade is unencumbered. For the analysis in the remainder of this chapter, a minimum of two plants per firm is assumed for the majority of manufacturers, so that the industry, under free trade, would comprise 15 to 18 multi-plant firms.

Under conditions of open trade, exports across the Atlantic or Pacific would occur in one of three situations, assuming no export subsidies or incentives. In one situation, there is a sudden increase in demand which cannot be met by domestic manufacturers. Transformers would be imported. In a second case, prices are increased, in America, for example. As long as the price rise is sufficient to allow overseas manufacturers to sell in the United States at full cost prices plus transportation, they would export. And finally, the third situation is that in which a producer's superior design would yield him a cost advantage that could offset transport costs.

The influence of transportation cost on trade in very heavy equipment is evident. Even now, for medium-size equipment, such as 50-megavolt-ampere transformers, transportation across the Atlantic is a large part of value. ASEA, unable to offset the cost of transporting smaller units to the United States, has agreed to build a plant in the United States jointly with RTE, an established American manufacturer of distribution transformers. ASEA believes it can offset the potentially high United States cost of production with its lighter, less expensive transformer design. ASEA is also building a Canadian plant for large power transformers.

Britain's transformer industry has argued that two-way trade in transformers is ludicrous, that the United Kingdom should not import transformers from the United States because the latter exports other types of electrical equipment to Britain.[85] Trade would be ludicrous when and if costs of production are equalised. Then, shipping large and heavy equipment both ways across the Atlantic, other than to fill peaks in demand, just adds to costs on both sides. Costs are not apt to be similar, however, until trade is opened

[85]*Electrical Review*, October 31, 1969, p. 633, and interview with BEAMA, London, January, 1970.

up and inefficient firms either merge with others or drop out of the industry.

Industry Structure and Barriers to Trade

In a climate of free and open trade, six to seven turbine producers, about 15 multi-plant transformer firms and from six to eight circuit breaker firms would maintain manufacturing facilities capable of meeting the average demand for their respective products in the areas in which they are located. Trade among industrialised areas would take place primarily in response to fluctuations in demand, and no manufacturer would be plagued by continuous excess capacity.

If trade continues to be restricted by purchasing policies that give preference to domestic firms, the amount of excess capacity in the world industry will increase as it has in the past. It will rise with the number and efficacy of protective devices. Two situations are considered—no trade and trade blocs.

Closed Domestic Markets

A situation in which domestic markets are closed to imported power equipment is similar to that which existed throughout the 1960s. Manufacturers in each country were required to have sufficient manufacturing capacity to meet peak demand. This resulted in chronic excess capacity. With each peak in demand, manufacturers invested in new plant and equipment, in anticipation of continuing prosperity and because, in times of peak sales, investment capital is available both from internal and external sources. By the second half of the 1960s, West European firms had production capacities 35 per cent and 100 per cent greater than their domestic demand for power transformers and for steam turbine-generators, respectively (see Table 1 on Page 7). Export demand was insufficient to support all of the surplus capacity, so merger activity intensified throughout Western Europe. The most notable characteristic of this activity was that it occurred along national lines, in accordance with the nationalistic preferences described in Chapter 3.

In the United Kingdom, 15 firms merged into four significant companies. West Germany saw the formation of joint turbine and transformer firms by its two electrical giants, AEG and Siemens. Similarly, the two main French companies, Alsthom and CGE, merged their heavy electrical equipment companies, and two French mechanical engineering companies, Rateau and SFAC, formed a joint turbine concern, Rateau-Schneider. One of the remaining French manufacturers, Jeumont-Schneider, has merger options under discussion. The French Government has refused to let Westinghouse acquire a controlling interest, has rebuffed a West German offer to buy the company, and is now even discarding the suggestion that CEM, the French subsidiary of Brown Boveri, take it over. The only solution acceptable to France seems to be the merger of Jeumont-Schneider into the CGE-Alsthom complex. In Switzerland, Brown Boveri bought-out Oerlikon Engineering and Escher Wyss. In Sweden, ASEA acquired a 100 per cent interest in Stal-Laval. Finally, in Italy, national mergers are still taking place.

The continuing accent on national industries was highlighted by the granting of new licences within EFTA and the EEC. Brown Boveri granted turbine licences to Stal-Laval, a Swedish manufacturer. Brown Boveri had already granted a licence to the Netherlands turbine producer, Rotterdamse Droogdomaatschappy. A second Dutch firm, Stork, concluded a turbine licensing agreement with Kraftwerk Union.

As long as nationalistic preferences persist, the build-up of excess capacity cannot be avoided. The outcome could be further mergers until each closed domestic market in Western Europe has only one turbine manufacturer and one or two transformer plants. When domestic demand slows, these domestic monopolists could seek to increase exports to open world markets. If adequate overseas business is not secured and survival of domestic firms is deemed to be in the national interest, then perhaps each of the West European countries would decide to support, by direct or indirect subsidy, its own domestic industry.

Trade Blocs

One alternative trade situation for the next decade is the formation of a larger European community comprising the present members of the EEC, and at least three of the EFTA members. Switzerland and Sweden may join the Community as associates, but because of their respective neutrality, they are less likely to become full members. If domestic utilities continue nationalistic purchasing policies, industry structure would be the same as that described in the previous section. Let us assume, therefore, that purchasing preferences are extended to all members of an enlarged

European Community, and denied to Japan and North America.

Within a few years after the removal of all trade barriers within the enlarged European Community, mergers would be expected to reduce the size of the industry. The extent to which excess capacity is reduced might, again, depend on trade between Community and non-Community countries.

Complete economic integration, including extensive mobility of capital and labour, absence of all internal trade barriers, and harmonised, or at least co-ordinated, fiscal and monetary policies, would tend to reduce differences in timing of national business cycles among West European countries. The lagged peaks of United States and West European cycles would most likely continue. If the only barriers to external trade are import duties comparable to or lower than those already in effect, the structure of the industry could approach that which is expected under conditions of free trade. The West European and American industries each would operate production capacities approximating the average demands in their respective regions. Peaks would be met by imports.

As the number and protectiveness of barriers to trade with outside countries increase, the West European firms could move farther from their most efficient position. The reason is that as the possibilities for imports are foreclosed, firms will tend to maintain production capacity closer to that required for peak demand. In downturns, exports will be sought.

The implication of these propositions concerning future industry structure is that as the possibilities for trade grow, the total volume of excess capacity in the industry will tend to decrease. The consequences with respect to profitability and survival may be determined by the reaction of United States firms to West European protectionism and by the commercial policies and behaviour used to support firms with unused capacity. These aspects of the outlook for the 1970s are discussed in Chapter 10.

10 COMMERCIAL POLICY AND PRACTICE

During the 1970s world capacity for producing heavy electrical equipment is expected to exceed the most optimistic projections of demand. The probable reactions of firms to the forecast excess supply capabilities is the subject of this chapter. It is proposed that the commercial reactions will be patterned after those of the past: High fixed costs will cause firms to seek to retain their shares of the market by offering low prices, especially in export markets. Efforts by national and international cartels to prevent deep price cuts are likely to be less and less successful. Finally, firms most weakened by poor sales and profits will be acquired by others. Each of these steps, evident throughout the history of the industry, is explored in succeeding sections.

Pricing Heavy Electrical Equipment

The importance of technical personnel and capital equipment in the manufacture of heavy electrical equipment results in fixed costs of production representing over 40 per cent of the total costs of production and sale of this equipment. A representative breakdown is given in Table 25. Many of the costs, particularly indirect labour and engineering staffs, are virtually fixed for different sizes of plants as well as for the range of production of a given plant.

Manufacturers seek to set prices based on full costs. First, variable costs are calculated per unit of output. Then overhead is added as a percentage of direct labour. To the total, profit is added.

$$\text{price} = \text{materials} + \text{direct labour} + \text{overhead} + \text{profit}.$$

The firm's objectives in its pricing policy, and its commercial policy as a whole, appear to be to retain a constant share of market and to achieve a target long-run rate of return on investment—frequently about 15 per cent, after taxes.

There appear to be three reasons for the selection of the long-run rate of return as a goal. First, the period of production ranges from 18 months to four years. This, in itself, urges producers to plan in at

TABLE 25
ANALYSIS OF PRICE BASE FOR HEAVY ELECTRICAL EQUIPMENT

	Full Cost	*Variable Cost*	*Fixed Cost*
Materials	50	50	—
Direct labour	13	7	6
Overhead	37	10	27
Shop cost	100	67	33
Drawing and engineering	5	—	5
Factory cost	105	67	38
Recovery for development	5	—	5
Special development	1	1	—
Commercial and administrative charges	22	—	22
Factory and internal commercial costs	133	68	65
External costs, such as freight and insurance	17	17	—
Total commercial cost	150	85	65

SOURCE: Typical breakdown compiled from discussions with several manufacturers.

least two-year periods. Second, fluctuations in demand are chronic and anticipated. Manufacturers are forced to consider average profits over the duration of a cycle. And third, capacity is added in discrete units and frequently written off rapidly. Depreciation charges, therefore, are very high when capital is first added and then decrease. Profits tend to move in the opposite direction.

During interim periods, usually one year, share of market is the area of concern. Where domestic markets are virtually closed to outsiders, and particularly in markets controlled by one major customer, manufacturers strive to divide the market according to their respective production capacities. Each firm then can cover approximately the same proportion of fixed costs, when total costs and prices are comparable. Efforts to enlarge market shares in home markets are more apt to be encountered where these markets have several customers and entry is not barred.

During periods of peak or stable demand, firms vary home market prices in response to changes in direct costs. This is so because such changes tend to be common across the industry. In several West

European countries, the manufacturers decide together when and by how much to vary prices when costs rise. In the United States, one firm will announce its intention to raise or lower prices and by what per cent. Whether or not others follow depends on the strength of demand.

Another means of including changes in direct costs in prices is to write sales contracts that include "escalation clauses". In such contracts, the final prices paid include a factor to cover increases in labour and material costs between the date of order and the date of delivery. Typical of price escalation formulae is that used by the EdF in France for power circuit breakers. Escalation is given for 90 per cent of the rise in costs. The index is weighted 52 per cent labour and 38 per cent materials. Generally, United States utilities will not accept escalation and require firm prices.

Price increases during periods of rising demand also may reflect increasing profits. The extent to which this can occur will depend on conditions of entry. For all the reasons cited in Chapters 5 and 7, it is highly unlikely that a new firm will enter the industry. A new entrant into the market generally would have to be from another country. One recent example of entry is into the United States. After a period of losses in the early 1960s, American manufacturers faced very strong demand in the second half of the 1960s. Their response was to raise prices, in part to offset rising costs, but also to recoup their losses and increase their rates of return. Power transformer and steam turbine prices both increased about 35 per cent between 1963 and 1968. Power equipment customers turned to West European manufacturers and invited them to bid for United States contracts. In the five years between 1963 and 1968, import orders went from 0.5 per cent to 9.1 per cent of total United States turbine-generator orders, from 2.3 per cent to 15.1 per cent of total power transformer orders, and from 0.3 per cent to 7.1 per cent of total power circuit breaker orders. Increases in United States manufacturers' prices were slowed.

Similar examples in Western Europe are rare. One case, the CEGB purchase of two Canadian transformers, was mentioned in Chapter 3. The EdF also has imported transformers when price discipline has been required.

These examples are applicable to periods of stable or rising demand when profit rate and market share objectives should be compatible. The more interesting situation, and one more relevant from the point of view of the 1970s, is that in which growth in demand falls short of the expansion in production capacity. In this case, which is considered next, all firms cannot hope to meet their profit goals, and the maintenance, then enlargement, of market share becomes most critical.

Commercial Reaction to Decline in Orders

For the reasons described in Chapter 8, total demand facing the heavy electrical equipment industry changes imperceptibly with a change in price of equipment. At the same time, the demand facing any one firm can be highly responsive to price changes, unless utility purchasers seek to allocate orders to insure a particular industry structure. Thus, when there is a drop in total demand, each firm is more concerned with its rivals' reactions than its customers', because any firm that fails to follow a price decrease will lose its share of the market. Also, if a firm raises its price and has no followers, it will suffer the same fate.

When demand falls, firms often yield to the temptation to cut prices and take larger shares of the market in order to keep their factories full. The competition may be subtle at first and entail offering a more efficient machine or improved credit terms for the same price. Since efficiency and credit are evaluated in comparing prices, these offers act as indirect price cuts.

If the fall in demand is severe enough, an all-out price war may occur, with firms cutting prices down to materials and labour—that is, variable or direct costs of production. This has occurred frequently in the past. A prominent example was the 1954–55 "White Sale" of electrical apparatus in the United States. Prices were cut as much as 40 per cent. Another example was the destructive competition in Italy in 1964–65, during which the Italian firms were operating at less than half of capacity. Similarly, in the United Kingdom, when domestic demand fell to less than one-third of the 1963–64 demand, prices of low and medium voltage transformers fell 25 to 30 per cent.

Price Floor

The intensity of price competition and the depth of price cuts are affected by the high proportion of fixed costs of production. (See Table 25.) Fixed costs are incurred whatever the level of factory output, even if it is zero. If no part of fixed costs is covered by price, it is still advantageous to take orders if only to continue to utilise fixed factory facilities and engineering and administrative talent. This fact, that is, the need to cover high fixed costs, encourages firms to compete for orders even when prices fall 20 to 30 per cent. The minimum price level, therefore, tends to be the total of variable costs for each unit produced. Firms can minimise losses by accepting orders at prices that at least cover variable costs.

In such harsh competition, the largest-scale plants may have an advantage. Whereas the total cost of production for various size plants may be the same, the relative proportions contributed by fixed and variable costs may differ. The larger-scale plant may use more capital and less labour, so that a greater proportion of its costs are fixed. When price cutting occurs, the large firm can cut its prices further. This is illustrated in the following chart, showing cost curves for two different scale plants, large (l) and small (s).

FIGURE 7
FIXED COSTS AND SCALE OF PLANT
(Dollars per unit of output)

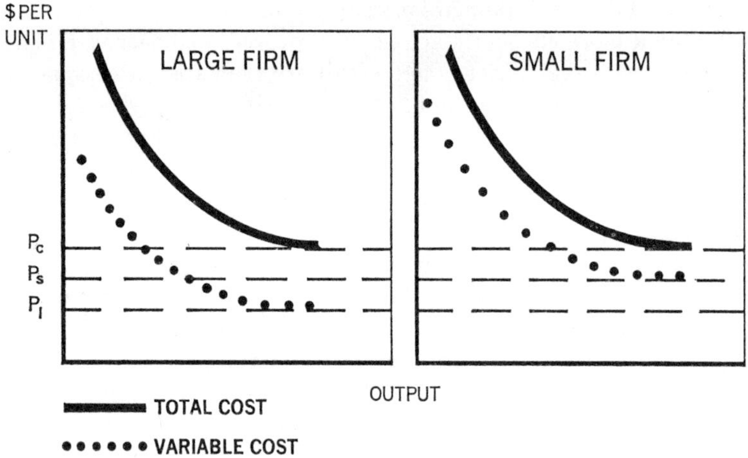

At a price, P_c, both firms cover their total costs and realise the same profit margin. Then prices fall. The lowest price the smaller firm can afford to offer is P_s, its minimum average variable cost. At this level, all variable costs are covered, but no contribution is made to fixed costs. At any price below P_s, variable costs would not be covered, so the smaller firms would be losing less money by not producing. The larger firm can continue to reduce prices to P_1, its minimum average variable cost. This can give the more capital-intensive firm an advantage in severe price competition. The advantage is increased if larger, more capital-intensive firms have lower total costs. It is also true that the firm with the highest proportion of fixed costs is also under the greatest pressure to cut prices to seek orders because the cost of under-utilised capacity is greater.

The possible advantage for large firms was recognised in the United States in the early 1960s. In response to a rapid decline in American utility orders, the price index for turbine-generators fell more than 30 per cent between August of 1959 and early 1963 when they were at an all-time low. During the years of sparse orders, many United States companies operated at 50 to 60 per cent of capacity. Those least able to finance manufacture at marginal cost prices were the small specialist manufacturers. When prices hit bottom, General Electric and Westinghouse were virtually the only two manufacturers taking orders. For this reason, the United States Department of Justice claimed that selling at "unreasonably low prices" was an unfair trade practice designed "to injure, suppress or stifle competition or tend to create a monopoly".[86]

The Justice Department, particularly interested in preserving the number of competitors, was stating that it is an unfair trade practice to cut prices below the variable cost of the least mechanised firm. The irony of this demand is that the consent decree was the outcome of anti-trust cases in which the same firms had been indicted for attempting to maintain and increase prices. The implication is that without restrictions on price competition only the largest firms may survive in an industry characterised by surplus manufacturing capacity.

Price Discrimination

Preferable to lowering domestic prices to obtain orders to fill factories is a vigorous search for export sales. Often, when home markets are insulated from outside competition, exports can be priced at whatever level is required to take an order. Such prices

[86]Proposed consent decree for defendants in the 1960 Electrical Equipment cases: This first proposal, for switchgear assemblies, was to be a prototype for the other types of electrical equipment. "Unreasonably low" was not defined. This was a significant factor in General Electric's refusal to sign the consent decree.

may be below domestic price levels. This pricing phenomenon, called price discrimination, is particularly applicable to the sale of heavy electrical equipment because of the unusually high fixed costs of production and the prevalence of closed domestic markets.

Look at the British market in the mid-1960s for an example of incentive to discriminate. After a boom ordering period in the early 1960s, domestic orders collapsed in the United Kingdom. As is indicated in Table 26, total demand for power transformers fell 73 per cent within three years. Five manufacturers received no orders in 1965–66, whereas at least two had received substantial orders in both prior years.

The first response of British manufacturers appeared to be more serious bidding in overseas markets. In the United States, for example, from mid-1962 through 1964, British firms submitted 33 bids on contracts awarded by federal power agencies. In only eight cases were these bids within 20 per cent of the award winning prices. By contrast, from 1965 through 1967, all but ten of 51 bids to these same utilities were within 20 per cent, and most were within 10 per cent, of the winning price.[87]

TABLE 26
CEGB ORDERS (IN MVA) FOR TRANSMISSION TRANSFORMERS

Companies	*1963–64*	*1964–65*	*1965–66*
Associated Electrical Industries	7,500	3,330	90
Bonar Long	660	730	—
Bruce Peebles	4,545	2,980	—
Brush Electrical	700	630	1,230
Crompton Parkinson	3,885	2,700	—
English Electric	4,440	2,940	720
Ferranti	4,250	4,515	2,300
Fuller Electric	3,960	2,620	1,770
General Electric	1,890	780	690
Hackbridge and Hewittic	4,200	3,270	3,500
Johnson and Phillips	375	255	—
C. A. Parsons	7,950	3,030	2,170
Yorkshire Electric Transformers	1,455	840	—
Total	45,810	28,620	12,470

SOURCE: Central Electricity Generating Board, London.

[87]Tabulation and analysis of bids on power transformer contracts awarded by Bonneville Power Administration, Bureau of Reclamation, and Tennessee Valley Authority from 1961 through 1969.

The prices bid by British manufacturers for United States orders in 1965 and 1966 are claimed to have been 25 to 45 per cent below those at which they sold comparable equipment in their home market—Britain.[88] The success of the British export drive in the United States and other markets is seen in the fact that exports rose from a low of 6.6 per cent of power transformer shipments in the mid-1960s to 20 per cent by 1968 and were expected to be even higher thereafter.

Export orders were not sufficient, however, to offset the effects of reduced domestic demand. By 1967, price competition broke out in the United Kingdom, first, for smaller transformers, and later, for larger ones. This, in addition to the devaluation of the pound sterling, served to reduce the differential between home and export prices. Since all prices were low, however, British power equipment manufacturers reported poor profits in the late 1960s. In October, 1970, hearings on a price and market sharing agreement, with the CEGB a party, were undertaken. A major purpose of the arrangement was to prevent further price deterioration in the face of continuing excess capacity.

International Price Agreements

In addition to domestic price agreements, manufacturers have attempted to eliminate or reduce the severe price competition that often results from their drives to obtain export orders by entering into international price agreements. The first restrictions on international competition were built into licensing agreements which carried the obligation not to sell in markets where there was another manufacturer using the same patents or licence. Consequently, there was little or no competition throughout the 1920s, according to the United States Federal Trade Commission's 1948 *Report on International Electrical Equipment Cartels*.

With the business collapse of the 1930s, pressure developed to export to non-exclusive areas—that is, those not covered by licence agreements. Competition in these areas became fierce and it was decided to formulate an agreement to divide export markets. The International Notification and Compensation Agreement (INCA)

[88] The pricing data used in this example has been under investigation in the United States under the Anti-dumping Act of 1921. As of this writing, July, 1971, no decision has been reached.

was signed on December 13, 1930, in the Paris offices of International General Electric.

Eight companies joined the INCA cartel: AEG and Siemens of West Germany; British Thompson-Houston, English Electric, GEC and Metropolitan-Vickers of the United Kingdom; Brown Boveri of Switzerland; and International General Electric and Westinghouse Electric International of the United States. They agreed to notify the association's secretary of all inquiries for bids in countries outside Western Europe, USSR, Canada, United States, Japan, and the French and Spanish colonies. The secretary would determine whose turn it was to take the order and the price which the winner was to bid. All other members bid above this price. The winner of an award was required to make a payment into a "compensation fund" held by the secretary of the INCA. The payment was designed to help defray the costs of preparing tenders by the losers. The members stated that such a procedure helped to maintain "the competitive power of each".

The probable effect of the agreement was to aid firms that otherwise would have failed due to lack of "competitive power". Some firms had not been obtaining orders, either because they lacked technical ability or because they were less efficient. These manufacturers probably would have closed down in the depression of the 1930s. The agreement to share the export business most likely sustained marginal firms throughout this period.

In order to facilitate their participation in the INCA, American firms, as did their West European counterparts, formed a domestic cartel, the Electrical Apparatus Export Association (EAEA). The objective was to divide the United States industry's share of world export business—allocated to it by the INCA—among American manufacturers.[89] If the association had been used solely to compete in export markets, it would have been legal under the provisions of the Webb-Pomerene Act. The United States Administration claimed, however, that the EAEA was created for the sole purpose of facilitating membership in an international cartel, the purpose of which was to set prices and allocate market shares. This is unlawful under the Sherman Act of 1890, and on March 17, 1947, United States firms were required to dissolve the EAEA and to end their membership in the INCA.

[89]*Report on International Equipment Cartels* (Washington: Federal Trade Commission, 1948), p. 8.

Shortly thereafter a new international agreement was established under the auspices of the International Electrical Association (IEA). Members now include almost all West European producers of heavy electrical equipment and exclude most Canadian firms and United States firms. As did the INCA, the IEA agreements are designed to eliminate the effects of "cut-throat competition" on sales to countries in which there are no domestic producing industries.

The methods used to reduce price competition differ for the various power equipment products possibly to cater to differences in numbers of manufacturers and contracts. For power transformers, there are relatively many manufacturers as well as numerous contracts, so the procedures are quite explicit. Excerpts from Transformer Agreement P(H)C illustrate its operation. Section 4 reads as follows:

> Every Member who obtains an order for plant shall forthwith submit to the Secretary in such form and with such particulars as he may require the following information:
>
> (i) the price at which the order has been placed by the ultimate producer—inclusive of (where payable):
>
> agency fees;
> charges for complete erection on site;
>
> but exclusive of:
>
> all financing costs and charges;
> all costs and charges (other than those included in the Appendices) payable in respect of spares, tools, special tests;
> all local costs and charges payable beyond the point of entry into the country of destination in respect of such items as customs duties, local taxes, local insurance, local transport;
>
> (ii) in terms of delivery (for example, c.i.f., f.o.b.) and point of delivery stipulated in respect of the price in (i) above;
>
> (iii) wherever ascertainable, the reference price of the plant ordered.

The "reference price" is calculated from extensive and comprehensive price lists contained in Appendices I and II of the agreement. If the price obtained by an IEA member is less than the reference price, he must contribute to the association pool an amount set forth in Section 5. The pool is distributed annually to members according to the total kilovolt-ampere capacity of transformers ordered from each.

The penalties become progressively stiffer as the amount increases by which the order price deviates from the agreed price.[90] It is anticipated that at least one company will find it more profitable to take orders at penalty prices rather than lose a contract, especially if domestic demand is slow and its factory under-utilised. It is hoped, however, that the increasing severity of penalties will deter deep price cutting and, thereby, raise the price floor.

A similar philosophy appears to underlie the turbine agreement. Here, the fewness of orders in non-producer countries permits the manufacturers to meet every time an invitation to bid is announced. Individual agreements are made for each order and cover efficiency, credit terms and extent of supply, as well as price. Penalty schedules are also established for prices bid below the agreed prices. In practice, the deepest price cuts are on the smaller size turbines for which competition is the greatest. This is evident in a comparison of desired and actual prices for turbine-generators shown in Figure 8. For sets in the 200-megawatt range, prices have frequently been below total cost.

If a manufacturer cuts turbine prices severely, a special meeting might be held by the IEA after the contract is awarded. At this time, it is possible that additional penalties could be assessed.

The effect of the penalties appears to be that they act as an addition to variable costs. In this case, the impact of the IEA agreements is probably to raise the price floor by an amount equal to the size of the penalty. A second benefit of the association meetings is the diffusion of market information. The secretary sends quarterly reports to all members containing the total number of inquiries and the number of orders reported by each member and each non-member. Annual reports divide orders taken by territories, and then by recipient, technical specifications, and award price as a percentage of reference price. In addition, meetings provide a forum for

[90]Section 5a of Agreement P(H)C reads:

(i) where the order price is not less than 90 per cent of the reference price, the pool shall be calculated at the rate of 0.25 per cent of the f.o.b. reference price per 1.0 per cent by which the order price is less than the reference price;

(ii) where the order price is less than 90 per cent of the reference price, the pool shall be 2.5 per cent of the f.o.b. reference price plus an additional amount calculated at the rate of 0.75 per cent of the f.o.b. reference price per 1.0 per cent by which the order price is less than 90 per cent of the reference price.

FIGURE 8
ACTUAL VS. DESIRED PRICES
(*Turbine-Generator, Condenser and Feed Heaters*)

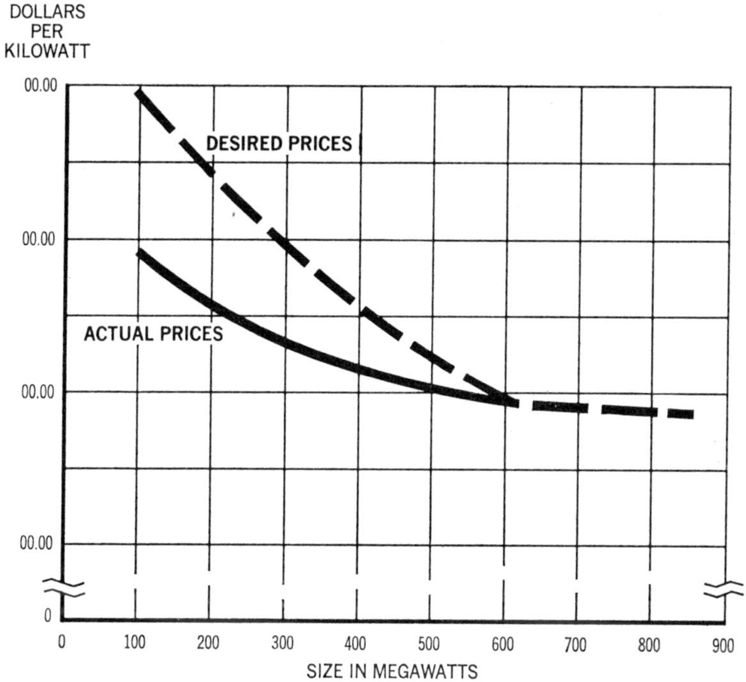

SOURCE: Unpublished reports and bids.

discussing technical specifications and terms of sale, as well as price.

The impact of the IEA is difficult to assess. With little or no planned market allocation, firms still compete for orders and sell at less than full profit prices. At the same time, the industry's potential for fierce price competition may be harnessed by the diffusion of current market information. Also difficult to assess is the impact in the North American markets. Here, the most severe competition is likely to be found in the 1970s, yet this area is specifically excluded from the agreements.[91]

[91]It would appear that the terms of the agreements could influence sales in the United States and Canada. Certainly, there is no reason to expect manufacturers to refrain from mentioning North America in their meetings or from applying reference prices to their bids.

Competition in North America

To understand which of the past commercial policies will operate in the 1970s and how they will work to change industry structure, it is useful to look first towards the North American markets, which already have begun to open to trade. (See the discussion on Pages 22–24 and 108.)

The Canadian and United States markets are particularly attractive due to (a) their large size, (b) the diversity of requirements, and (c) their demand for equipment that is among the most advanced used anywhere in the world. The popularity of these markets is illustrated by bidding on a power transformer contract for the Bureau of Reclamation (Invitation No. DS-6620). On March 26, 1968, the bureau opened bids for four 250-megavolt-ampere, 345/230-kilovolt auto-transformers. Eighteen bids were received from manufacturers in eight countries—five British, three Japanese, two American, two Italian, two Swiss, one Austrian, one Canadian and one French.

The situation in turbines is tending to be even more competitive. As indicated in Chapter 7, United States utilities are the only ones ordering a significant number of very large turbine-generators. Manufacturers that have adapted their plants to produce these large units are forced to sell in the United States. The result is that seven firms have announced their goals of capturing a combined total of 150 per cent of the expected American market demand in the 1970s.

Protectionism

Severe and successful foreign competition has forced American firms to re-evaluate their policies on trade. The two largest manufacturers are multi-national companies with large stakes in world trade and investment. Their recent actions have been these: (a) An anti-dumping complaint was instituted against West European and Japanese transformer manufacturers, similar to the complaint filed by Canadian transformer producers. (b) The possibility that the United States could impose quotas on imported power equipment has been explored. (c) The United States Administration has been petitioned to help American firms gain access to the major foreign markets, and if this cannot be accomplished, to close the public part of the American market to competitors from countries whose power equipment markets are closed to the United States—France, Italy, Britain, Japan, Switzerland and possibly West Germany.

If firms are successful in closing all or part of the American and Canadian markets, a rapid increase in mergers in Western Europe is likely to ensue. Even if some firms, such as Rockwell-Parsons, were to accelerate plans to build manufacturing facilities in the United States, this would tend only to increase world production capacity, and thereby hasten the pressure to reduce capacity.

Protectionist action in the United States, even if successful, consumes at least three years in hearings and debates. It is unlikely that the situation in power equipment markets will remain static for that long. The more probable occurrence is the onset of direct competition by United States firms.

Price and Non-Price Competition

Competition among American firms in the United States power equipment market in the past six or seven years has been along non-price lines, such as service, reliability and performance characteristics. The prices charged by each company appear on printed price lists, and changes in discounts from the lists are announced publicly. Given the strength of demand, American manufacturers' prices have moved upward.

West European manufacturers entered the United States market in the late 1960s, first, by offering prices 20 to 40 per cent below the domestic level. This tended to dampen the rise in American prices. As competition stiffened in the American market, particularly among West European firms, indirect price cuts in the form of better credit terms, exclusion of escalation clauses, and improved machine efficiency, have been offered. The most prevalent have been liberal credit terms.

The high cost of capital in the United States has affected American utilities that are trying to float new issues to finance power station construction. West European producers have found that they may gain an advantage in bidding in the United States by offering American utilities credit rates at below those prevailing. Here, two examples will illustrate the way in which this occurs.

As interest rates have risen in the United States, the Tennessee Valley Authority has agreed to higher prices for deferred payment privileges. In 1967, for example, Delle-Alsthom quoted two prices to TVA for 500-kilovolt air blast circuit breakers—$235,000 for payment on delivery and $245,000 for deferred payment.[92] The terms of payment, as accepted by TVA, called for 30 per cent to be paid 30 days after delivery and 70 per cent 24 months after installation, maintenance and repair. TVA paid only 3 per cent per year for this capital, an obvious advantage. In 1969, Delle raised this to 4 per cent ($250,000 price with deferred payment on Contract 69C-619222). This was still a big saving for TVA, considering the high rates of interest that prevailed in the United States market.

A second example of an advantage realised through offering low interest rates is that of English Electric's bid to the San Diego Gas and Electric and the Southern California Edison companies. English Electric's award-winning bid for two 1,100-megawatt nuclear turbines was backed by British bank financing of 80 per cent of the contract price of $47m at an interest rate of 6.72 per cent per year.[93] This represents a saving of $4.3m, equivalent to a price discount of nearly 10 per cent, to the California utilities.

The difference between the 6.72 per cent rate and the market rate of interest in Britain was subsidised by the British Government under their export credit programme. Although such credit is usually reserved for sales to developing countries (see Chapter 4), it was used in this case by a British company as a means of non-price competition.

Barring immediate success of protectionist moves, a possible move for United States firms might be to begin cutting prices to meet foreign competition. American firms would have to lower prices at least 10 to 20 per cent to meet current import levels that are from 20 to 30 per cent below domestic prices. It is generally believed that most United States utilities are willing to extend a 5 to 10 per cent preference to domestic firms. Another cut might be necessary if West European firms lowered their prices in order to maintain their shares of the American market.

The results of such competition are likely to be influenced by these variables: (a) The volume of demand in West European markets: a sudden and unplanned spurt in orders in Western Europe could relieve the pressure in North America. (b) Relative rates of inflation: the more rapid rise in costs in the United States certainly im-

[92]TVA Contracts 68P5–7331 (October 13, 1967); 68C5–61502 (October 20, 1967); and 68C5–61804 (October 12, 1968).

[93]Will B. Johnstone, Vice-President (Finance), San Diego Gas and Electric Company, as reported in *The Wall Street Journal*, New York, August 21, 1970.

paired the cost position of American firms in the second half of the 1960s. There is now some question as to the level of variable costs of United States firms compared to West European firms and, therefore, how low each could cut prices. (c) Sources of capital: sales at less than full cost for an extended period require subsidies from some source. European firms operating from closed domestic markets can use higher returns on home sales to help defray the cost of price discrimination in North America. United States firms and West European firms with inadequate home market business eventually might be dependent on product divisions other than power equipment to carry them. Here the salient considerations are the willingness and ability of each company to carry its power equipment division.

It appears reasonable to assume that American firms will not close down their power equipment divisions. If vigorous price cutting is necessary to retain market shares, American firms will cut prices. What can be anticipated, however, is that West Europeans will win some share of the United States market. There are only two turbine-generator manufacturers, now, while the market can support three. It is possible that after a price war, General Electric and Westinghouse could end up with two-thirds of the market, the remaining third being supplied by imports.

What also might be expected is that not all West European firms will endure in the United States market and the longer they are shut out—by protectionist measures or by severe competition—the more difficult it will be to survive at all.

Competition in Western Europe

The most important force retarding the concentration of the heavy electrical industry in Western Europe has been the nationalistic procurement policies in individual countries. As demand for equipment has changed from many small power stations to fewer large ones, the subsequent economies in the development and production of power equipment have caused the number of firms that can survive to decrease. In accordance with nationalistic preferences, however, mergers during the 1960s have occurred along national lines.

As national companies have been created, any pretence at or possibility of effective competition within each country has been reduced or eliminated. The EdF has attempted to compensate for the lack of price competition by using prices in other countries as a guide in negotiations with French firms. Poor technical performance is penalised by reducing the manufacturer's share of market. West German utilities have also used market share to stimulate competition. Since the AEG-Siemens merger, the shares of the West German market held by Brown Boveri-Mannheim and M·A·N appear to have been augmented. The CEGB in England and Wales has yet to devise a means of obtaining competition from few firms. As of this writing, they are entering into new pricing arrangements with British manufacturers.

West European utilities are finding themselves in positions similar to United States utilities with respect to competition. With only one or two domestic firms and no import competition, each West European country is a sellers' market. In the United States, where there is price leadership through published price lists, power equipment customers found the only way they could gain a measure of purchasing power was to invite West European manufacturers to bid in the United States. The outlook for Western Europe is a similar breakdown of national purchasing preferences if utilities want the most efficient and least costly equipment and do not decide the national interest is better serviced by supporting and, in effect, subsidising domestic industries.

In summary, excess production capacity in the 1970s, combined with the competitive situation in the United States market, should serve to hasten further concentration of the heavy electrical equipment industry. While a few protected markets may persist, firms will be forced to compete in many markets, particularly North America. The result may be that severe competition will eliminate those firms that are financially unable or unwilling to improve efficiency and, at the same time, secure capital to keep up with the requirements for continuous research and development expenditures.

11 OUTLOOK FOR CHANGE

The structure of the heavy electrical engineering industry is strongly influenced by technological requirements, economies in production and barriers to international trade. Each of these helps to determine the number and size of manufacturers in the industry. If the barriers to trade could now be removed, the optimum industry structure would consist of relatively few multinational firms. Production economies would dictate the minimum size plant; and technological requirements, the minimum size firm.

TABLE 27
OPTIMUM INTERNATIONAL INDUSTRY STRUCTURE: 1970s

	Annual firm output[a]	*Number of firms*[b]
Turbines (100 MW and larger)	10,000 MW	6 or 7
Transformers 10 MVA and larger)	12,000 MVA	15 to 18
Circuit breakers (30 KV and higher) Number of equivalent 220-KV units	200 units	6 to 8

[a]It is emphasised that these numbers are not absolutes and minima are higher in high-labour cost countries.
[b]Single-plant firms for turbines and circuit breakers; multi-plant firms for transformers.

Set forth in Table 27 above is an optimum industry structure under conditions of free trade. Under such conditions, the firms would all be multinational and would operate internationally, according to demand and transportation costs.

The merits of such an industry structure have been recognised by the EEC Commission which has advocated that the West European section of the industry should be restructured into two or, at the most, three multinational companies.[94] To accomplish this, the

[94]"Restructuring the Community's Electrical Engineering Industry", Commission of the European Communities, Brussels, April 22, 1970.

Commission urges: (a) the gradual opening of Community markets by co-ordination of the purchasing policies of the governments and electricity producers of member countries; (b) the promotion of multinational European groups which could reconcile efficiency and competition while helping to open up the market; and (c) steps to ensure that agreements, both government and private, in the electro-mechanical and nuclear fields do not impede the achievement of the first two aims.

Since the conclusion of the Kennedy Round negotiations in 1967, the difficulties of attaining an optimum industry structure worldwide have enlarged due to the development of protectionist trends on both sides of the Atlantic. The prospects, then, for a countervailing initiative in the direction of free trade in heavy electrical equipment cannot be said to be bright. If the United States succeeds in holding to a liberal trade course, the objectives of any new international trade negotiations under the General Agreement on Tariffs and Trade—whatever form they take—are likely to include the elimination of substantially all industrial tariffs.[95] More importantly, they are likely to be concerned with non-tariff distortions of international competition, besides such other contentious issues as the operations of multinational corporations and trade in temperate-zone agricultural products.

As observed in Chapter 3, tariffs are *de minimus* in international trade in heavy electrical equipment when compared with two categories of non-tariff protection, namely public procurement policies and technical standards. Thus the attention now being given to ways of overcoming non-tariff barriers to trade is of considerable relevance to the heavy electrical engineering industry. Since there is no suitable method for measuring their distorting effect, non-tariff devices do not lend themselves to bargaining on a reciprocal basis, in the way that tariffs have done in the past. Instead they are likely to be confronted on an *ad hoc* basis. It may be possible to negotiate the elimination of certain non-tariff restrictions. An elaboration of existing rules may be enough in other

[95]For a discussion of optional negotiating strategies for further freeing world trade, see Hugh Corbet, "Trade Strategy for an Open World", in Corbet *et al.*, *Trade Strategy and the Asian-Pacific Region* (London: Allen and Unwin, 1971; and Toronto: University of Toronto Press, 1971), pp. 15–17.

cases.[96] For still others it should be possible to work out rules of competition—alternatively described as "codes of good conduct", "rules of behaviour" and so on.[97]

In their review of non-tariff barriers affecting trade between developed countries, Gerard and Victoria Curzon, of the University of Geneva's Graduate Institute of International Studies, concluded that public procurement policies designed to discourage imports are "probably not very easy to abolish", if only because they are practised so widely.[98] That general conclusion is borne out in this paper by the examination of the political factors influencing trade in power plant. (Professor and Mrs. Curzon are more optimistic about the prospects for dealing with public procurement policies that encourage exports.) Even if progress is slow at first, however, the international development of the heavy electrical engineering industry would be greatly aided by appropriate modification of public procurement policies according to an agreed set of guidelines.

It is a finding of this study that, because of the economics of the heavy electrical equipment industry, pressure to formulate appropriate procurement guidelines will come first from the firms in the industry. The beginnings of a breakthrough may very well start with those companies that are now multinational and are trying to operate internationally as well.

(1) Brown Boveri, which has been multinational since its establishment, has extended its policy with the conclusion of a licensing agreement for steam turbines with Stal-Laval, ASEA's turbine division, and the construction of a repair and partial manufacturing plant in the United States. The relations among Brown Boveri companies no longer cover simply technical exchange, but also include co-ordinated ordering and production for export. It remains

[96]The protectionist pressures which have recently developed in the United States were partly motivated by what are seen to be the "unfair trade practices" of other countries. Rules of competition, however, are a feature of the Stockholm Convention, the "constitution" of EFTA, as they are of the EEC's constitution, the Treaty of Rome. They have been a feature, too, of contemporary proposals for a free trade treaty among developed countries, providing an institutional framework within which might be pursued a broad strategy for further freeing world trade.

[97]This approach is discussed in Curzon and Curzon, *Hidden Barriers to International Trade* (London: Thames Essay, Trade Policy Research Centre, 1970) and in Robert E. Baldwin, *Nontariff Distortions of International Trade* (Washington: Brookings Institution, 1970; and London: Allen and Unwin, 1971).

[98]Curzon and Curzon, *Hidden Barriers to International Trade*, *op. cit.*, pp. 15–17.

for the managements of the various divisions to accept further co-operation for domestic production and specialisation.

(2) Kraftwerk Union's links with Allis Chalmers of the United States and Fuji Electric of Japan have instituted a second multinational tie that includes co-ordinated production. Expansion of the proposed collaboration on power stations for export between Kraftwerk Union and the Nuclear Power Group of Britain could provide Parsons, a member of the group, with added strength in world markets. Until now, Parsons has relied heavily on its affiliation with James Howden and Parsons of Canada and on the advantage of Commonwealth preference (see Table 4 above) to export generating equipment. Parsons' attempted joint venture in the United States was doomed to fail. The venture could contribute nothing to restructuring the world industry or to opening trade since North American Rockwell, itself, was a newcomer to the market with no particular strengths for Parsons.

(3) A third multinational group, comprising Rateau-Schneider of France, M·A·N of West Germany, Breda of Italy and La Meuse of Belgium, is dissolving (at the time of writing) because no one of these firms has the facilities or financial strength to support the group. Rateau was acquired by Alsthom of France in 1971.

(4) The Westinghouse attempts to form a multinational organisation among its Italian, Belgian and Spanish companies and Japanese licensee are incomplete. Significantly, these affiliates all appear to be comparatively weak and domestically dependent.

(5) General Electric has yet to try to draw its licensees closer in co-operative production. The company's main connection is still the technology given to two Japanese affiliates as well as its Italian and French licensees.

One major firm, GEC, remains unattached.

Groups: Basis for Free Trade

A crucial characteristic of most of these groups of multinational firms is that they bridge the trade blocs of the 1960s—the EEC, EFTA, Japan and North America. In this respect they provide an excellent basis for free trade among industrialised countries because the firms have substantial economic incentives to urge removal of trade barriers.

Firms operating internationally would find it less costly to build equipment to common standards than to limit competition on a national level through the continuation of diverse technical requirements. These firms, therefore, could be expected to advocate the removal of prohibitive and restrictive technical standards and specifications, and before they become more widespread a problem than they are at present.

The longer multinational firms co-operate, the clearer the advantages of division of labour and the opportunities for specialisation on a world-wide basis should become. While France, for example, might be required to concede its turbine industry, it could become the centre of circuit breaker production. In order to facilitate such specialisation, the international industry would press for the end of residual tariffs and non-tariff devices.

Isolation No Answer

The prerequisite for more rapid harmonisation and specialisation is recognition by the CEGB and the EdF that the interests of Britain and France may be better served by accepting the international nature of heavy electrical equipment manufacture than by defending national prestige. (By the nature of their technically dependent industries, ENEL in Italy and the Japanese utilities will be forced to accept the dictates of the world industry.) EdF has taken one step by urging the restructuring of the French industry into two firms with strong international ties. It has not yet gone the next step and accepted specialisation by these firms. The CEGB has made no similar concessions.

Significantly, British manufacturers have not discouraged an isolationist policy. Their Commonwealth preference has been eroded by the Kennedy Round agreement, and they have no important ties on the Continent, in North America or in Japan. Yet only Parsons has recognised the need to join a multinational group. (Ferranti has limited ties with Legnano, its Italian licensee.) On their own, British manufacturers of heavy electrical equipment will have neither the economic nor the market power of their multinational competitors. If the long and rich backlog of British engineering expertise and manufacturing skills are to be preserved and utilised, it is imperative that Britain initiate action to open power equipment markets by starting with its own. Such action would encourage its manufacturers to become multinational.

The situation British firms face will be the same whether or not the United Kingdom joins the EEC. Their competitors in EFTA—

primarily ASEA and Brown Boveri—have already made moves towards internationalisation without formal entry into an enlarged Common Market. The formation of an Atlantic free trade association between Canada, the United States, Britain and any or no other EFTA country would include manufacturing affiliates of Brown Boveri, ASEA and Kraftwerk Union. Any free trade treaty among all the major trading countries would include all manufacturers. There is therefore no way in which British firms can avoid competition within the United Kingdom with larger multinational concerns if it wants trade access to other industrialised countries.

It is the conclusion of this study that the economics of developing and producing heavy electrical equipment, particularly large steam turbine-generators, will eventually transcend the problems of national pride as manifested in public procurement policies. Through the formation of international firms, free trade will be promoted and consumers of electric power will obtain energy produced by the most reliable and advanced equipment—and at the lowest possible cost.

Part II

CHEMICALS UNDER FREE TRADE

by

Duncan Burn

1 THE FREE TRADE TREATY PROPOSALS

This study sets out to assess how the formation of a multilateral free trade association embracing North America and Western Europe, and possibly Japan, would affect the British chemical industry. When the study was first projected it was envisaged that the free trade treaty that was being advocated would initially include only North America and the countries of the European Free Trade Association (EFTA) and perhaps Japan.[1] For the United Kingdom this provided an alternative to membership of the European Economic Community (EEC).[2] Some of those who supported the free trade treaty option thought it offered Britain greater economic gains than the EEC, while involving only very limited political commitments; and in any event, it seemed that British entry into the EEC might remain blocked. The free trade treaty proposal, even in its most limited sense, was always thought of though as a step which was consistent with, and would lead towards, a broader free trade association embracing all developed countries, including EEC. When the United Kingdom and other EFTA countries entered again into negotiations with the EEC, interest and discussion focussed increasingly on the broader strategy.

In this study the possible impacts on the chemical industry of these various Atlantic free trade options, narrow and broad, are considered and the probable effects for the British chemical industry of joining the EEC are compared with those of joining a limited free trade arrangement initiated by North Atlantic countries (and hence NAFTA) from which the EEC abstains. The data needed to analyse all these three options were of course in most particulars identical. For simplicity the term NAFTA is used throughout this paper to refer to the limited area that does not include the EEC.
include the EEC.

[1]See *A New Trade Strategy for Canada and the United States* (Washington and Montreal: Canadian-American Committee, 1966).

[2]Although the European Economic Community (EEC), the European Atomic Energy Commission (Euratom) and the European Coal and Steel Community (ECSC) have merged into the European Communities, the more familiar abbreviation, the EEC, will be used in this paper when referring to the signatory countries to the Treaty of Rome.

Within a free trade association, whatever its extent, all trade between member countries would be freed from import duties. But the member countries would retain duties on imports from countries outside the association and, exercising full sovereignty, the members would determine these duties individually. In this respect a free trade area differs from a customs union like the EEC which has a common external tariff. In a free trade area the external tariffs of member countries do not have to be uniform and, as in EFTA, some member states may have much lower tariffs than others. Under a free trade treaty which embraced all of North America, all of Western Europe and Japan, this would have much less significance than in an association of lesser extent.

Preferences in Free Trade Schemes

Wherever import duties are eliminated between countries with different tariff levels, exporters from the low-tariff countries will inevitably gain more in duty reductions than those in high-tariff countries, whether in a free trade area or a customs union. But whereas in a customs union exporters from one member country to another member country have the same preference over exporters from third countries to the same market, in a free trade area those exporting from a low-tariff member country have a higher preference against "third country" exporters in the high-tariff member countries than those exporting from the high-tariff member countries have in those with low external tariffs. In EFTA, for instance, the United Kingdom manufacturers have a much smaller preferential advantage in competing with American chemical manufacturers in Scandinavia than the Scandinavians have in the United Kingdom. Furthermore, the differences in external tariffs give rise to the problems of "origin". If duties on particular commodities are much lower in one member country it might be profitable to import these commodities into a low-tariff member country and then send them as "area" products to a high-tariff country. Or an import which pays a low duty may be used by manufacturers in a low-duty member country in goods subsequently exported to a high-duty member country. For these and analogous problems origin rules have been developed in EFTA.[3] Obviously these problems are

[3]They were discussed earlier in the paper under the Atlantic Trade Study Programme by Hans Liesner, *Atlantic Harmonisation* (London: Atlantic Trade Study, Trade Policy Research Centre, 1968), pp. 48-50.

likely to be less important the wider the extent of the free trade area: in an area which included all Western Europe, all North America and Japan they would have little significance.

The formation of a free trade association, whatever its scope, should, like a customs union, increase trade and accelerate the growth of industry within the association as a whole for two reasons. First, firms in each member country would be able to compete on more even terms with firms in the other member countries. As a result, those with relatively low costs, whether from natural advantages or acquired skills, would be able to increase sales partly by attracting new buyers by lower prices and partly by taking business from firms with higher costs. This should give scope for large-scale methods and more specialisation and in general raise efficiency—including that of the higher cost producers. Secondly, all firms in member countries would compete in the market on preferential terms against firms from outside the association, whose imports to member countries would still be subject to import duties. Increases of sales by firms in member countries arising from this preference would also give scope for larger scale methods, more specialisation, lower costs and greater efficiency—even though some firms inside the association who benefit from preference may be less efficient than the firms outside the association from whom they take trade.

The extent of the preferences enjoyed by firms in member countries in competing with firms from outside depends upon the level of the external tariffs. The higher the tariff, the higher the preferences. Thus in effect in a free trade association those firms which are located in the low-tariff member countries have a greater preference to enjoy over firms in non-member countries in selling in the high-tariff member countries than do the firms in the high-tariff member countries have when selling in the low-tariff member markets. This particular differentiation does not occur in a customs union.

Acceleration of industrial expansion following the creation of a free trade association will not be uniform in all regions or all industries. With the distorting influence of tariffs partly removed, and with new preferences established, comparative production and transport costs would play a more determinant part; and changes in the geographical distribution of industries would be expected. This would not be identical in character for all industries.

To identify the type of change which formation of a particular area of free trade is likely to bring about is easy; to assess the probable extent of changes in particular industries and regions is much more difficult. This is what must be attempted in forecasting the effect which the formation of NAFTA, or a broader free trade association, would have on a particular industry—in this case the chemical industry. We would like to know not only the direction but the degree of change to be expected in imports and exports, outputs, regional distribution of production, rates of expansion and innovation, and the extent of specialisation. We want also to know the probable timing and sequences of changes, since obviously they will not all take place overnight when the association is created. It is only possible to answer these questions in very general terms.

It would be necessary also to consider what minimum of associated changes in laws and administrative practices, other than the tariffs which distort competition, might be found necessary to make a free trade association acceptable. However, it could only be appropriate in a study concerned with one industry to deal in detail with such laws and practices where they affect this one industry mainly or exclusively. In the chemical industry this situation is extremely rare; so that in this study while the main associated changes needed will be referred to in the conclusions and summarised, they will not be discussed in detail.

Outline of Study

Before these questions can be asked it is necessary to provide a brief survey of the chemical industry in the main producing countries which may be affected. This is done in Chapter 2. The next step is to establish the size of the duty reductions which the formation of a free trade area of broad or limited scope would bring in chemicals, which is done in Chapter 3. Chapter 4 sets out to show what light is shed by experience in the last decade on the extent to which such reductions may be expected to change the flow of trade. Chapter 5 compares prices and price movements in the United States, Britain and West Germany. Chapter 6, necessarily much the longest, examines the trends of comparative advantage, the probable movements of factor costs in different countries. This provides the basis for the main conclusions of the study set out in Chapter 7.

2 SCOPE, PRODUCTS, MARKETS, GROWTH AND EXPORTS

The definition of the chemical industry adopted for this study is the one used by the Organisation for Economic Co-operation and Development (OECD), with the addition of synthetic fibre production. It includes (1) the manufacture of basic or "general" chemicals, organic and inorganic, and (2) the manufacture of what may be called more finished products: industrial gases, plastic materials and resins, synthetic fibres and rubbers, explosives, fertilisers, pesticides, dyes, pigments, paints, printing ink, drugs, pure chemicals, detergents, toiletries, adhesives and polishes and photographic chemicals. Many of the basic or "general" chemicals, possibly from 20 to 25 per cent of sales in the United Kingdom,[4] are used in making the more finished products in the other sectors. Most are produced as joint products.

Size of Industries

The sectors which make the more finished products are for many purposes reasonably regarded as industries on their own. Their production and marketing problems are very diverse. But large "chemical" firms invariably participate in several of these sectors; the largest firms in the main industrial countries participate in all or nearly all of them. There are clearly good reasons for this[5] and it provides one of the strongest arguments for treating the group of activities as "one" industry. On many points, however, it is necessary to look at particular sectors separately.

The size of the industry (under its wide definition) in the countries with which this study is mainly concerned is shown in Table 1.

Of the sectors of the industry, the basic or general chemical sector is not only essentially the key sector; it is also much the largest. This is shown in Table 2.

[4]Based on *Input-Output Tables for the United Kingdom, 1954* (London: HM Stationery Office, 1961) and *Reports on the Census of Production*, HM Stationery Office, London (various years).

[5]See, for example, W. B. Reddaway, "The Chemical Industry", in Duncan Burn (ed.), *The Structure of British Industry* (Cambridge: Cambridge University Press, for the National Institute of Economic and Social Research, 1958).

TABLE 1

OUTPUT AND EMPLOYMENT IN THE CHEMICAL INDUSTRY[a] IN 1968

	Net Output of the Chemical Industry $m	*Net Output of Chem. Ind. as % of Gross National Product (1967)*	*Total Employment in the Chemical Industry ('000)*
United States	25,760[b]	2.9	1,043
West Germany	5,475	4.5	479
Japan	4,780	3.2	417
United Kingdom	3,335	3.3	410
France	2,895	2.5	265
Italy	2,540	3.3	240
Canada	1,209[b]	2.0	70

[a]*The Chemical Industry*, 1968-9 (Paris: OECD Secretariat, 1970). The United Kingdom figures, however, are taken from the *Provisional Census of Production* which was published after the OECD figures were compiled. (*Board of Trade Journal*, London, December 31, 1969.) The United Kingdom exchange rate is £1 = $2.4.

[b]Calculated on the assumption that the ratio of net to gross output was the same in 1968 as in 1967.

The industry is based on several major (and many minor) raw materials. The early heavy chemical industry was based primarily on salt, sulphur, limestone, phosphate rock, potash and coal. Coal was first a fuel, but later became an important raw material for hydrocarbons and organic chemicals. Other raw materials—ilmenite and borates for instance—have become important for particular sectors. The major development since World War II has been the increasing use on a vast scale of mineral oil refinery products, some liquid, some gaseous, and natural gases as raw materials for the manufacture of organic chemicals, in which the greatest expansion in the industry has occurred. The petrochemical industry has made many old products by new "routes", new series of processes using the new raw materials as "feedstock", but even more it has introduced many new products, and thus typifies the two-fold pattern of innovation in the industry: (1) the development of new processes, which are cheaper or permit more expansion, for making known products; and (2) the development of new products which may be substitutes for known materials or may have properties hitherto not available.

TABLE 2

NET OUTPUTS OF MAIN SECTORS OF UNITED KINGDOM AND UNITED STATES CHEMICAL INDUSTRIES[a]
(in $m)

	United States (1967)	*United Kingdom (1968)*
Basic chemicals	7,175	1,058
Pharmaceutical preparations and chemicals	4,035	526
Manmade fibres	1,754	403
Toilet preparations	1,743	163
Plastic materials	1,657	468[b]
Soap and detergents	1,428	163
Paints	1,330	220
Polishes[c]	654	48
Fertilisers	636	140
Agricultural chemicals[c] (other than fertilisers)	610	72
Dyes and pigments[d]	531	167
Synthetic rubber	399	[e]
Explosives	375	161
Adhesives and gelatine	211	51
Printing ink	166	41

[a]Based on the most recent Census of Manufactures (United States) and Census of Production (United Kingdom) figures available. The *gross* output of the whole United States chemical group of industries was almost 10 per cent higher in 1968 than in 1967.
[b]Includes synthetic rubber (probably about $45m).
[c]"Polishes" are combined in the United States statistics with "sanitation goods" which in the United Kingdom statistics are included with "formulated pesticides" (that is, agricultural chemicals).
[d]The United States figure is an estimate; organic dyes and pigments are included with cyclic intermediates and crudes. Gross outputs of dyes are given separately, but not net output.
[e]Included in plastic materials.

The number of substantially different products (excluding merely different grades and qualities of single products) made by the industry runs into thousands and the number is constantly growing. Only a few, such as the bulk acids and alkalies, ammonia, carbide, chlorine, benzine, glycerine, acetylene, aniline, and PVC, are familiar household words. The products listed in the Census of Production and in tariff schedules, especially for general chemicals, are mostly meaningless to the layman. Many of the products are relatively new. Among these, the expanding ranges of plastics, synthetic rubbers and man-made fibres are conspicuous. But this gives a misleadingly simple view. Firms in the chemical industry often claim that half the products they sell have been newly introduced in, say, the last five or ten years.

All the sectors, except those making drugs, detergents and toiletries, produce for the most part raw materials or processing materials for other industries. A substantial part of the output of many chemical firms is sold to other chemical firms for further processing. Of the products of firms in the British chemical industry which were sold outside the "industry"—in its widest sense—in 1963, almost 60 per cent went as intermediates to other industries. About 20 per cent was exported. Only the remaining 20 per cent was in the form of products for the "final buyer", individual consumers or public authorities.[6]

This means of course that one cannot study the possible effect of a free trade association on the British chemical industry without taking a view of its likely impact on several other industries. The industries with the largest consumption of chemicals in the United Kingdom in the mid-1950s were (in order of importance) agriculture, building and construction, motor car making, textile manufacture and finishing, electrical engineering, paper and board, the rubber industries, mechanical engineering and radio and television. These took about two-thirds of the total sales of chemical intermediates in 1954. The pattern was largely similar in the United States and West Germany.

Growth Record

All these consuming industries, except agriculture and textiles, have expanded faster than industry in general. In all of them, including textiles and agriculture, and in many other manufactures, the use of chemicals is becoming more intense. Synthetic materials are being used increasingly as substitutes for older materials, either (1) because the supply of older materials has lessened or cannot be rapidly and cheaply expanded, or (2) because newly developed materials are relatively cheap to make or use, are more precisely adaptable and predictable in performance, or have other useful properties which older materials lack. New chemical treatments

[6] *National Income and Expenditure, 1967* (London: HM Stationery Office, 1968), pp. 24-25. (Input-output tables for 1963—the most recent available at the time of this study.)

are giving new qualities to old products: for example (to refer to two which affect familiar consumption goods) crease and fire resistance to textiles, greater durability to razor blades. In the sectors whose product is in forms used for final consumption, it is found that in their markets, too, the use of chemicals is more intensive: synthetic drugs are used increasingly in medicine; synthetic detergents have taken much of the market for soap; synthetic materials have replaced vegetable oils in paint, and so on.

As a result of these market conditions, the chemical industry is everywhere a "growth" industry. Its output has been increasing in the major industrial countries—with occasional interludes in some and with the notable exception of Japan—at a rate higher (often much higher) than the rate at which the aggregate output of all industries has been increasing, as Table 3 shows.

The ratio between the growth indices for the chemical industry and all industry varies considerably from country to country and it has varied much from year to year in individual countries. It is not a stable function. It varies greatly also for different sectors of the

TABLE 3

INCREASES IN OUTPUT OF (A) CHEMICAL INDUSTRIES (B) ALL INDUSTRIES IN MAIN PRODUCING COUNTRIES, 1958-68

	A Production Index for Chemical Industries in 1968 1958 = 100	*B Production Index for All Industries in 1968 1958 = 100*	*A ÷ B*
United States	220 (7½)[a]	175 (5¼)[a]	1.3
West Germany	294 (10¼)	177 (5¼)	1.7
Japan	393 (13¼)	422 (14)	0.9[b]
United Kingdom	197 (6½)	139 (3¼)	1.4
France	247 (8½)	162 (4½)	1.5
Italy	344 (11½)	227 (7¾)	1.5
Canada	189 (6)	180 (5½)	1.1

SOURCE[a]: *The Chemical Industry 1968–69* (Paris: OECD Secretariat, 1970) and the *National Institute Economic Review*, London (various issues).

[a]Figures in brackets are annual percentages growth rates.
[b]For the period 1963-68 the ratio was unity: chemical industry output in 1968 was 191 (1963 = 100), output of all industry was 190.

chemical industry; in some, the rate of growth has been below that of "all industries". Table 4 shows the position in the British industry.

Within the sectors of slow overall growth, outputs of some particular products have grown remarkably: synthetic detergents, for example, in the last sector shown in Table 4.

TABLE 4

PRODUCTION INDICES FOR SECTORS IN THE UNITED KINGDOM CHEMICAL INDUSTRY, 1965-67
(1958 = 100)

	1965	*1966*	*1967*
All industries	133	133	139
Chemical industry	163	169	177
Index for			
Plastic materials	241	255	278
Organic chemicals	232	246	262
Pharmaceutical preparations	187	206	220
Photographic supplies	158	169	172
Toilet preparations	154	161	169
Other general chemicals[a]	147	151	158
Dyestuffs	171	158	151
Fertilisers	133	129	139
Paint, varnish, etc.	124	125	128
Soaps, detergents, glycerine	106	107	108

[a]Other, that is, than organic chemicals.

The chemical industry has had the highest rates of growth normally where industry in general has had the highest rates, as Table 3 shows. This does not mean, however, that growth in the chemical industry has been completely determined by the rate of growth of other industries. The position is one of interdependence, the growth of industry in general depending greatly on the provision of new products by the chemical industry and the reduction of the price of chemicals; that is, on the quality of the chemical industry itself.

Rapid growth in the output of chemicals has been accompanied by an even faster growth in international trade in chemicals. The major producing countries have greatly increased their trade with each other as is shown in Table 5. Their imports of chemicals have grown faster than their exports although all except Canada, Italy and Belgium have had a substantial net export. Net exports grew only slowly in the United Kingdom and France, but rapidly in West Germany, the United States, the Netherlands and Switzerland.

TABLE 5

INTERNATIONAL TRADE IN CHEMICALS IN 1968[a]

	Exports		*Imports*		*Net Exports*	
	$m	*Average annual increase 1958-68* %	$m	*Average annual increase 1958-68* %	$m	*Average annual increase 1958-68* %
United States	3,289	8¼	1,135	11½	2,154	7½
West Germany	3,114	11½	1,192	14¼	2,022	10½
United Kingdom[b]	1,438	6	997	10½	441	1
France	1,361	7¼	1,148	16	222	1
Netherlands	1,108	13½	754	12¾	354	15½
Switzerland	811	11	452	12¼	358	9½
Japan	805		690		115	
Italy	780	15	770	15¾	10	
Belgium	636	9½	609	10¼	27	
Canada	408	5¼	616	6½	− 208	−10¼

[a]Based on OECD Reports in *The Chemical Industry* for 1958 and 1968-9. The tables used cover only SITC5, and so exclude synthetic rubber, photographic chemicals, man-made fibres.

[b]The United Kingdom figures are affected by devaluation. The British figures in 1967 were: Exports 1,449 (7¾ per cent); Imports, 978 (12¾ per cent); Net Exports 470 (1¾ per cent).

Export Performance

The United States remained the largest exporter in 1968, though not in every sector; but the increase in the West German industry's exports was more significant as an index of current competitive strength. Exports equalled nearly 35 per cent of the West German industry's total output in 1968, whereas American exports were not quite 8 per cent of turnover. The British firms exported 21 per cent of turnover, roughly midway between the United States and West German figures, but the British net export grew relatively slowly.[7]

West German exporters had a new preferential advantage in these years through membership of the EEC (where the progressive elimination of tariff barriers between member states was completed in 1967), and the United Kingdom had a similar but smaller new preference through membership of EFTA. Table 6 shows that in both instances exports increased exceptionally in the new preference areas.

TABLE 6

EXPORTS IN 1967 BY AREA OF DESTINATION WITH PERCENTAGE GROWTH, 1961-67

	Total Exports[a]		*Exports to* *EEC Countries*		*EFTA Countries*		*Remainder*	
	$m	*% growth 1961-7*	*$m*	*% growth 1961-7*	*$m*	*% growth 1961-7*	*$m*	*% growth 1961-7*
West Germany	2,705	95	855	139	633	72	1,217	85
United Kingdom	1,360	48	261	72	189	97	910	36

[a]In this table synthetic rubber, fibres and photographic materials are not included.

British exports to the EEC were also expanding much faster than British exports to markets outside the two European blocs. One can reasonably argue that part of West Germany's additional exports to her EEC partners may be attributed to the exceptionally rapid general expansion of the EEC economies. But in markets outside the two blocs, West German exports grew much faster than British exports. In 1961 the total of British exports to these markets was slightly above the West German total; in 1967, the West German was one-third higher. It would be wrong to attribute the major part of West German export success in these years to new preferences.

[7]Exports as percentages of turnover for the other countries in Table 4 were: Switzerland, 80; Belgium, 62; the Netherlands, 55; France, 21; Canada, 21; Italy, 13; and Japan, 9.

For the analysis of trade prospects under different tariff conditions the scale and trend of trade in individual sectors of the chemical industry is important as well as the aggregate. Broad features of this are given in Table 7 for the United States, Britain and West Germany.

TABLE 7

EXPORTS AND IMPORTS OF CHEMICALS BY SECTOR[a] IN 1967
($m)

	United States		*West Germany*		*United Kingdom*	
	Exports	*Imports*	*Exports*	*Imports*	*Exports*	*Imports*
Organic chemicals	749	219	613	249	200	263
Plastic materials	473	60	544	187	260	179
Inorganic chemicals	299	216	248		118	109
Medicinals and pharmaceuticals	288	72	288	83	216	44
Fertilisers	232	142	154	29	23	73
Photographic materials	180	49	89	63	61	36
Synthetic rubber	170	21	89	43	61	36
Soap, detergents, toiletries	140	69	111	65	120	46
Pigments, paints	74	6	128	30	94	21
Radioactive materials, etc.	51	16	12	31	7	5
Synthetic dyes	32	37	195	22	63	21

[a]Excludes fibres. Changes since 1967 are examined later.

Some points stand out immediately: (1) the much greater exports, gross and net, of the United States and West Germany in basic chemicals and plastic materials; (2) the British net import of fertilisers; (3) the high level of pharmaceutical exports from all three countries; (4) Britain's relative strength in soap, detergents and toiletries; (5) the smallness of the United States export of dyes and West Germany's strength in this area; (6) the higher proportionate importance of exports of more finished products for the United Kingdom and (to a less extent) for West Germany. But the figures have to be studied in relation to growth rates and the performance of other countries in some trades, and this, together with a study of most recent trends, comes in later sections.

The proportion of American exports sold in Western Europe was much greater than the proportion of West European exports sold in the United States. The United States had a large export balance in its trade in chemicals with Western Europe. The figures for 1966-8, with details for the main sectors, showing the rapid growth in these years, are in Table 8.

Exports of Technology

The United States firms not only had the largest aggregate exports. They also licensed manufacturers abroad extensively to make many of their products or use some of their processes. They manufactured extensively overseas, either in wholly-owned subsidiaries or in companies owned jointly with indigenous companies. Naturally, these companies helped to spread the use of American technology.

There are no statistics of American chemical firms' transactions in licences. The annual expenditures on plant and equipment by their foreign affiliates rose from $237m in 1960 to $863m in 1965 and $1,472m in 1968. The increase in the most recent years was most rapid in the EEC, where the annual investment averaged $400m in 1967 and 1968. The sales of the United States' foreign affiliates in the chemical and allied industries rose from $3,290m in 1960 to $6,857m in 1965 and approximately $9,000m in 1968—almost three times the direct export of chemicals from the United States. Moreover, the foreign affiliates had large exports themselves.[8] They also imported semi-products (or "intermediates") from the United States which they processed and they sometimes act as agencies for some of the parent-firm products; but on this there are no published statistics.[9]

[8]In 1963 exports by United States affiliates in Europe, whose total sales were $2,040m, were $450m. Figures up to 1963-64 are published in John Backman, *Studies in Chemical Economics* (Washington: Manufacturing Chemists Association, 1965). For later, less complete figures, see *Hearings on Foreign Trade and Tariff Proposals* (Washington: US Government Printing Office, for the Ways and Means Committee, House of Representatives, United States Congress, 1968), pp. 547-48 (June 5-10, 1968).

[9]Backman, *op. cit.*, pp. 47-48. George Hegeman (of A. D. Little Inc.), "Impact of Tariffs, Trade and Investment on the US and European Balances of Payments", Paper at a Seminar on Management of Marketing in the Chemical Industry, Frankfurt, June 27, 1967, said that about 20 per cent of US chemical companies' exports were to affiliates abroad.

TABLE 8

UNITED STATES TRADE IN CHEMICALS WITH OECD EUROPE, 1966-68

($ m)

	Imports from Europe			*Exports to Europe*			*Net Export/ (+) Import (—)*
	1966	*1967*	*1968*	*1966*	*1967*	*1968*	*1968*
Organic chemicals	147.3	130.4	185.2	310.3	313.5	416.1	230.9 +
Inorganic chemicals	58.0	59.3	63.4	79.9	78.2	95.7	32.3 +
Dyes, pigments, paints, etc.	43.1	43.2	58.3	25.9	27.8	36.6	21.7 —
Pharmaceuticals	40.7	37.8	44.8	71.3	79.7	94.2	59.4 +
Toilet preparations	38.7	39.1	42.8	21.0	21.7	24.5	18.3 —
Soaps and detergents	3.8	4.5	5.4	20.7	21.5	25.5	20.1 +
Plastic materials	37.6	36.7	60.2	206.5	197.1	256.4	196.2 +
Synthetic rubber	3.2	1.8	3.8	86.2	85.5	88.7	84.9 +
Photographic supplies	40.5	43.2	50.4	72.0	82.6	97.9	47.5 +
Total (including products not included above)	463.7	454.8	570.9	1072.0	1081.9	1352.9	782.0 +

The American industry was the largest exporter of technology, enterprise and capital in these ways. But firms in other large producing countries—for example, West Germany, the United Kingdom, Switzerland—did the same things on a smaller scale. There are no comprehensive statistics. For large individual firms information on some of the activities is often available. Imperial Chemical Industries (ICI), for example, spent £52m ($146m) on capital projects abroad in 1966, and the expenditure dropped to £34m in 1968 but rose to £48m ($115m) in 1969, and a further expenditure of £76m had been sanctioned. The sales of ICI's overseas affiliates were almost £460m ($1,100m) in 1969 compared with the firm's export sales from its United Kingdom plants of £244m ($526m). The large West German and Swiss companies also have invested heavily in plants outside their homeland; but for the West German firms direct exports have been proportionately more important in comparison with the sales of their foreign subsidiaries than for ICI.

A significant recent development has been the decision of the three major West German chemical firms to build large plants near Antwerp and Rotterdam. Sites in these areas have also been selected and developed by American and British firms. ICI, for instance, has a plant near Rotterdam. For them the location is predominantly important as giving access to the EEC market. But for the West German firms, Bayer, Badische-Anilin and Hoechst, the location is designed to maximise their advantage from the EEC for trade not only in Western Europe but overseas. These deep-water plants have the advantage of the two major ports for raw material imports and for exporting overseas; they have a good labour supply, and access to relatively cheap gas. The sites are large. Bayer, for instance, could build on its site at Antwerp a plant as large as their main plant at Leverkusen near Cologne where some 35,000 people are employed; and might do so, it has been said, within ten years. Investment in the chemical industry in Holland and Belgium, by all firms, Dutch, Belgian, West German, American and British, was collectively as large in 1967 as the investment in the United Kingdom in the same year, and was equal to 56 per cent of the net output of the chemical firms in the two countries (compared with 21 per cent in the United Kingdom). It was the most important locational development in the West European industry.

Statistics on licensing have been published for both the United

Kingdom and West Germany.[10] Those for West Germany are fuller and more up-to-date. The British chemical industry had a favourable balance in 1965—expenditure on foreign licences was $21m, receipts from foreign firms with licences to use United Kingdom processes were $46m. In West Germany the position was reversed; receipts in 1969 were $45m, expenditure $85m. The United Kingdom spent more, however, on United States patents ($14.5m) than the United States spent on the United Kingdom licences ($11.9m). So did the West German industry and the total of transactions was higher. The balance of the West German industry's transactions with its six main customers or suppliers is shown in Table 9.

TABLE 9

WEST GERMAN LICENSING TRANSACTIONS: 1969
($m)

	Receipts	*Expenditures*
United Kingdom	2.6	11.9
United States	14.4	33.2
Switzerland	2.2	23.2
Japan	2.7	0.8
France	2.8	7.3
Italy	4.7	1.9

Many of the processes in the chemical industry require costly and sophisticated plant which has to operate at extremes of high or low temperatures and pressures and has to process materials that are often highly corrosive. There are thus great hazards. Modern technologies increase what is demanded of plant. They depend upon and respond to great advances in chemical engineering skills and in the development of new constructional materials, particularly metals—and of new controlling and monitoring devices, largely electronic. The provision of this plant has itself become the

[10]The British figures are in *Statistics of Science and Technology* (London: HM Stationery Office, 1968). The oil company figures were not included: several have chemical plants attached to their refineries. The West German figures come from the *Monthly Report of the Deutsche Bundesbank*, May, 1970, pp. 23-30. The Bundesbank points out that the statistics are not a complete account of transactions in technical know-how. Know-how which is transferred when enterprises are sold, or plants are erected, is not included. Nor are transfers under mutual exchange arrangements.

object of an extensive international trade, which again is dominated by American firms. Many constructors in other countries participate in this trade; but it is estimated that United States contractors had two-thirds or more by value of the export orders for chemical process plant between 1960-66.[11] This is another important factor in spreading technology—especially American technology.

[11]Cf. Christopher Freeman, "Chemical Process Plant: Innovation and the World Market", *National Institute Economic Review*, National Institute for Economic and Social Research, London, August, 1968, p. 32 *et seq*.

3 TARIFFS BEFORE AND AFTER FREE TRADE

The first step is to establish both the scale of the tariffs on chemical imports which a multilateral free trade association—broad or narrow in scope—would remove and the scale of those which would remain against imports from non-member countries and in countries outside the area, particularly those in EEC, if the association were geographically limited in scope (as in the original free trade treaty concept).

This cannot be done either simply or precisely. The tariff schedules are very complex. Duties are prescribed for an enormous number of individual products. The American duties are often specific (cents per pound) or part specific and part *ad valorem*. To turn them into percentages of value exclusively, which is necessary for comparisons, involves attributing a price. Prices, however, are not always known, not always uniform and not stable over a run of years. Hence conversions are approximations. Where American duties are *ad valorem* the value on which the duty is calculated by the customs authorities is normally the f.o.b. invoice value of the goods imported (most countries take the higher c.i.f. value). But for "benzenoid" chemicals it is the price which American manufacturers would charge—the American Selling Price (ASP). This is sometimes notional, where United States manufacturers do not in fact make the product, and it is often, though not invariably, considerably above the f.o.b. value, which may be below the home price in the exporting country. So in effect it often raises the duty although it can also occasionally lower it.[12]

Finally, the Kennedy Round of tariff negotiations resulted in large reductions of duty whose full extent is not yet determined. Some reductions were unconditional and either have been made, or

[12]According to the calculations by H. G. Grubel and Harry G. Johnson, "Nominal Tariff Rates and United States Valuation Practices: Two Case Studies", *The Review of Economics and Statistics*, Harvard Department of Economics, Cambridge, May, 1967, pp. 138-42, the nominal tariff rate for a sample of benzenoid chemicals was from 23.9 per cent to 26.4 per cent (according to the estimating method), but the real rate was from 40.9 per cent to 53.2 per cent. ASP raised the real duty above the nominal by from 71 to 102 per cent.

are being made, on a phased programme which ends in 1972. But other reductions are conditional on the removal of ASP to which the United States Congress had not agreed by March, 1971.

Hence in Table 10 two columns are given for the duty levels in the United States, Britain and EEC, those which will persist if ASP is kept, those which will be reached if ASP is abandoned. Duty levels are given separately for the main sectors of the chemical industry because there are significant differences between sectors. United States duties which are wholly or partly specific are given as *ad valorem* percentages based mainly on 1966 prices. American duties on benzenoid chemicals, based on ASP, are based on calculations given by the President's Special Representative for Trade Negotiations.[13] Duty levels are mainly given in terms of ranges, because there are great variations within particular sectors. Averages, on whatever basis they are made, are unsatisfactory and conceal differences within some sectors which must be taken into account. When it seems appropriate one or more figures of a range are underlined as a guide to relative importance. These are the duties in force for a large number of important products. Below, then, in Table 10, is the position. A few salient conclusions may be drawn at this point.

(1) Few import duties on chemicals will be very high if the ASP package is accepted by the United States (or indeed if it is not: the importance of ASP is exaggerated by all the disputants). Many will be very low, 5 per cent or below. Nevertheless, duties of 10 per cent and more will still be charged on a wide range of products, including some in most sectors. In some sectors the general level in some countries will be substantially over 10 per cent. Therefore the removal of duties, whether between all the "Atlantic" countries (including Japan) or between some of them, would be likely to have significant effects on trade flows and the structure of the chemical industry.

(2) The duty levels in the United States will be higher after the Kennedy Round agreement has been implemented than in Britain in most sectors, although slightly less than the table suggests because American figures are on f.o.b. prices, the

[13] *Foreign Trade and Tariff Proposals*, Part 2 (Washington: US Government Printing Office, for the Ways and Means Committee, House of Representatives, United States Congress, 1968), pp. 528 and 530-46 (June 5 and 10, 1968). Most of the figures were from US Tariff Commission reports.

TABLE 10 IMPORT DUTIES AFTER THE KENNEDY ROUND (AS PERCENTAGES OF VALUE)[a]

I—after unconditional reductions (ASP not abolished) II—conditional on removal of ASP (ASP abolished)

	United States		*United Kingdom*		*EEC*		*Canada*	*Japan*
	I[a]	II	I	II	I	II		
Inorganic chemicals	0–*5*–14	0–*5*–14	*8*–17½	*5*–12½	2½–13½	1½–11	0–15 0–10[c]	5–10
Organic chemicals	9–20–27[b]	9–20	0–*23*	0–*12½*	2½–18½	1½–12½	0–15 0–10[c]	2½–12½
Plastic materials	12[b]	12	*10*–23	6½–*10*	7–16–18½	5½–*10*–11½	7½–17½ 7½–17½[c]	*10*–17½
Dyes	17–49[b]	30	8–16	5–*15*	7–*12*–17	4½–*10*–13½	0–15 0–10[c]	5–*12½*
Paints	4–7½	4–7½	10½–12½	7½	12	7½	15 10[c]	7½–*10*–12½
Drugs	9–*23*–53[b]	9–*20*–27	7–23	5–12½	8–17½	6–12	15 0–15[c]	7½–15
Synthetic rubber	3	3	4	4	*0–5*	0–5	0	0–7½
Synthetic fibres	7½–25	7½–25	13	13	9	9	15–16	7½–12½
Fertilisers	0	0	0–*12½*–23	0–7½–12½	0–8	0–6	0	*0*–10
Pesticides	15–24[b]	15–20	8	5	6½–9½	4–6	0–7½ 0[c]	10
Soap and detergents	3–15[b]	3–11	13–20	10–12½	12	7½	15–17½ 10–15[c]	10–17½
Photographic chemicals	5–30[b]	5–14–20	12	7½	9½	6	15 10[c]	10

[a]In the United States the value taken is the f.o.b. price (except where ASP applies); in other countries it is the c.i.f. price. Hence a given percentage rate of duty in this table is in fact lower in the United States than in the other countries since freight and insurance add from below 5 to 20 per cent and more to prices—least for high value products. (See Pages 89-92.)

[b]Sectors marked by an asterisk include some benzenoid products. The sectors where the importance of ASP is greatest are dyes, drugs and organic chemicals. [c]British Preferential Tariff.

Italic figures indicate rates which within a wide range apply to a large number of important products.

British figures on c.i.f. prices. The position varies much between sectors. Dyes will have a protection of 30 per cent in the United States if ASP goes—more for many dyes than if it does not go. Most drugs, photographic chemicals and pesticides will have about 20 per cent protection; organic chemicals from 9 to 20 per cent (some large volume products indeed much more); plastic materials about 12 per cent; inorganics from 4 to 6 per cent, synthetic rubber 3 per cent, fertilisers nothing.

In dyes, drugs, photographic chemicals and pesticides the British duty level will clearly be much lower than the United States. It may be slightly lower in organics. There is little difference in inorganic chemicals. In rubber and fertilisers, the United Kingdom figure is higher.

If, therefore, duties were wholly removed in the chemical trade between the United States and Britain the advantage derived by the British industry from this would be significantly greater in a few sectors—notably dyes and drugs—than the corresponding advantage to the American chemical producer.

(3) If a limited free trade association which excluded the EEC were formed, the level of American duties would in several sectors be sufficiently high to give the British chemical industry a substantial advantage in this respect over EEC countries in exporting to the United States.

(4) The external tariff of the EEC after the Kennedy Round agreement has been implemented will be markedly lower in most sectors of the chemical industry than either the American or British tariffs. Thus British entry into the EEC would bring a lesser advantage to Britain in chemical tariff reductions than membership of a free trade arrangement with the United States and the net gain in this respect of the EEC countries would exceed that of Britain (though the margin of difference would not be large).

(5) If the ASP package is not accepted by the United States then duty reductions in the United States, Britain and the EEC will be limited to those which are unconditional. The extent to which duties will be higher percentage-wise will be in general, though not in all sectors, greater in the United Kingdom and the EEC than in the United States.

The formation of a multilateral free trade association would make ASP inoperative in trade between member countries

—where there are no duties there is no question of valuation. However, if ASP remained, then because duties would be more above the ASP package level in Britain than in the United States it can be argued that the United States would gain more additionally in the British market through duty elimination under the proposed free trade treaty than the United Kingdom would gain in the American market. But the advantage of the new preference for Britain against the EEC in the American market, if the EEC declined to adhere, would be greater than if ASP were eliminated. This would be of most importance in regard to products most affected by ASP—in particular dyes, dyestuff intermediates, and some drugs (for example, sulpha drugs).

If Britain became a member of the EEC then the new preference against the United States would be higher for the United Kingdom in other EEC countries, and for these countries in the United Kingdom, than if ASP had been eliminated.

(6) Elimination of tariffs by Canada in a free trade association agreement would give a greater *new* advantage to the United States or the EEC or other EFTA countries than to Britain because the United Kingdom has a preference in the Canadian market which would be lost.

EFTA does not have a common external tariff. The tariffs of member countries do vary greatly. But in most of the EFTA countries, apart from the United Kingdom, and for most of the sectors, duties after the Kennedy Round will be substantially below those in the EEC and still more below those in the United States. The fact that the level of duties on chemicals was below the British level in the other EFTA countries has given rise to "origin problems" in EFTA—but they have been problems which fell into the categories referred to earlier, not problems which call for special discussion in the chemical industry context.

4 WHAT THE TRADE FIGURES FORETELL

It is customary in analysing the probable impacts of a free trade treaty to forecast the effect of duty reductions by using a "price-elasticity" which is intended to indicate the percentage increase or decrease of imports which will be induced by a 1 per cent fall or rise in the price of imports due to a change in import duties. Multiply the existing volume of import by the number per cent of duty reduction and by the import elasticity and you have the addition to imports which the duty reduction will bring. Where there is a "round" of tariff reductions, like the Dillon and Kennedy rounds under the GATT, you can, it is averred, compare in a rather mercantilist fashion the relative "gains and losses": increases of exports and increases of imports which the participants may expect, and which the negotiators can bargain over with each other, being able to put values on the concessions they offer and those offered in return. The national income forecaster, too, who must have a figure, can feel on solid ground.

Tariff Reductions in 1960*s*

Having established the range of import duty changes which Atlantic free trade would bring, how far could it be established from recent trade statistics what the effect of these changes would be? The main object of this chapter is to examine this, primarily in relation to British experience. The study is for practical reasons limited to the direct effects on trade in chemicals and primarily on imports of chemicals. It was pointed out earlier that since most chemicals, apart from those exported, go to consuming industries a full study of the impact of a free trade association would require an analysis not only of its direct effects on overseas trade in chemicals but of its effects on the purchases of chemicals from home producers by consuming industries whose growth would also be affected—in different ways—by the formation of a free trade association. The industries which are the main consumers of chemicals were listed in order of importance above. It is quite beyond the scale of this study to assess the impact of free trade associations of different scopes on all these industries, and no attempt is made to do it.[14]

It is only practicable to consider the position from 1960 onwards, because during the 1950s trade was restricted both by tariffs and by quantity restrictions particularly designed to limit dollar imports. In 1953 Britain had "liberalised" 82 per cent of her chemical imports: there was thus a significant margin still to be freed from quantitative restrictions, and the United Kingdom restrictions were important in most sectors—particularly in organic and inorganic chemicals, dyes, pigments, paints and varnishes, medicinal and pharmaceutical products, fertilisers, explosives and plastics.[15] The other countries with large outputs of chemicals, with the exception of France, had liberalised (that is, removed quantity restrictions) much more. The completion of "liberalisation" occurred in 1959: it may account for part of the striking increase of imports of chemicals —by 20 per cent—which occurred in that year. There is thus only a short period of relevant experience during which quantitative restrictions have not disturbed the effect of tariff and analogous changes.

Since 1960, as has been seen, there have been two "rounds" of tariff reductions. As a result of the Dillon Round agreement import duties on many chemicals (though of a rather small proportion of the whole range) were reduced one-fifth or less in October, 1962. The Kennedy Round agreement brought reductions of two-fifths in import duties on virtually all chemicals in July, 1968—with a possibility of bigger reductions later. Sandwiched in between these there was for two years—from November, 1964, to November, 1966 —a surcharge on imports. It was 15 per cent for the first six months to April, 1965, and 10 per cent thereafter. In November, 1967, devaluation gave a temporary competitive advantage to the United

[14]Some broad estimates on simple hypotheses were published in Maxwell Stamp and Harry Cowie, *The Free Trade Area Option* (London: Atlantic Trade Study [Trade Policy Research Centre], 1967), re-published as "Britain and the Free Trade Area Option", in Johnson (ed.), *New Trade Strategy for World Economy* (London: Allen and Unwin, 1969; and Toronto: University of Toronto Press, 1969), pp. 204 *et seq.* Even such broad figures would presumably require revising in the light of subsequent growth experience and comparative developments of productivity, inflation, currency values and the like.

[15]For the details, see *The Chemical Industry in Europe* (Paris: Organisation for European Economic Co-operation, 1954), pp. 89-97. This study was carried out for the OEEC's Chemical Products Committee.

Kingdom, comparable at the outset to a tariff increase.[16]

In November, 1968, moreover, the United Kingdom introduced a new temporary restriction on imports, the Imports Deposit Scheme, which required importers to deposit 50 per cent of the value of the imported goods before customs released, repayable after six months. It amounted to an addition of from 2 to 3 per cent on the price of the import. Some raw materials, and therefore some but not all chemicals, were exempt. It was to last initially for one year, but was prolonged at a reduced rate to the end of 1970.

It is thus not possible to observe the effect of either round of relatively small duty reductions (averaging roughly from 1 to 2 per cent in the first round and 5 per cent in the second) for several years of uninterrupted operation. The increased protection offered by the surcharge and the price advantage from devaluation were closer in scale to the average duty reduction which the proposed free trade treaty would bring, but neither could be expected to have the same impact as an import duty change which reflected long-term policy. That the surcharge was going to be short-lived was likely to change its impact, and that it was suddenly imposed meant that it could not be prepared for by traders stocking up in the way that a pre-announced tariff cut could be prepared for when traders can delay imports. It cannot be assumed that an increase in a tariff or analogous restriction on trade would have an effect of the same magnitude (in reverse) as a previous downward movement of equal size. Devaluation is too recent for a long-term result to be observed—and its effect was quickly modified by that of the Kennedy Round agreement.

Other Impacts on Imports

In Figure 1 the course of aggregate imports of chemicals into the United Kingdom in the period 1960–69 is shown, together with the course of the output of manufactures. There was, it will be seen, a sharp upward movement in imports after both the rounds of duty reduction: and the introduction of the surcharge was followed by a sharp, but short-lived, reduction in imports.

But the most impressive characteristic of chemical imports shown in Figure 1 is the strong upward trend whenever industrial output

[16]But not to a tariff increase corresponding to the extent of devaluation, which would have been 16$\frac{2}{3}$ per cent. Devaluation, for example, quickly raised the prices of imported raw materials. The cost of materials and fuels for the chemical industry rose by 5 per cent within a few months after devaluation.

FIGURE 1
IMPORTS OF CHEMICALS INTO THE UNITED KINGDOM
(Volume Index: 1963 = 100)

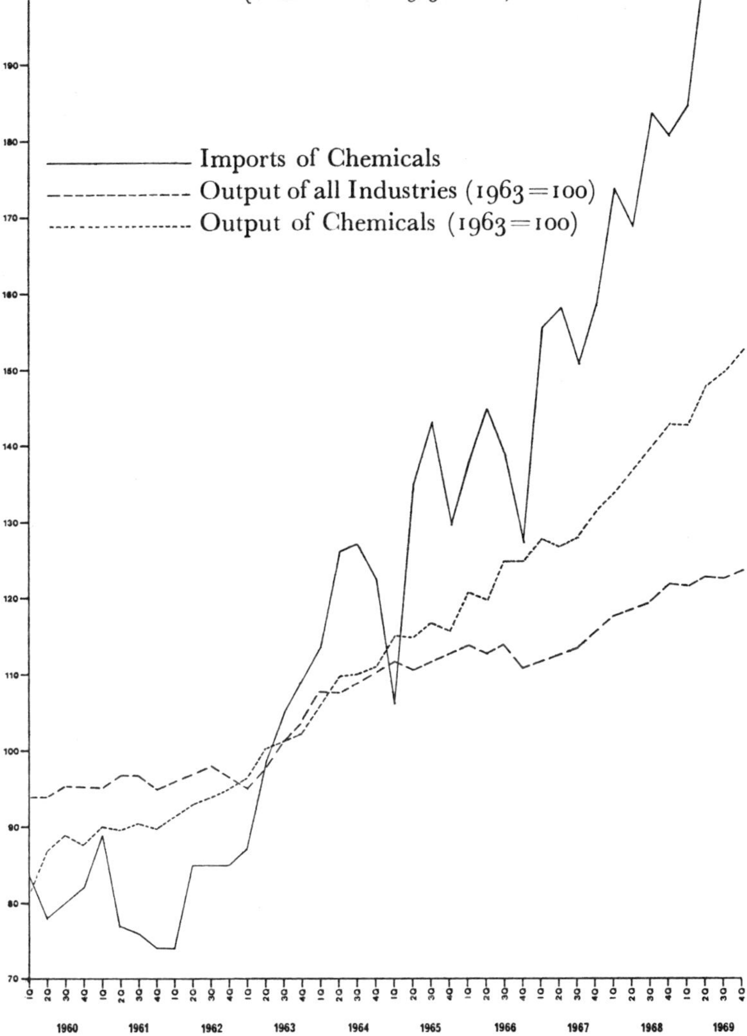

has moved up. Thus, although there was initially a sharp fall of imports, by 12 per cent, when the 15 per cent surcharge was imposed, there was during the period of the surcharge as a whole a substantial increase in imports. The average volume of imports from April, 1965, to September, 1966, which fluctuated within a narrow range, was 14 per cent above the previous import peak of April-September, 1964. It fell sharply, however, in the last quarter of 1966, during which the surcharge was removed, but during which also total industrial output dropped back to its 1965 level. As industrial output began to rise again after November, 1966, so chemical imports resumed their rapid increase. Devaluation a year later was followed by a slight check to this increase—appropriately, it might be thought—but this coincided with a slowdown in industrial growth. The rise in imports was resumed after the first stage of Kennedy Round duty reductions—again, it might appear, appropriately—but it was not for long. The drop at the end of the year could possibly reflect the Import Deposit Scheme. Imports rose again in the second quarter 1969—not as fast as in the first quarters of 1965 and 1967; the impetus could have been the resumed increase—again not for long—of industrial output.[17]

On the experience of the 1960s, therefore, changes in the volume of imports in response to changes in industrial output have been much greater than those in response to changes in the level of protection (or analogous changes like the temporary surcharge which in the short run affect import costs similarly). If one wanted to quantify this it is a workable hypothesis that a 1 per cent change in industrial output resulted—in the short run—in a rise in chemical imports of from 4 to 5 per cent, whereas a 1 per cent change in the rate of import duties resulted in not much above 1 per cent change in the volume of imports.

If the elasticity of imports to changes of import duties is assumed to be between −1 and −2 for the United Kingdom, then removal of all duties on all imports of chemicals from all sources would lead to an increase of annual imports of chemicals into the United Kingdom from the 1969 level of approximately £37m to £75m.[18] The free trade treaty proposal, however, as initially conceived, assuming the abstention of the EEC, would only remove the duties

[17]The index rose from 131 in November, 1966, to 134 in March, 1967.

[18]The total import including synthetic rubber and fibres in 1969 was approximately £490m, of which over £90m was duty free from EFTA or Canada. Clearly the reduction if a free trade treaty is formed will be related to a larger import—larger both as a result of the completion of the Kennedy Round (if the full change is made) and of the general forces promoting growth of imports. The estimates in the text assume that ASP is eliminated. To project the increase for a later year a percentage addition corresponding to the recent average rates of increase of imports could give a rough approximation.

on United States and Canadian imports. EFTA imports are already free, and Canadian imports pay only low preferential duties. If the duty reduction applied in effect only to the imports from the United States, and the general elasticity was applied to the particular—a dubious procedure—the increase in imports would be from about £9m to £18m. It is probable that firms in countries not benefiting from NAFTA would bring some of their export prices down, and imports into Britain might grow on this account. The £9m to £18m is a lower limit; but the upper limit of £37m to £75m would clearly not be reached. The figures are small in relation to the turnover of the British industry, considerably below the annual increase in turnover.

But there is a risk in such quantification of giving an illusory sense both of precision and of permanence which the limited experience and the high aggregation of the figures do not warrant. The sharp upward trend in imports of chemicals, as already seen on Page 139 above, was not peculiar to the United Kingdom, although in the other major producing countries it was counterbalanced by a bigger growth of exports than in Britain. It has multiple origins.

Since demand for chemicals grows much faster in most countries than industry in general grows, wherever the supply of chemicals depends partly on imports such imports will, other things being equal, rise faster than aggregate industrial output. Some chemicals are imported because they cannot be obtained from the home industry—they are in a narrow and basically misleading sense non-competitive. Not all the thousands of chemical products are made in all countries; many are new developments, including many patented and branded products. The United States, with its enormous relative scale (and for other reasons), has the greatest flow of new products: but all the big producing countries have some.

Some chemicals are imported because they are cheaper in the importing country than they are when supplied by home producers, either because domestic prices are sufficiently lower in one country than another at the current rates of exchange, or because manufacturers sell in export trade at discriminatingly low prices. Often both circumstances coincide.

Products are sometimes cheaper in one country than another because raw materials or power are cheaper. Thus, Britain in the past has not made potassic fertilisers, because the raw material has been much cheaper in West Germany and the United States than it could be in Britain. New mining projects in Yorkshire are expected to change this. The production of phosphorus is being phased out in the United Kingdom and future supplies will come from Canada, based on exceptionally cheap electric power.

The rapid expansion of imports described earlier has both made possible and depended upon dramatic price reductions—which have come first where manufacture of particular products is expanding most, where the market gives most scope for the use of giant units, and where there is most competition. The United States has clearly been the most favoured area in these respects collectively. Where the largest units have been installed in expectation of rapid market growth there has periodically been for a time much unused capacity which manufacturers have sought to use by selling exports at prices below the domestic level, close if need be to incremental cost. The probability of such sales is presumably larger because so many chemicals are joint products: it is difficult in planning new plants which will take two or three years to build and commission to choose a balance of capacity for two or more products which proves perfectly judged as markets develop.

At the other extreme—this has been conspicuous in Britain—provision of capacity for indigenous supply of some products has not invariably kept pace with the rise of demand (which even in the United Kingdom has often exceeded 10 per cent a year in the fast growing sectors). This may be because the forecasts of growth have been underestimates, or because the addition to demand has correctly been seen to be small in relation to the capacity a new unit having low costs by international standards would have, or because of delays in completing new plants and making them work efficiently. There have been gaps in supply frequently which domestic producers of the products wanted have themselves filled with imports which they have organised, paid for and distributed. This has occurred conspicuously with plastics and fibres in Britain.

Firms who are introducing into their home market the manufacture of a product hitherto developed abroad often import the product while they are building a plant to make the product in order to establish a market for it by the time they start production.

International firms have at times increased the volume of imports by developing specialisation in works in different countries and using the products of such specialisation (which results in larger scale operations and lower costs) in the combined market. A plant in Holland, for example, has regularly supplied a chemical intermediate of one type to an associated plant in the United Kingdom for further processing and received back an intermediate of another type. Firms with foreign manufacturing subsidiaries often send intermediates to the subsidiaries to make into more finished products. American pharmaceutical firms, for example, send substantial quantities of intermediates to their subsidiaries in Britain and on the continent of Western Europe. ICI send intermediates from their Wilton works in the North of England to their plant near Rotterdam.

UK Import Fluctuations

It is not possible to assess with precision (at least from the outside) the relative importance of the various forces encouraging growth in chemical imports. But obviously one would expect that the various sectors of the chemical industry would be differently affected by them, and would exhibit different elasticities, which was indeed what happened. This is illustrated in the diagrams in Figure 2 which broadly trace the fluctuations in the volumes of selected groups of imports into the United Kingdom in nine finished product sectors.[19]

The products dealt with in five of the six diagrams on the left—all except potassic fertilisers—and the top one on the right were not the subject of any reductions of duty under the Dillon Round agreement. There were, however, some temporary exemptions from duty on some medicaments (not all of those to which the diagram refers) from 1961 on, and on some pesticides from 1964 onwards. I am not able to quantify them. Potassic fertilisers (with exceptions which are for our purpose unimportant) were duty free and were exempted from the surcharge. Some of the imports represented in each of the three lower of the right-hand diagrams did benefit from duty reductions under the Dillon Round agreement. For cellulose plastics there was a reduction of 4 per cent in one of nine categories imported: the crude average reduction was thus below 0.5 per cent. In condensation plastics the highest duty—$33\frac{1}{3}$ per cent—in one category was reduced to 25 per cent: in two other categories there was no reduction; the unweighted average reduction was thus

[19]In all cases except Medicaments the percentages are based on weights of imports: but for Medicaments it was only possible to use values. In the case of synthetic organic dyes the weights are not available from 1963 to 1965.

FIGURE 2
INDICES OF IMPORTS OF PARTICULAR PRODUCTS
(1961 = 100)

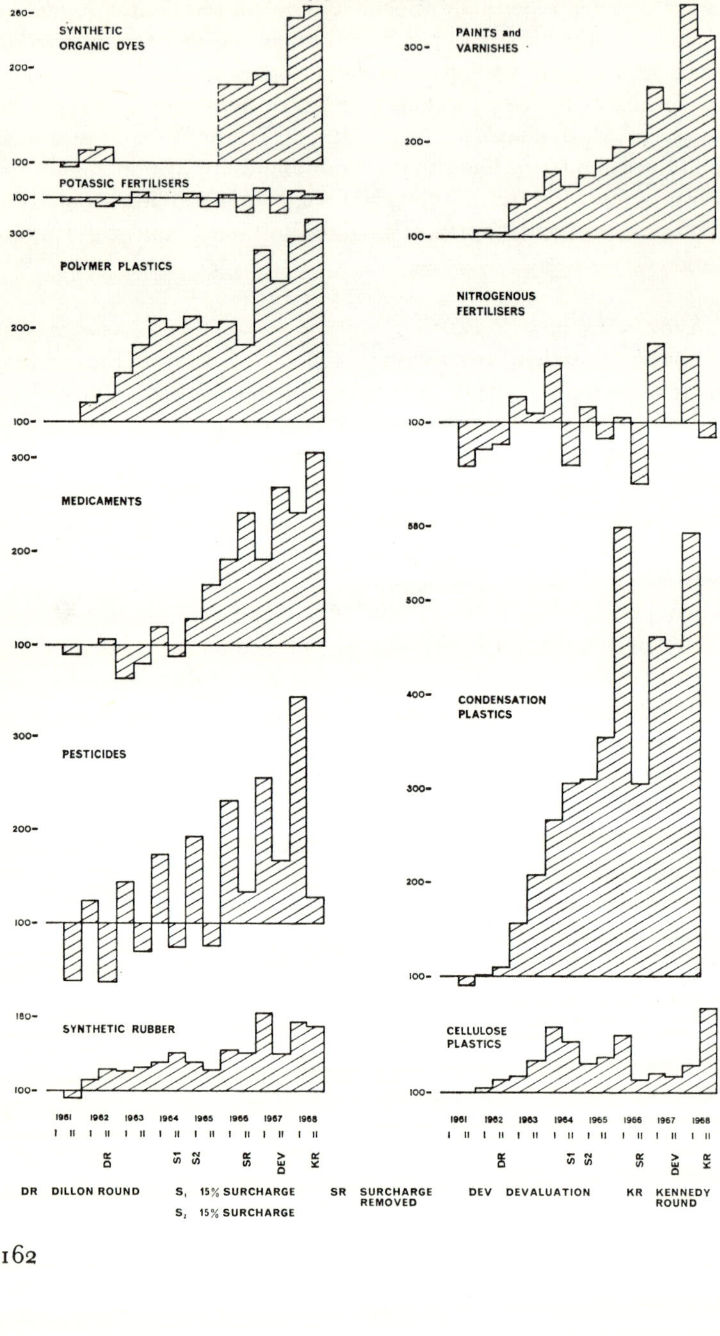

about 3 per cent. Two out of three categories of nitrogenous fertiliser were subject to reductions; the unweighted average reduction was 4 per cent. Here there was also a temporary suspension of duty in 1965. All the products except polymerisation plastics were subject to Kennedy Round reductions in July, 1968.

It will be observed that the increase of imports over the eight years varies from nil for potassic fertilisers (on which there was no import duty) and not much more for nitrogenous fertilisers, to over 500 per cent for condensation plastics, with the other products falling in between at various intermediate points: synthetic rubber and cellulose plastics, 80 per cent; synthetic organic dyes, 170 per cent; polymerisation plastics, paints and varnishes, pesticides and medicaments, each a little over 200 per cent. The distribution of growth during the eight years also presents sharp contrasts. The highly seasonal import of pesticides rose smoothly to a new peak year by year, showing hardly any response to the surcharges. Devaluation was followed by faster growth of imports, but the first reduction of the duty on pesticides (apart from a temporary suspension on a limited range), in July, 1968, was followed by a sharper than usual seasonal fall of imports.

Imports of polymerisation plastics, paints and varnishes and synthetic rubber all rose conspicuously in 1963-4 without any reduction of duties. Imports of condensation plastics rose fast in 1963-4 and for some of these products duties had been reduced. But the imports continued to rise with only a brief slowdown during the surcharge and reached their highest point in the first half of 1966 while the surcharge was still in force. They fell by over 40 per cent in the second half of 1966 and in 1967, after the removal of surcharge, they were still 20 per cent below the 1966 peak. After devaluation they rose immediately close to the former peak.

The only imports included in Figure 2 which were reduced significantly during the surcharge were those of cellulose plastics and nitrogenous fertilisers. Imports of synthetic rubber and polymerisation plastics were on a plateau in 1965-6; their increase was interrupted, and it was renewed after the surcharge was removed. Imports of medicaments, which showed no firm trend from 1961-4, rose fast during the surcharge. Imports of paints and varnishes continued to rise during the surcharge. Imports of all the products except medicaments and cellulose and condensation plastics were higher immediately after the removal of surcharge than they had been in any earlier six months' period. But it is much more remarkable that imports of all except medicaments rose immediately after devaluation, in most cases quite substantially, whereas increases immediately after the Kennedy Round duty reductions were in all cases moderate or small, and imports of some products fell.

It is not possible on the scale of this study to set out separately the reasons for each of the divergent trends illustrated in Figure 2. They do strongly reinforce the view, however, that tariff and analogous changes have been less important than the other factors described above in determining the growth of imports. They also emphasise the danger of trying to use elasticities for the chemical (or any other) industry as a whole based on much earlier trade experience (or even the experience of another country.)[20] The diagrams in Figure 2 refer to only a small number of products, chosen largely because appropriate figures were available.[21] An "industry" average would need to be based on a greater range of examples, but the significance of the aggregation would be hard to assess. There seems no reason to suppose that the mix at different periods of time would give a uniform answer. One cannot look for a "normal" elasticity for the industry as a whole with all its various sectors.

Import Changes in Other Countries

If it is not possible here to assess the relative importance of the various factors in the individual product situations in Britain reflected above, it is still less possible to do so for the other major producing countries. It is of interest that for the Kennedy Round talks the American negotiators used elasticities of from − 1.5 to − 3 per cent for products where the volume of imports was expected to be "relatively elastic", from − 2.2 to − 4.5 for products where it would be "elastic", and from − 3 to − 6 per cent for products where it was expected to be "highly elastic".[22] These figures are substantially higher than those which appear most consistent with

[20]These practices are often followed. See, for example, M. F. G. Scott, *A Study of United Kingdom Imports* (Cambridge: Cambridge University Press, for the National Institute for Economic and Social Research, 1963), pp. 167-76.

[21]That is: figures giving (save in one case) quantities and referring to relatively homogeneous products. It should be emphasised that they are not a rigorously selected representative sample.

[22]The upper and lower figures were regarded as indicating the limits within which changes would occur.

British experience in the 1960s (see Page 156 above), but there is no reason to look for uniformity. I do not know the basis on which the American figures were founded, but it is probable they were not the outcome of precise calculation.

On these United States assumptions, if duties at the post-Kennedy Round level were removed on all imports of chemicals into America, the imports would be increased by from \$250m to \$500m. But a free trade treaty not embracing the EEC would only open the American market duty free to imports from Canada, Britain and other EFTA countries, which together provided below 40 per cent of the total imports. The elasticity assumptions would imply an increase in imports from these sources of from \$80m to \$160m. The British share of this "potential" would be from \$22m to \$44m (£9m to £18m). To the extent that Britain, other EFTA countries and Canada made the products imported by the United States from the EEC, Japan and other sources, and had capacity which they were able and prepared to make available, they might of course expand exports to the United States at the expense of these other exporters. These in turn, by reducing prices to meet competition, might stimulate a further increase of United States imports. There is no means of quantifying this, but the initial \$250m to \$500m should be treated as an upper limit which, like the upper limit for the United Kingdom, would not be reached. Again, it is extremely small in relation to the turnover of American industry, much less than the normal annual growth.

The additional imports into the United States from the United Kingdom and into the United Kingdom from the United States arising immediately from free trade would on these projections be almost in balance, but this is merely a coincidence and partial balances of this kind are not significant. NAFTA would of course have other repercussions on the trade of the members. The United States would obtain free entry to the "other EFTA" markets (where American sales of chemicals had already thrived well in the 1960s while Britain had enjoyed a preference); and free entry to Canada would mean that the British industry no longer had a preference there. Canada would obtain free access to the United States and all EFTA markets: but loss of preference in the United Kingdom would remove the attraction of Canada for American investment there in the chemical industry as a means of obtaining the advantage of this preference. It is not proposed to attempt to quantify these effects.

The balance, to repeat, is not important. The fact that the impact would be initially small is of course significant. But since a free trade association is likely to promote more specialisation in the member countries on activities where comparative advantages are greatest (or comparative disadvantages least) there is no reason why, within any particular aggregation of activities, changes should result in a balanced change in trade flows. If for two member countries the overall outcome was an unbalanced change this could be quite consistent with a movement to better use of resources within each. The imbalance in one industry might be matched by an imbalance in the opposite direction in another industry. If not, the situation would merely call for some general adjustment, possibly a change in parities.

Returning to the elasticities which are postulated, and whose implications have been analysed, it is important that they refer to the probable impact of competitive imports from all possible suppliers. When a free trade association is instituted this is not the situation. The new competition free from import duties will only come from within the area. In NAFTA, as conceived without the EEC, this would be important. In the calculations made above it has been assumed that an elasticity can be applied equally to a part of a trade or to the whole. The figures involved are so relatively small that the procedure is unlikely to give a misleading order of magnitude. But it clearly can be important that increased competition will only come from specific countries, because it cannot be assumed that the competitive strengths of all are equal and likely to have the same competitive impact.

Comparison of Competitive Strengths

Considerable differences in competitive strengths are suggested by the trade figures given in Chapter 2. The American and German chemical industries had much larger exports—gross and net—than the industries in any other country, and the rate of growth of their exports was greater than that of the British industry (See Table 5 on Page 139 above). Their exports of basic chemicals (organic and inorganic), plastic materials, and fertilisers were much larger than those of the British industry. The United Kingdom's industry was not the biggest exporter in any sector, and in all except medicinals, soaps, detergents and toilet goods and paints, its exports were relatively small compared with those from the United States or West Germany or both (see Table 7 on Page 141 above).

It is useful to examine some of the sector figures more closely to form a slightly more comprehensive judgment. In Table 11 the value of trade between the three countries in four different sectors of the chemical industry in 1961 and 1968 is set out, together with the value of the imports into the three countries in these sectors from Switzerland. Changes in imports are used as the basis for this Table.[23]

The top group of figures (Table 11-1) underlines again the relative strength of the United States and West Germany in basic chemicals. It is true that the British exports to the United States in this sector more than trebled, but the West German exports to the United States grew still faster and were almost three times the British figures in 1968. American exports to Britain grew more, at a much higher level, than West German exports to Britain; and they grew slightly more than American exports in this sector to West Germany itself, which is striking because the West German market was increasing much faster than the British. This may be taken to point to the greater relative strength of the West German industry compared with the British in this sector, which made the West German market harder to penetrate and gave the West German industry more thrust in the American market. United Kingdom exports in this sector to West Germany were not one-sixth those of the United States and were far below the Swiss figure. The Swiss industry exported as much in this sector to the United Kingdom as to West Germany.[24]

British exports of plastic materials (See Table 11-2 on Page 166 below) to the United States grew fast in 1961–68, but remained

[23]Since United States imports are measured in f.o.b. prices (prices of goods at port of departure before freight and insurance are paid for) and the rest on c.i.f. prices (prices at the port of arrival after freight and insurance are paid), the figures giving imports into the United States should be increased (see Pages 217-20). At a guess, the additions should be somewhat below 10 per cent. Freight and insurance charges on cheap bulk products can be as much as 30 per cent of the selling price, but on high-value chemicals they fall to below 5 per cent. This would be more important if the changes and differences shown in Table 11 were small.

[24]The Swiss imports of organic and inorganic chemicals (chemical elements and compounds) from West Germany were double the West German imports from Switzerland.

TABLE 11

SELECTED SECTOR IMPORTS, 1961 AND 1968
($m)

Into:	United States 1961	United States 1968	United Kingdom 1961	United Kingdom 1968	West Germany 1961	West Germany 1968
1. Chemical Elements and Compounds						
From: United States			44.1	97.9	61.9	116.0
United Kingdom	9.9	31.6			11.4	21.4
West Germany	26.1	92.0	27.3	55.1		
Switzerland	4.1	14.1	10.3	32.1	15.6	32.0
2. Plastic Materials						
From: United States			31.0	61.6	25.0	50.2
United Kingdom	1.2	17.3			5.8	10.6
West Germany	2.3	23.9	15.6	34.5		
Switzerland	0.4	1.3	1.9	5.4	5.0	8.7
3. Dyeing, Tanning and Colouring Materials						
From: United States			3.2	9.8	3.1	9.0
United Kingdom	1.7	7.7			3.2	6.7
West Germany	5.4	24.3	6.1	15.2		
Switzerland	8.1	19.7	6.9	16.8	13.9	17.1
4. Medicinal and Pharmaceutical Products						
From: United States			3.6	7.6	7.8	12.4
United Kingdom	3.6	8.8			1.3	9.2
West Germany	8.8	6.8	2.3	12.6		
Switzerland	5.6	4.0	1.3	5.6	10.8	26.0

below the West German figure; West German exports of plastic materials to Britain were over three times British exports to West Germany—and American sales both in the British and West German markets were impressively large. The exchanges in dyes, tanning and colouring materials (Table 11-3) are dominated by the West German and Swiss industries; if synthetic organic dyes are isolated within this group the dominance is greater—as Table 7 would lead one to expect in respect of West Germany. In the trade in medicinals and pharmaceuticals (Table 11-4) British exports were more expansive than American exports, and they made headway in the United States whereas West German exports lost ground. The figures leave a confused impression, however, because the American industry exported more than the British industry into West Germany and these exports greatly exceeded West Germany's exports to the United States. But West German exports to Britain exceeded those to Britain from the United States. Swiss exports to West Germany in this sector exceeded the British and American sales combined. In both these highly finished sectors, dyes and pharmaceuticals, West Germany imported considerably more from Switzerland than Switzerland imported from West Germany.

These sector figures show fairly conclusively that in most products either the American or West German industry or both were more thrusting and more competitive exporters than the British industry between 1961 and 1968. But of course the end of the period covered by Table 11 (1961-8) was marked by devaluation in the United Kingdom and by the first stages of the Kennedy Round tariff reductions.[25]

In 1969 there were further Kennedy Round tariff cuts—the American and EEC second set of 10 per cent reductions came in January. The franc was devalued by 11.1 per cent in August; West Germany introduced a 4 per cent tax on exports in March and raised the value of the mark by 9.3 per cent in October (cancelling the export tax). On balance these changes might have been expected to encourage British exports, discourage imports into Britain, and strengthen the British chemical industry *vis-à-vis* its competitors and especially those in West Germany. Should the 1961-8 trends be regarded as significant? Are there indications of radical post-devaluation changes in the competitive strength of British, American and West German—and other—industries?

Although the British industry did improve its relative performance in some respects after devaluation the vigorous growth of the American and West German industries continued, as the output and trade figures show. Production in both the United States and West Germany continued to increase in both years faster than in Britain; in West Germany, much faster. Exports also grew much faster in the United States and West Germany than in the United Kingdom in

[25]In the United States and the EEC the 10 per cent reduction came in January; in the United Kingdom, a 20 per cent reduction came in July.

TABLE 12

PERCENTAGE INCREASES IN PRODUCTION, EXPORTS AND IMPORTS IN UNITED STATES, UNITED KINGDOM AND WEST GERMAN CHEMICAL INDUSTRIES, 1967-69[a]

	Increases over preceding year of:								
	Production			*Exports*			*Imports*		
	1967	*1968*	*1969*	*1967*	*1968*	*1969*	*1967*	*1968*	*1969*
United States	6	9	8	5	17	3	1	19	10
United Kingdom	5	7	6	4	15	10	10	14	13
West Germany	9	17	15	12	17	15	7	28	27

[a]These are estimates of changes in volume. For imports and exports value figures in dollars, sterling and Deutschmarks respectively have been roughly adjusted for changes in prices. For the United Kingdom the Board of Trade (succeeded by the Department of Trade and Industry) provides indices of volume for exports, but not for imports.

1968, and in West Germany in 1969. Exports of chemicals increased relatively slowly in the United States in 1969, substantially less fast than British exports; this probably reflected not British competition (West German competition was clearly stronger) but first the two-month dock strike and later the serious inflationary situation in the United States. In April-May, 1969, exports were 20 per cent above the 1968 level.

Imports of chemicals into the United States and West Germany also grew much faster than into Britain in 1968; and in West Germany again in 1969. The high rates of growth of imports of chemicals into West Germany and the United States reflected the increase of total industrial activity in both. The increase was more continuous and at an exceptionally high level in West Germany. In the United Kingdom in 1968-9 total industrial output grew relatively slowly (being 5 per cent higher in 1968 than in 1967 and 3.3 per cent higher in 1969 than in 1968), partly as an outcome of deliberate policy, and unemployment increased. In West Germany the increase of all industrial output was 12 per cent in 1968 and 13 per cent in 1969 and resources were very fully employed.[26] The

[26]For the United States, the percentage increases were 4.6 and 4.4 per cent respectively—not very different. But in 1968 output rose steadily month by month throughout the year whereas in 1969 it reached a peak in May and then fell.

rate of growth in West Germany was much lower from the end of 1969, because "with domestic resources working still nearer capacity", as the Bundesbank put it, and "despite immense efforts in the production field industrial output could not be raised much further".[27]

The 15 per cent growth of British chemical exports in 1968 over the 1967 level was faster than at any earlier period in the sixties—the highest previous rate of growth had been 11.5 per cent from 1963 to 1964.[28] The acceleration after the slow expansion of exports in 1967 may no doubt be attributed partly to devaluation, since chemicals were among the products which could be offered quickly after devaluation for fairly early delivery at lower dollar prices. But as the much faster growth of American and West German exports at the same time showed market conditions for exports were very favourable in 1968—less so in 1969.

Much of the expansion of British chemical exports since devaluation, it has often been pointed out, has been to the continent of Western Europe and particularly to EEC countries. Imports from some of these countries have, however, also grown strikingly. Both movements are illustrated in Table 13 which compares the trades in 1968 and 1969.

Net imports into Britain from the EEC were reduced between 1968 and 1969 by £3.6m—about 7 per cent. The figures for Netherlands and Belgium in this table are of particular interest—these trades collectively were more important than the trade with West Germany, and reflect the vast international investment there.

It is significant that the increase in British exports to West Germany from 1968 to 1969 was 21 per cent: much below the average increase in West German imports of 27 per cent. West Germany's imports from other EEC countries were substantially above the average.[29] Imports from the United States into West Germany

[27]*Monthly Report of the Deutsche Bundesbank*, June, 1970, p. 5.

[28]Board of Trade volume figures are being used here. In *sterling* exports rose by 21 per cent in the period 1967-68; in dollars, by only 5.8 per cent. In dollars, British net exports *fell* in 1968.

[29]West German imports of chemicals from other EEC countries in the first half of 1969 were 37 per cent higher than in the first half of 1968; imports from the United Kingdom were 21 per cent up; those from the United States, 12.5 per cent up.

TABLE 13

UNITED KINGDOM TRADE WITH EEC, 1968-69

	Exports to 1969 (£m)	*Imports from 1969 (£m)*	*Net Export(+) Import(−) 1969 (£m)*	*Percentage Increase for 1968 to 1969*	
				Exports to	*Imports from*
West Germany	24.2	70.8	− 46.6	21	12
Netherlands	42.0	58.2	− 16.2	11	14
Belgium	20.6	16.3	+ 4.3	28	32
France	30.1	24.6	+ 5.5	35	6
Italy	18.2	14.1	− 4.1	30	8
EEC	135.1	184.0	− 48.9	21	14

(Based on United Kingdom foreign trade statistics.)

increased more than those from Britain in 1969: but imports from the United States into Western Europe as a whole had increased by 25 per cent in value—slightly more probably in volume. In the other direction, exports from West Germany to the United States rose by 30 per cent in 1968 when American imports were rising fast; those from Britain rose by only 22 per cent.

It would certainly be premature to argue from trade and production statistics of 1968-9 that post-devaluation trends invalidate conclusions based on the 1961-8 trends, or to suggest that devaluation had changed the balance of dynamic forces in the chemical industry, not merely provided a transitory accommodation to them. In its *Economic Assessment* for the industry to 1972, the Economic Development Committee of the Chemical Industry, a subsidiary body of the National Economic Development Council, gave no suggestion that the competitive situation had improved. It emphasised the disadvantages which still beset the British industry and the need, also, for continuous financial assistance from the British Government without which investment in the industry would be less attractive and remunerative than investment in competing countries.[30]

[30] *Economic Assessment to 1972* (London: HM Stationery Office, for the Economic Development Committee for the Chemical Industry, National Economic Development Council, 1970).

The main conclusions of this chapter may be summarised thus:

(1) It is not possible to forecast with precision from available data the extent of the impact which the introduction of a free trade treaty, whether broadly or narrowly based, would have on the international trade in chemicals. Insofar as the trade figures of the last decade are a sound guide, however, it can be inferred that the removal of all remaining import duties by the creation of a free trade association embracing all developed countries would have a relatively small direct and immediate impact on the chemical industry in the main producing countries. For Britain and the United States and probably the other major producers the increase of imports would be substantially smaller than the annual increase of turnover. Increased exports would be roughly equal to the increased imports in the area as a whole, but not in individual countries. In the United Kingdom the increase of imports might be expected from the trade figures to be from £37m to £75m by the time duties were fully eliminated. The annual increase of turnover in the British chemical industry averaged £200m between 1963-8; at 1969 prices the average increase is rather above this.

(2) For a free trade association including the EEC, North America and EFTA these would be the relevant figures to indicate the probable scale of changes. For the free trade treaty idea, as it was originally more narrowly envisaged to include only North America and the EFTA countries, the increase of imports which would be generated would be substantially smaller. For the United Kingdom it would be between £9m and £18m.

(3) Formation of a multilateral free trade association would produce indirect effects on the chemical industry through its impact on other industries which are large markets for chemicals. Insofar as this would change imports, it is in some measure taken into account in the figures for direct effects. To the extent that the formation of a free trade association increased or decreased rates of growth in consuming industries, the home market for chemicals would be increased or decreased. The indications which trade statistics give of the scale of such changes is beyond the scope of this study.

(4) The fast growth of imports of chemicals into the United Kingdom since 1960, which has its parallel in all major chemical producing countries, has been due mainly to factors other than the tariff: in particular to the rapid expansion and creation of demand,

the great extent of innovation in product and processes, and great cost and price reduction through the improvement and enlargement of plants and (secondarily) of transport equipment. This will all continue, and these non-tariff factors are likely to result in a larger, more continuous increase of imports than the removal of tariffs would bring about. Removal of tariffs will, however, increase the effect of these other factors.

(5) The trade flows examined in this chapter show first the American, and second the West German, as the strongest initiators in the chemical industry hitherto, both with great penetrative power in international trade.

(6) It is not possible to identify from the trade statistics any radical rapid changes in competitive strengths of major producers. To identify the scope for such changes and the *effect* which formation of a free trade treaty—broad or narrow in scope—might have on trends it is necessary to study the trends of comparative costs. This is done in Chapter 6, but as a necessary preliminary the comparative levels and movements of prices in the three main producing countries are analysed in the next section.

5 PRICES OF CHEMICALS IN AMERICA, BRITAIN AND WEST GERMANY

In the first part of this chapter movements of price indices for various groups of chemical products in the United States, Britain and West Germany are compared. This is followed by a comparison of the absolute levels of home prices of different classes of product in the three countries.

The price indices for the whole chemical industry (as defined in Chapter 2) which are shown in Figure 3 rose sharply both in the United Kingdom and the United States in the early 1950s (much

FIGURE 3
PRICES OF CHEMICALS AND ALLIED PRODUCTS
(1958 = 100)

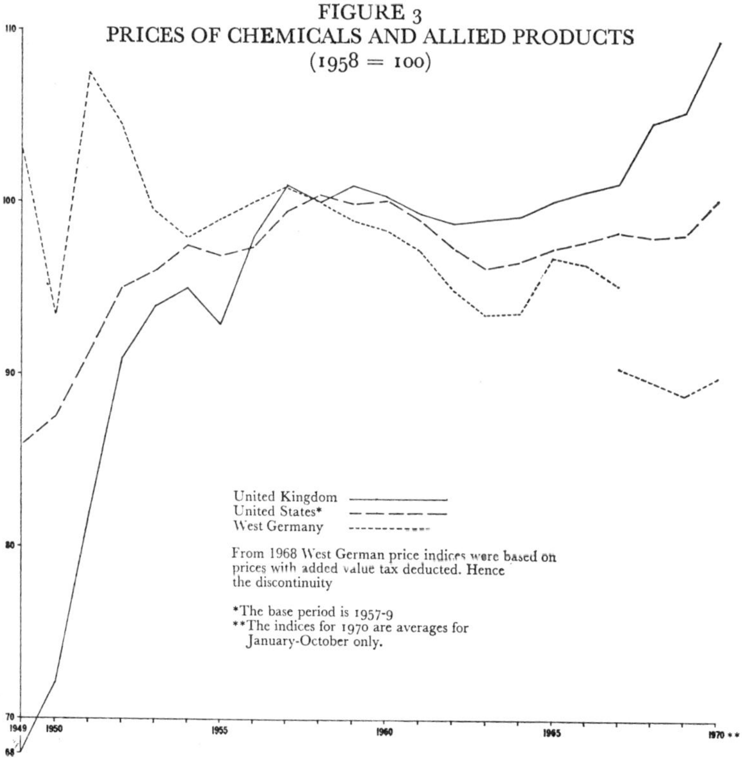

more steeply in the United Kingdom), but after 1952 they rose relatively slowly. From 1958 to 1969, the period of greatest interest for this study, the index rose 5.3 per cent in Britain, more than half of this after devaluation, and fell 2.1 per cent in the United States and 6.4 per cent in West Germany (an adjustment has been made here for the change introduced in 1968 whereby the indices were based on prices less added value tax). In all these countries prices of industrial products in general changed more in the same period: upwards—by 31 per cent in the United Kingdom, by 13 per cent in the United States, and by 14 per cent in West Germany.

This is of course the most familiar picture of chemical prices, relatively stable, and falling in relation to the general level of prices. While the British chemical price trend looked appreciably less favourable in the period 1958-67 than that in the other two countries, its fall in relation to industrial prices in general was greater.[31]

The price indices for the whole chemical industry are in some respects deceptive. The smoothness and relative stability of their movement conceals sharply divergent movements in different sectors of the industry. Since the relative importance of different sectors is not uniform in the three countries, the more finished products, for instance, being proportionately more important than basic chemicals in the United Kingdom and basic chemicals being most important in the United States (see Page 135 above) different movements of sector prices would necessarily lead to divergent movements of the price index for the whole chemical industry, even if within each sector price movements were identical in all these countries.

Price indices exist for a number of sectors in all three countries, but the products grouped together for these sector indices are not identical in all three countries. The contrasts presented by the sector price indices are nevertheless useful and are shown in Table 14. The sector price indices are set out above and below the average for the whole industry, with those which have fallen most at the top. Although there are some dissimilarities in the different countries the trends in the same sectors are in general broadly alike. Prices of plastic materials and organic chemicals have fallen most. Inorganic chemical prices have risen significantly: and the prices of most chemicals sold to the final consumer have risen.

[31]In the years when prices rose sharply, in 1949-52, prices of chemicals and allied products rose *more* in the United Kingdom than prices of manufactures in general.

TABLE 14
INDICES OF PRICES OF CHEMICAL PRODUCTS IN 1967
(1958 = 100)[a]

	United States	West Germany	United Kingdom
Plastic materials[b]	89.1		80.4
Organic chemicals	89.5	73.0	
Special chemicals for further processing		92.4	
Pharmaceuticals	94.0		102.6
Synthetic rubber	97.4		
Chemical and allied industries	98.4	95.25	100.2
Soap }	105.7		126.2
Synthetic detergents }			100.4
Dyes			107.7
Chemicals for consumption		107.9	
Fertilisers	106.4		94.1
Paint	109.3[c]		107.1
Inorganic chemicals	110.1	123.0	
Toilet preparations	110.7		134.0

[a]For the United States, 1957-9 = 100.
[b]The West German statistics include these in special chemicals for further processing.
[c]This is the index for prepared paint. The index for paint materials was 90.9. The combined index in 1966 was 106.7.

There is no United Kingdom price index for organic chemicals on a 1958 base and no West German index for plastics. But prices move fairly uniformly; it may be assumed these fell.

Just as the relatively stable general price level for all chemicals conceals divergent trends in sector prices, so within particular sectors prices of particular products often diverged sharply from the sector trends. In sectors where the index falls, for instance, there were falls for particular products which at certain periods far exceeded the average. To give two examples out of many, the United States list price of phthallic anhydride fell by 75 per cent between 1958 and 1963; that of polypropylene was halved between 1962 and 1965. Both reductions were sustained.

The sector figures other than for organic, inorganic and plastic materials present a somewhat confusing picture. This is partly because the sub-divisions are not identical for the different countries. Even the content of organic chemicals varies significantly. The American figure includes dyes, for instance;[32] the West German does not.[33] It is more important, however, that the products covered by these more finished product sectors vary from those like SBR synthetic rubber which (1) is made to standard specifications by capital intensive processes in large quantities from organic chemical intermediates (whose prices have moved down) and (2) is bought by large, technically well-informed buyers, to pharmaceutical products and toilet preparations where (1) the ultimate buyer is not technically well-informed, (2) the product must be packed to be sold in very small lots, (3) brand names are important and (4) production of part of the output, at least in the final stages, is likely often to be relatively labour intensive. The first set of conditions favours price movements below the average trend; the second set favours movements above the average. There are many intermediate stages between the extremes.

Comparison of Absolute Price Levels

Persistent divergences between price trends in the three countries, though clearly significant in assessing changes in relative competitiveness, do not provide a comparison of actual prices. It is possible, however, to get a broad indication of actual price differences between the United States and Britain by linking the indices to a comparison of actual prices in 1950 which was published by the OEEC in 1959. It was part of a study of output and productivity in the two countries.[34] The authors compared some prices in eight sectors of the chemical industry and concluded that the appropriate exchange rate for the chemical and allied industries in 1950 was $3.5 = £1, while for general chemicals alone (organic and inorganic chemicals, fertilisers and plastic materials) it was $3.22 = £1. These were exchange rates arrived at by comparing prices of appropriately weighted samples of broadly identical products. At the then current exchange rate of $2.8 = £1 the United States prices were therefore on average above United Kingdom prices.

But international prices were clearly not in equilibrium in 1950. The influences of sterling's devaluation in 1949 and of the subsequent Korean War had not worked themselves out. As Figure 3

[32]This would probably make the index fall less than it would if dyes were not included.

[33]Dyes in the West German indices are among the "chemicals for further processing".

[34]Deborah Paige and Gottlieb Bombach, *A Comparison of National Output and Productivity in the United Kingdom and the United States* (Paris: OEEC Secretariat, 1959.).

shows, prices of chemicals rose sharply in the United States and Britain from 1950-52, but much more in the latter than in the former. The exchange rate for chemicals, which would have been established by comparisons a few years after 1950, would have been much closer to the then current exchange rate. In Table 15 the exchange rates established in the 1950 comparisons have been adjusted to allow for the changes recorded by the relevant price indices for 1958, 1963, 1965, 1968 and 1969.

TABLE 15

DOLLAR/POUND EXCHANGE RATE FOR CHEMICAL PRODUCTS

	Chemical and Allied Products	*General Chemicals*
1950	3.50	3.22
1958	2.97	2.70
1963	2.87	2.78
1965	2.88	2.74
1966	2.87	2.69
1968	2.76	2.70
1969	2.75	2.65

According to these figures, therefore, a comparison of American and British prices in the decade after 1958, similar to the OEEC study of 1950, would show that American prices of general chemicals have been on average slightly below the British prices. But American prices over the whole range of chemical and allied products have been on average slightly higher than British prices. That is, basic chemicals were on average cheaper in the United States than in Britain, but prices in many of the more finished sectors were substantially higher than in the United Kingdom. Devaluation naturally changed the position. The dollar/pound exchange rate for chemicals dropped in 1968 and 1969 but was above the new parity of 2.4. The position had not stabilised, however. As Figure 3 shows, British prices rose substantially faster than American prices from January to October, 1970—the exchange rate for chemical and allied products on the July indices would have been about 2.66—and West German prices rose less than American.

International comparisons of prices of chemical products are hard to make, and the authors of the OEEC report did not show

how (or whether) they overcame the difficulties. Price indices for individual countries, moreover, are particularly difficult to construct for the chemical industry, partly because the price data are difficult to establish and partly, too, because it is an industry making thousands of products in varied qualities, with many new products coming in and some going out of production, and with constant shifts in the relative importance of different products. It would be unreasonable to regard the figures in Table 15 as precise guides to the position in the 1960s. But their broad indications are probably right. British prices certainly moved upwards towards (or above) American prices for chemicals in the 1950s, very sharply at the outset, and this continued but more slowly in the 1960s. If the American/British price ratio in 1950 was properly represented by the OEEC study, the subsequent price trends would have brought the ratio nearer to the current exchange rate, a little above or a little below, and lower for general chemicals than for the whole range of products covered in "Chemical and Allied Products".

The analysis of actual prices in the three countries from 1958 onwards broadly confirms these conclusions. Prices of a great many chemical products—not, of course, nearly all the thousands of products which are made—are quoted regularly in journals.[35] These are for the most part home prices of products which are made in relatively large quantities to standard specifications by several firms in each country and bought for further processing by informed buyers. They include a wide range of intermediates and also the standard plastics, synthetic fibres and rubbers. Some of the intermediates are products of which a large proportion is used by the maker—the part sold on the market, to which the quoted price refers, may be much smaller than the "captive" use of the product.

These price quotations provide a useful starting point for a survey of chemical prices, and they have been used as such for this study. But buyers and sellers alike state that the quoted prices are not the prices at which sales take place—except for spot sales, usually of small quantities. The prices quoted are normally (though this is not always printed in the journals) for delivery in certain minimum

[35]*European Chemical News* carries comparative price data for many chemicals in many countries presented in cents per pound. In the United States the *Oil, Paint and Drug Reporter* has a wide coverage for general chemicals. Many specialist journals cover prices in particular sectors: for example, the *Textile Monthly* in the United Kingdom and the *Modern Textile Magazine* in the United States for man-made fibres; and *Modern Plastics* in the United States for plastics.

quantities, in tank cars, barrels or packages of specified sizes or weights, which are not always uniform in all countries. There are normally quantity discounts in addition, and discounts for long contracts. Most sales of chemicals to industrial users are on long contracts and for fairly large quantities. Discounts commonly range from 10 to 25 per cent—but they are sometimes more than 25 per cent. Discounts tend to reflect the state of trade, the extent of unused capacity. Different makers may offer different discounts and the discounts are not stable. They are not systematically published, and there is an effort at secrecy although in the course of competition they tend to get known, and when they become very substantial they are prominently discussed. This may lead to a reduction of the list prices.

In the case of new products, protected by patents, or the subject of licence, this discounting procedure will not occur (and prices may not be quoted). This is the stage when high margins are hoped for. Nor will discounts occur where there is monopoly and no close substitute and therefore no need for discounts.[36]

It is not possible therefore to accept the published prices without qualification and modification. But there are supplementary sources of information which often make it possible to correct or confirm published prices for many products, though it may only be spasmodically. It has been possible to obtain specific information from sellers or buyers in regard to some products. Average values published yearly by the United States Census Bureau give a check for products which are sufficiently homogeneous. The United Kingdom Census of Production gives similar data at less frequent intervals. Average values of exports are less useful because export prices are normally below home prices—but they can sometimes provide a guide.[37] There have been from time to time investigations for groups in the chemical industry by consultants (Arthur D. Little Inc. for instance) which are well informed. On particular ranges of products some official inquiries, such as the Kefauver inquiry into the drug industry in the United States, have provided useful data. Many of the more reliable sources of price data do not unfortunately provide continuous series, and some of the best cannot be quoted.

[36]It is understood that there is no discount on rayon prices, for example, in the United Kingdom, but discounts are significant on rayon prices in the United States and in West Germany.

[37]Average values for total sales will be a little below home prices where exports occur: but the American export percentage is low.

Conclusions from Price Analysis

The number of chemical products is vast. The number whose prices it has been practicable to study and check for this limited exercise is small. A list of the products covered and some particulars of the sources and dates of information on them are given in Appendix I. The extent to which the sample is representative cannot be established. The results arrived at are inevitably tentative. But while it is impossible on this basis to establish a quantitative comparison, the data appear adequate to support two general conclusions:

(1) In bulk chemicals and intermediates, organic and inorganic, synthetic rubbers and fibres, plastic materials and fertilisers, prices are not uniformly lower in the United States than in Britain or West Germany, but during the 1960s American prices have been more often the lowest in the three countries. For some products the difference has been small. The position is not stable; the relation of prices for individual products in the three countries has not remained uniform over a long period of years. Real prices charged vary more in West Germany and the United States than in Britain, being more influenced by the state of trade and more subject to competition. In West Germany there is domestic competition, and competition from firms in all the EEC countries as well as (behind protection) from the United States and Britain; in the United States prices respond primarily to strong domestic competition, although in some sectors there is pressure from West Europe (West German pressure is found to be the strongest) and Japan.

It is most probable then that in this range of products the price level in the United States, certainly until Britain's devaluation, was slightly below the level in West Germany, and the West German slightly below the level in the United Kingdom.[38]

(2) In regard to dyes, pharmaceuticals and probably perfumes, toilet materials and cleaning materials, American

[38] An unpublished report, *Petrochemical Feedstock Imports and Their Effects on the US Balance of Payments*, Vols. 1 and 2 (Stanford: Stanford Research Institute, 1967), came to the general conclusion (Vol. 1, p. 105) that "prices for petrochemicals in Western Europe and Japan are generally comparable, but slightly higher than in the United States". The report is cited hereafter as the Stanford Institute Report of 1967.

prices are above, sometimes substantially above British and West German prices. With regard to dyes, the average values for analogous groups of dyes in census reports show United States values 30 per cent above United Kingdom values. The Kefauver Report and a Canadian inquiry into drug prices provides many instances where American drug prices are above British and West German prices by a still greater percentage. It cannot be assumed, however, that these drug prices are representative: the drugs whose prices are quoted in these reports are drugs which had been fairly recently developed at the time of the reports. They were products of American research and enterprise, their production or sale in other countries being commonly by subsidiaries of United States companies. The Canadian report showed the British price normally below the West German: the Kefauver Report showed the British price more usually above the West German. But both were always much below the American price.

These conclusions accord well with those suggested by the OEEC comparison of 1950 adjusted to changes in the price index.

The inquiries into pharmaceutical prices showed that profit margins on new drugs are often above average. The wide margins are a result of innovation. This does not occur only in the pharmaceutical sector. It is probable that in most sectors of the United States chemical industry there is a greater proportion of new products than in the British or West German industries which earn premium prices for a few years.

It is likely that if home prices were identical in the United States and Britain the American firms would have a higher average price because they export a smaller proportion of their output than the British ones. The latter would have a similar advantage over West German firms who export still more. This is because export prices tend to be lower than home prices.[39]

[39] Exports also involve additional costs.

6 FACTOR SUPPLIES AND RELATIVE COSTS

In this chapter the relative costs in the main producing countries, and the changes which are occurring or are likely to occur in them in the next decade or so, are analysed as a basis for estimating the probable impact of a free trade treaty on flows of trade in chemicals, on the scale of the chemical industry in different areas, on regional specialisation, distribution of investment and employment, and on the development of company structure. Considerable changes in relative costs are taking place. The relative competitive strength of the United States is being reduced in some respects, and that of other producers is increasing, but not uniformly in all respects in all countries. The crucial problem is to establish the spread and extent of change: it is a problem of degree and time.

The problem has been much discussed publicly in the United States during the last decade in connection with the preparations for the Kennedy Round negotiations and with criticisms of their outcome. Two reports by Arthur D. Little Inc. were of particular importance. The first was a study made in 1962 of the probable effect of completely removing all duties on imports of organic chemicals into the United States.[40] Their conclusions were that if this happened: (1) direct imports of organic chemicals would probably increase from the then current level of 2 per cent to 10 per cent of the sales of organic chemicals in the United States; (2) American firms who consumed organic chemicals of their own making would probably make some abroad to import for their own use; and (3) imports of more finished chemicals—paints, drugs, fibres—which were based on organic chemicals, would rise more than direct imports of organic chemicals because the relative competitiveness of those manufactures would prove even less than that of the organic chemical manufactures.[41]

All told, possibly 20 per cent of the American market for organic chemicals would—the report suggested—be supplied by imports.

[40] *The Impact of Proposed US Tariff Changes on Organic Chemical Imports* (Cambridge, Mass.: Arthur D. Little Inc., 1962), an unpublished report prepared for the Synthetic Organic Chemical Manufacturers Association, hereafter cited as the 1962 Little Report.

[41] *Ibid.*, pp. 57 and 58.

This would seriously reduce the growth of the market for indigenous supplies of organic chemicals and their derivatives, and it greatly exceeded the increase of imports postulated by the import elasticity figures used by the State Department. (See Pages 162 and 163 above.)

This assessment was based on the judgement that the American chemical manufacturers no longer had advantages sufficient to offset the much higher price they paid for labour. Labour productivity was higher in the United States than in competitor countries, but the margin was stated to be relatively small when foreign manufactures had identical plants—about 25 per cent—and was steadily declining. When foreign manufacturers built new plants they built them similar to those in the United States and they obtained them more cheaply. The American makers had no monopoly in innovation, and their innovations were quickly introduced in competing countries, under licence or by American firms who manufactured abroad. Foreign manufacturers now had raw materials for organic chemicals as cheap as those available in the United States. The United States still had cheaper fuel and power, but this was a minor advantage. All told, the costs of production for foreign producers using new plants would, according to the report, amount to only 80 to 85 per cent of costs in the United States. Italy would have the lowest costs.[42] Foreign firms had more experience of export selling than the American makers, and this it was expected would allow them to exploit their cost advantages by selling in the United States.

The second report by Arthur D. Little[43] argued—in 1966—that raw materials for organic chemicals would progressively become dearer in the United States than in Western Europe or Japan, unless restrictions on the import of oil, gas and oil products into the United States were relaxed.

The implication of these reports is that if import duties on trade in chemicals between the United States and EFTA were removed, and still more if trade were freed between North America and

[42]The total unit costs of the main competitor countries in a new works making organic chemicals, assuming identical raw material costs, were given as: the United States, 100; the United Kingdom, 84.6; West Germany, 84.4; France, 83.9; Italy, 80.8; and Japan, 84.6.

[43]*Oil Import Quotas and the US Balance of Payments in Petrochemicals* (Cambridge, Mass.: Arthur D. Little Inc., 1966), an unpublished report prepared for the Dow Chemical Company and the Monsanto Company, hereafter cited as the 1966 Little Report.

Western Europe and Japan, then a large increase would occur in imports of chemicals into the United States and this increase would not be matched by a parallel increase of imports of chemicals from the United States into Britain and other West European markets and Japan. It is clearly important to establish in this section how far subsequent development of costs support these judgements. Global and sector figures for value added per man and for average earnings are analysed and then the main components of costs are examined individually. External factors which are to some extent (but not entirely) outside the control of the industry are considered first, the size of markets, raw material costs, fuel and power costs, the cost of equipment and construction, the cost of transport. Internal factors are then considered; the size of firms and plants, the extent of innovation, investment, research and development, the quality of labour and management, profitability and access to capital.

Value Added per Man and Cost of Labour

Figures 4 and 5 show the movements of (a) added value per worker (of all grades) from 1958-68 in the British, American, West German, French, Italian and Japanese chemical industries measured in dollars per year, as estimated by the OECD, and (b) the full cost of operative labour in the same industries for the same years, measured in dollars per hour and based on national estimates.

The graphs show that although according to these figures the margin between the United States and the other five became smaller in the decade it remained impressively wide. The added value per worker was more than twice as high in the United States as it was in Japan or West Germany in 1968, and nearly three times the British figure, and the cost of labour in the United States was twice as high as the cost in West Germany—and much more above the cost in the other five countries. The added value per worker and the average cost of labour per hour in 1968 are given in Table 16.

Added value per worker and cost of labour rose more slowly in the United Kingdom than in the other West European countries and Japan, and measured in dollars the British figures became sharply lower in 1968 as a result of sterling's devaluation. At the old parity the British figures would have been $9,772 and $1.84.

The dollar figures are useful where absolute comparisons are relevant. For some purposes they are also useful because they underline the effect of devaluation. Thus, the fall in the dollar

FIGURE 4
ADDED VALUE PER PERSON UNEMPLOYED, 1958-68
($'000 per year)

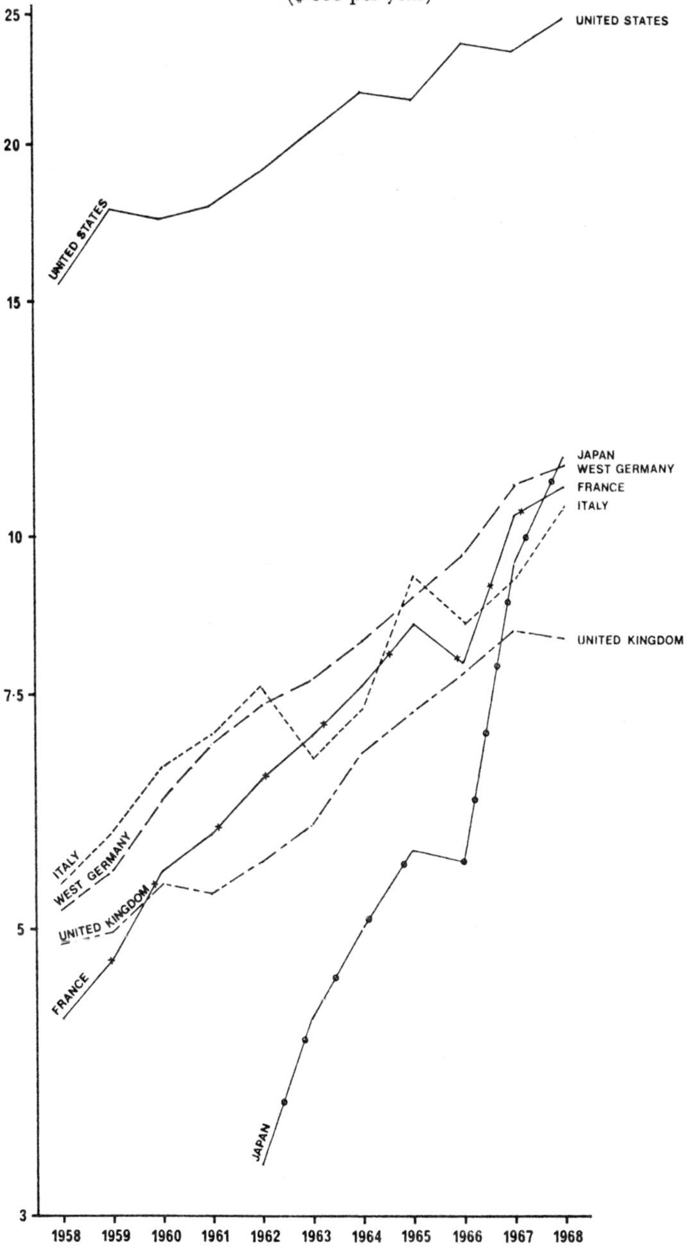

FIGURE 5
COST OF LABOUR PER HOUR, 1958-67
($ per hour)

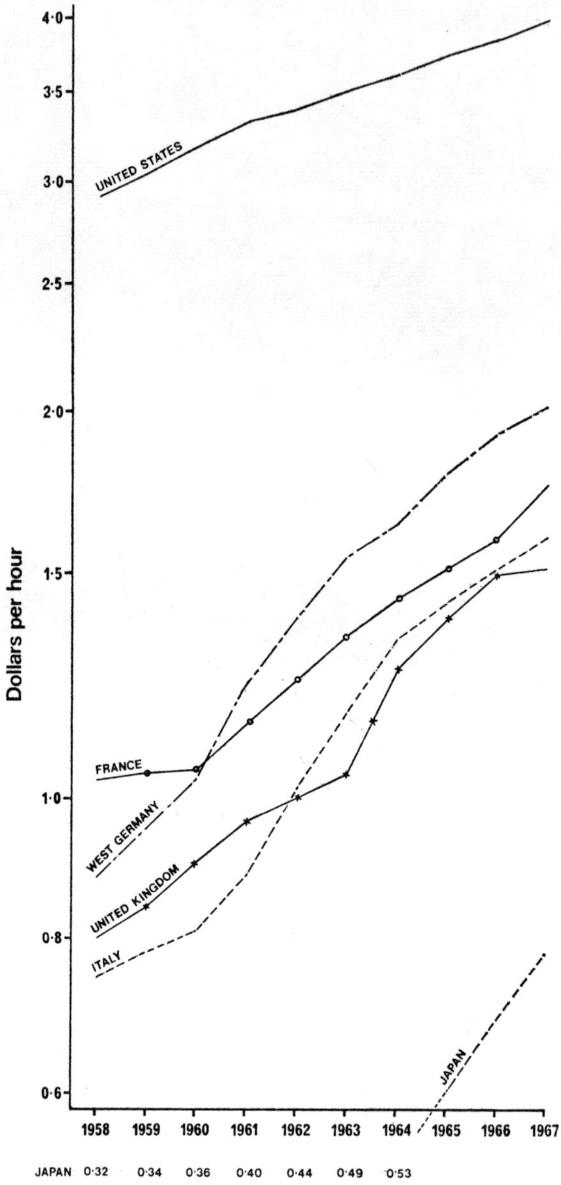

TABLE 16

ADDED VALUE PER WORKER AND AVERAGE COST OF LABOUR PER HOUR IN THE CHEMICAL INDUSTRIES IN 1968

	Added Value per worker (annual) $		*Cost of Labour per man hour* $	
United States	24,850[a] ..	100	4.25 ..	100
Japan	11,466 ..	46	0.87 ..	20
West Germany	11,440 ..	46	2.15 ..	51
France	10,933 ..	44	1.93 ..	45
Italy	10,578 ..	43	1.69 ..	40
United Kingdom	8,376 ..	34	1.61 ..	38

[a]estimated.

The added value figures are calculated from the figures published in *The Chemical Industry, 1968-69*, OECD, March 1970. The cost of labour figures come from *Direct and Total Wage Costs for Workers*, published by the Swedish Employers' Confederation; they are weighted averages for adult workers, men and women, and include fringe benefits. The EEC figures are provisional, partly estimated, and subject to revision.

cost of labour in the United Kingdom in 1968 shows the immediate cost advantage derived in international competition.

But for productivity trends within individual countries it is better to use production indices,[44] which is done in Table 17. This table gives (1) percentage increases in output per worker (including all "staff" workers) between 1958 and 1963, and 1963 and 1968, based on increases of output and numbers employed, and (2) percentage increases in the labour cost component of total costs in the chemical industry, based for the United Kingdom and for the United States where possible on figures from the industrial censuses and for the other countries on the cost per hour of the work of wage earners (including fringe benefits).[45]

[44]Production indices set out to measure in some sense the change in volume of output. Prices in national currency are used for assessing relative values of output when this must be done via price.

[45]The bases for cost of labour are thus not exactly comparable. But comparisons of the United Kingdom and the United States census figures with those which would have been derived from the average cost per hour of operatives' wages, show that the annual expenditure on labour rose *less* than the cost of labour increased by increases in hourly operatives' wages plus fringe benefits. Use of the wage figure basis would thus have given too high an index of the cost of labour for both the United States and the United Kingdom.

TABLE 17

CHANGES IN OUTPUT, EMPLOYMENT, PRODUCTIVITY AND LABOUR COST

	1958–1963 (1958 = 100)					*1963–1968 (1963 = 100)*				
	Output 1963	*Numbers Employed 1963*	*Output per Worker 1963*	*Cost of Labour per Worker 1963*	*Labour cost per unit of output*	*Output 1968*	*Numbers Employed 1968*	*Output per Worker 1968*	*Cost of Labour per Worker 1968*	*Labour cost per unit of output*
United Kingdom	141 (7)[a]	109	120 (5¼)[a]	129	100	140 (7)[a]	97	144 (7½)[a]	142	99
United States	149 (8¼)	109	137 (6½)	118	86	149 (8¼)	119	125 (4½)	120	96
France	162 (10)	109	148 (8)	153	103	157 (9½)	101	155 (9¼)	143	92
Italy	186 (13¼)	115	162 (10)	158	98	158 (9½)	126	125 (4½)	141	113
West Germany	171 (11½)	113	151 (8½)	167	111	172(11½)	110	156 (9¼)	143	92
Japan						191 (13½)	108	177 (12)	178	100

[a]The figures in brackets are the annual rates of change.

SOURCES: OECD, *The Chemical Industry* (1967-68 and 1968-69); *United Kingdom Census of Production*, 1963, and *Preliminary Results of the Census of Production* for 1968 (*Board of Trade Journal*, January 28, 1970); *United States Census of Manufactures* 1963, and *United States Annual Survey of Manufactures* 1966; and *Direct and Total Wage Costs for Workers*, international survey by the Swedish Employers' Confederation.

Thus the United States had, after Britain, the slowest growth of output and a much smaller increase in output per worker after 1963. But because the cost of labour rose much more slowly in the United States than elsewhere, labour costs per unit of output, in this global sense, fell substantially there between 1958 and 1963, but not elsewhere (except marginally in Italy). Between 1963 and 1968 labour cost per unit of output again fell in the United States, although by much less than in the previous five years, and less than in France and West Germany, though the difference was not great. In Italy a steeper rise in the cost of labour and slower rise in output per worker resulted in an *increase* in labour cost per unit in the second period.[46] In Britain and Japan there was no change in terms of domestic factor prices.

This table only compares apparent *rates of change*, not absolute quantities. On this level of aggregation "labour cost per unit of output" is a useful concept, but it cannot have a counterpart in absolute terms.

Since the "chemical industry" in its widest meaning is composed of many sectors whose economic characteristics differ, it is helpful and a safeguard in interpreting these global figures to break them down where possible into sector figures. This can be done for the United States, and to a lesser extent for Britain, but not at all for West Germany. Table 18 compares: (1) added value per head in most sectors of the chemical and allied industries of the United States in 1967 and Britain in 1968, and (2) labour cost as a percentage of added value for the same years. The sectors are ranked according to the labour cost percentage in the United States with the lowest at the top and the remainder in ascending order. The American sector figures differ from the global figures used above (see Tables 16 and 17 and Figure 1), because they exclude workers in purely administrative and auxiliary units.[47]

[46]This figure in Table 10 should be used with special caution. As mentioned above, the Italian statistics in the OECD reports have been subject to drastic revision in the last few years. The Italian Central Institute of Statistics kindly sent the author revised data on added value and the index of production from 1958-67. But the various statistics which must be used in combination with these are not all collected by one body. Problems of reconciling all the figures have not been solved.

[47]The administrative and auxiliary units include central offices of large companies which are not attached to manufacturing establishments and also units, such as central research units, not working for a specific manufacturing plant. They were not statistically negligible. In 1963 the relevant figures were:

Since the most recent published census data refer to different years—1967 for the United States and 1968 for the United Kingdom—allowances must be made for this in comparisons. First, and relatively simple, the American figures would all be higher for 1968. The average added value per head in the United States chemical industry probably rose by almost 4.5 per cent from 1967 to 1968.[48] Average payroll costs probably rose by slightly more—between 5 and 5.5 per cent. In Table 18, therefore, the American added value per head figures should be increased on an average by about 4.5 per cent (but the figure would not be uniform for all sectors), and both the added value ratios and the cost of labour ratios would be increased by a slightly higher percentage (which is likely, however, to be more uniform for all the sectors). This obviously will not greatly affect the comparison of the ratios in the two columns. A second more speculative allowance must be made in interpreting these figures because, as an outcome of sterling's devaluation, 1968 was a year in which there were considerable changes in relative prices. In Table 18 the ratios are given both before and after allowances.

Thus the rank of sectors according to added value per head is fairly similar in the United States and Britain, although there are a few striking differences. The important contrast is that the range of variation between sectors is much greater in the United

	No. employed ('000)	*Payroll* ($m)
Operating Manufacturing Establishments (available for sectors)	835.1	6,013
Administrative and Auxiliary Establishments (not available for sectors)	115.7	1,044

In the United Kingdom figures, firms "were asked to exclude from all sections of their returns particulars relating to any department not engaged in production for which they kept a separate set of accounts". This applied to merchanting, factoring, canteens, packing, manufacture of containers, buildings, maintenance, selling and transport departments. Where separate accounts were not kept for these, the activities were included whether carried on at the producing establishment or on a separate site. The British figures are thus not uniform in coverage. Particulars for head offices and common service departments (such as research) could be included in the return for a firm's main establishment or an appropriate proportion could be included for each establishment. *Particulars of head offices of firms with very diverse activities were not included.* The author does not know how the omissions from all the United Kingdom returns, and those from the United States sector returns, compare, but doubts if it is possible to establish this.

[48]This is based on the assumption that the average added value per head rose at the same rate as gross output per head (which was 4.5 per cent).

States. The ratio between added value in the United States and Britain ranged from 5.9 : 1 for toilet preparations to 2.1 : 1 for printing ink and synthetic fibres and 1.8 : 1 for fertilisers. Similarly labour cost, as a percentage of added value, varies much more between sectors in the United States than in Britain. It is impressive that despite the much higher level of American wages this percentage is normally lower, and often much lower, in the United States than in Britain.

To the extent that the added value ratio in a sector exceeds the ratio between American and British earnings (including fringe benefits) in the same sector, the labour cost per unit of output would be lower in the United States than in Britain and *vice versa*—subject to two conditions. First, that the items of labour cost covered directly are broadly the same in both countries; and, secondly, that the prices on which the added values depend are, at the current rates of exchange, broadly similar. These conditions, as has been seen, are not fully satisfied and the figures cannot be regarded as precisely correct. But the broad conclusion seems clearly to be that, in a majority of sectors, American labour costs per unit of output were below British costs or nearly identical with them—although the cost of labour per head was from 2.7 to 3 times as high in the United States in most sectors.[49] Labour costs per unit of output in the United States tended naturally to be most below the British costs in sectors where added value per head was very high and most above the United Kingdom figure; where also of course

Group I *United States labour cost below United Kingdom*	*Group II* *United States and United Kingdom labour costs broadly equal*	*Group III* *United States labour costs above United Kingdom*
Toilet preparations[a]	Pharmaceuticals[a]	Agricultural chemicals
Soap and detergents[a]	Adhesives and glues	Man-made fibres[b]
Polishes	Plastic materials[b]	Printing ink
General chemicals[b]	Fertilisers	Explosives
Dyes and pigments[a]	Paints	

[a] [b]See notes e and f, Table 18.

[49]The earnings figures in the censuses naturally reflect the actual mix of different grades of workers of all types in the sectors.

TABLE 18 LABOUR COST AND ADDED VALUE: UNITED STATES (1967) AND UNITED KINGDOM (1968)
(Exchange Rate: $2.4 = £1)

	Labour Cost as % of Added Value		*Added Value per head ('000 $)*		*Unadjusted Ratios*		*Adjusted Ratios*[d]	
	United States (1967)	*United Kingdom (1968)*	*United States (1967)*	*United Kingdom (1968)*	*Added Value Ratio C ÷ D*	*Cost of Labour per head United States ÷ Cost of Labour per head United Kingdom (COL Ratio)*	*Added Value Ratio*	*Cost of Labour Ratio*
	A	*B*	*C*	*D*	*E*	*F*	*G*	*H*
Toilet preparations	15	30	41.6	7.0	5.9	2.9	5.5[e]	3.0
Soap and detergents	17	29	47.1	9.8	4.8	2.8	4.4[e]	2.9
Polishes[a]	19	34	33.9	7.0	4.8	2.8	4.4	2.9
Pharmaceutical chemicals and preparations	23	28	34.3	9.2	3.7	3.1	3.4[e]	3.3
Agricultural chemicals	24	24	31.9	11.7	2.7	2.8	2.5	2.9
Syntnetic rubber	27	—	31.9	—				
General chemicals	27	34	31.8	9.5	3.3	2.6	3.1[f]	2.7
Fertilisers	33	39	15.6	8.5	1.8	1.7	1.7	1.8
Dyes and pigments[c]	33	41	25.0	7.5	3.3	2.6	3.1[e]	2.7
Plastic materials[b]	34	36	23.4	8.5	2.8	2.6	2.6[f]	2.7
Man-made fibres	33	35	19.8	9.5	2.1	2.2	1.9[f]	2.3
Adhesives and gelatin	35	40	21.7	6.6	3.3	2.9	3.1	3.0
Paints	37	39	19.9	6.6	3.0	2.9	2.9	3.0
Printing ink	44	47	14.9	7.1	2.1	2.6	1.9	2.7
Explosives	59	56	11.5	4.6	2.5	2.7	2.3	2.8

[a]The United States figures for Polishes include "sanitation goods"; in the United Kingdom figures "disinfectants" are included with agricultural chemicals (which are called "formulated pesticides").

[b]Synthetic rubber is included with plastic materials in the British figures.

[c]Dyes and pigments are not given separately in the United States figures. There is a sector for inorganic pigments, but organic dyes and pigments are included with cyclic intermediates. I have assumed that the net output of these (whose gross output is given) bears the same relation to gross output as the net output of cyclic intermediates. This may be wrong; it may be a smaller proportion. If so the estimated average added value per man is too high. If this is so the average added value per man for United States general chemicals is too low, because I have included the residual cyclic intermediate figures in general chemicals. I do not think the differences are substantial.

[d]The adjustments are (1) additions of 4.5 per cent approximately to the added value ratios and 5 per cent to the cost of labour ratios to allow for the increase of United States output and earnings in 1968 (2) deductions of approximately 12 per cent from the added value ratios to allow for the relative fall in United Kingdom prices in dollar equivalents resulting from devaluation. The immediate fall was naturally 16½ per cent but price adaptations soon began to occur, and the United Kingdom price index was slightly over 4 per cent higher in 1968 than before devaluation, whereas the United States index fell slightly. These indices must be recognised as guides rather than precise measures.

[e]Sectors where in general United States prices were normally above United Kingdom prices (above, Page 52); hence United States labour costs per unit would be less below (or more above) United Kingdom costs than the ratios suggest.

[f]Sectors where United States prices were normally below United Kingdom prices; hence United States labour costs would be more below or less above United Kingdom than the ratios suggest.

labour cost was a small percentage of added value. The sectors may for convenience be put in three groups on the basis of Table 18.

It will be noted that general chemicals, which accounts for one-third of the added value of the whole American chemical industry, is among the sectors whose labour costs fall below those in the United Kingdom and since prices in this sector tend to be below British prices the ratio probably underestimates the difference. With toilet preparations and soap and detergents, on the other hand, where American prices may tend to be above British prices, the situation is reversed. But both are sectors in which the supply of fairly standard goods in small packs for a mass market gives great scope for economies of scale in subdividing output, weighing, measuring, counting, packing, labelling and handling for stock and delivery. The gap between the ratios may slightly over estimate the difference in labour costs, but not sufficiently to alter the bearing of the figures. With dyes and pigments it may be different. The gap is narrower and—as mentioned above—there is a possibility that the added value ratio is too high as an indication of labour cost differences, not only because American dye prices were above British prices, but also because the American statistics do not isolate added value figures for organic dyes and pigments. Plastic materials (in Group II) and man-made fibres (in Group III) are both sectors where American prices have been more often below than above British prices and in both, therefore, the real labour cost comparison was probably more favourable to the United States than the figures in Table 18 suggest. Apart from man-made fibres, the sectors in Group III are small and, while agricultural chemicals is a growing sector, the definitions of the British and American sectors differ markedly.

The figures in Table 18 provide a cross-section of the industry five or six years after the Little Report of 1962. They underline the continued competitive strength of the American industry. Similar figures are available for 1963 and they make it possible to trace some of the changes which had occurred after the 1962 analysis was published. The broad features are shown in Table 19. Here the first two columns contrast the average annual rates of growth of added value per head in the various sectors from 1963-7 in the United States and from 1963-8 in the United Kingdom. In the next four columns the adjusted added value and cost of labour ratios in Table 18 for 1968 are put beside the analogous ratios for 1963.

TABLE 19

COMPARATIVE CHANGES IN ADDED VALUE PER HEAD IN UNITED STATES AND UNITED KINGDOM, 1963-1968

	Average Annual Growth of Added Value per head		*1963*[b]		*1968*[c]	
	United States (1963-7)	*United Kingdom*[a] *(1963-8)*	*Added Value Ratio*	*Cost of Labour Ratio*	*Added Value Ratio*	*Cost of Labour Ratio*
	%	%				
Toilet preparations	4¼	3	5.0	2.9	5.5	3.0
Soap and detergents	6½	9½	5.1	3.0	4.4	2.9
Polishes	7	8¼	4.8	3.1	4.9	2.9
Pharmaceutical preparations and chemicals	4¾	11¼	4.5	3.2	3.4	3.3
Agricultural chemicals	15	16	2.8	2.9	2.5	2.9
General chemicals	4¾	6½	3.3	2.6	3.1	2.7
Fertilisers	10	11½	2.4	1.9	1.7	1.8
Dyes and pigments	1½	8½	4.0	2.7	3.1	2.7
Plastic materials	4½	7¾	2.8	2.6	2.6	2.7
Man-made fibres	4½	6¼	2.3	2.5	1.9	2.3
Adhesives and gelatin	5¾	9	3.4	2.8	3.1	3.0
Paint	2¼	8¾	3.6	3.1	2.9	3.0
Printing ink	3¾	6¾	2.5	2.3	1.9	2.7
Explosives	1	5¾	2.7	3.1	2.3	2.8

[a]These are based upon sterling values; there is no devaluation effect.
[b]Here the exchange rate used is \$2.8 = £1.
[c]Here the exchange rate used is \$2.4 = £1 and the ratios are the adjusted ratios of Table 18.

The first two columns show that the average annual increase in added value per head was substantial in the United States in almost all sectors (4 per cent or more). But the average increase in Britain, measured in sterling, was considerably higher in almost all sectors—the average was 7.25 per cent. Since the American added value a a head was from 2.5 to 5.5 times the British figure in all save four sectors (only one of them of major importance) this difference in rates of increase was not enough to reduce the gap quickly. Indeed the excess of the American value added per head over the British figure in absolute terms had increased substantially between 1963 and 1968.[50] American productivity figures are often discussed as fixed targets at which competitors can aim and quickly reach: they are in fact fast-moving targets. To some extent the higher British *percentage* rates of growth may reflect the fact that economies of large scale are usually largest when the starting point is small scale and are likely to decline as the scale of production from which increase is initiated rises.

The remaining columns of Table 19 show that the added value ratio was lower in 1968 in all save two sectors (toilet preparations and polishes) than it was in 1963. But the cost of labour ratio was roughly the same in both years—except, again, in two sectors, both small, namely printing ink and explosives. The falls in added value ratios reflect the greater percentage rise in added value per head in the United Kingdom which is shown in the first two columns.

The falls in the added value ratio were not uniform. In general chemicals, which accounted for one-third of the added value of the whole American chemical group, it was notably small (6 per cent), and it was also low (7 per cent) in the plastic materials sector. The falls were in general lowest (not surprisingly) in sectors where added value per head was high in the United States. But pharmaceuticals were an exception due to an above average rise in added value per head in Britain. It is significant that the pharmaceutical industry is a sector of the British industry in which subsidiaries of American firms are particularly prominent. The added value ratio fell by 22 per cent in the dyes and pigments sector—due mainly to a much

[50]If the United Kingdom 1968 figures are compared with the United States 1967 figures at the exchange rate of \$2.4 to £1, the absolute increase of the gap since 1963 was 16 per cent; if the exchange rate of \$2.8 = £1 was used, the gap increased by 8 per cent. At the rates of growth experienced from 1963 to 1967-68 and neglecting devaluation effects it would take 40 years or so for the United Kingdom average added value per head to reach the United States average.

below average increase in added value per head in the United States. The other substantial falls in the added value ratio—in fertilisers (30 per cent), man-made fibres (17 per cent), paint (19 per cent) and printing ink (24 per cent) were all sectors where the added value per head in the United States was relatively low. The man-made fibres figures seem somewhat anomalous in this context and, as has been seen, more competitive prices in the United States in 1967-8 may distort this particular ratio.

The close similarity of the cost of labour ratios in almost all sectors in 1963 and 1968 is at first sight surprising because devaluation necessarily raised cost of labour ratios when it occurred in 1967. Earnings in the United Kingdom rose in sterling by 42 per cent per head from 1963 to 1968 whereas in the United States the rise was approximately 22 per cent for the same period.[51] When the British sterling figures are converted to dollars at the rates current in 1963 and 1968 respectively the United Kingdom rise becomes 22 per cent. The rate of devaluation in 1967 in fact just balanced the greater increase in average earnings and fringe benefits per head which occurred in Britain from 1963-68. Devaluation had broadly restored in the chemical industry the 1963 situation in regard to the comparative cost of a unit of labour.

These statistics of added value per man have been described by the Economic Development Committee of the Chemical Industry, a subsidiary body of the National Economic Development Council, as "so global and so crude that they give no guide to the reasons for their discrepancy".[52] This is to misconceive their function. They are a guide to differences of performance, but do not purport to explain the sources of difference. The appropriate question is: how accurate are they for the function for which they are designed?

Some of the "globalness" can, as has been seen, be removed. But there are, as has also been seen, deficiencies. They arise partly from the acute difficulties, which have already been referred to, of measuring price and output changes in an industry making thousands of different products, with many new products coming in and old ones being discontinued, and where the relative import-

[51]From 1963-7 the rise in the Census of Manufacturing Statistics was 17 per cent. Projected to 1968 this was 22 per cent. The increase in average weekly earnings from the United States Bureau of Labour Statistics supports this.

[52]*Manpower in the Chemical Industry* (London: HM Stationery Office, for the Economic Development Committee of the Chemical Industry, National Economic Development Council, 1967), p. 1.

ance of different products changes constantly in each country, and is not the same in different countries. Deficiencies also arise from the methods of collecting and calculating the figures. The OECD relies upon statistics provided by member countries. These are not based upon identical enquiries from firms in all countries. Most countries do not regularly collect statistics of added value but calculate it from production statistics, using ratios based on periodic censuses of production. The ratios progressively lose their validity and there are, from time to time, substantial revisions. As mentioned above, the sectors are not identically defined in different countries, and the range of activities covered in census of production statistics is not uniform. All this means that small differences and small short period changes cannot be regarded as significant.

But the large difference between added value per head in the United States and the competitor countries, and the persistent differences between trends within the competitor countries, in particular between the relatively slow growth in Britain and the faster growth in the others, remain reliable though not precise guides to comparative performance. It is of course plain that the great excess of the American wage levels over wage levels measured in dollar equivalents at current exchange rates in competing countries, about which there is no dispute, has to be offset mainly by a corresponding excess of added value per head.

The analysis turns now from the statement of the differences to the strength of the forces producing change.

Size of Markets

Considering that it was being argued in 1962 that if foreign competitors built new plants to make organic chemicals their costs of production in the new plants would be 10 to 20 per cent below American costs and that by 1970 these competing industries would be capable, given tariff relaxations, of deep penetration into the American home market, the persistence in 1968 of the wide difference between added values per head and average earnings in the United States on the one hand and the many competitor countries on the other is impressive. It is striking, too, that the keenest competitor in Western Europe, as revealed by these (and other) figures, has been not Italy, whose cost advantage was originally expected to be the largest (see Page 184 above), but West Germany.

GNP has been growing faster in most West European countries

TABLE 20

CONSUMPTION AND PROJECTED CONSUMPTION OF CHEMICAL PRODUCTS[a], 1960-75

	Consumption[b] *in 1960* (*1960 prices*)	*ADL*[c] *"Probability" for 1970* (*1962 prices*)	*Consumption*[b] *in 1968* (*1968 prices*)	*OECD*[d] *Projection of Consumption for 1975* (*1958 prices*)
EEC	12.4	35	23.4	(44)[e]
United Kingdom	4.9			
All Western Europe	19.4	45	38.9	65
United States	26.4	45	44.3	80

[a]The Table gives in columns 1 and 3 consumption based on sales less net exports. The net exports from the EEC, the United States and the whole of Europe were, in fact, relatively small. It is likely that the Little Report figures were for the *sales* of the chemical industry, not sales less net exports. If this were so the corresponding 1968 figures for the EEC and United States were $26,000 and $46,600m billions. The OECD projection was defined as consumption. The OECD noted that the most recent figure for the U.S. prior to their projection suggested growth might prove less than projected: but the 1968 figure turned out to be right on course. Prices in 1968 were slightly lower than in 1958. (Cp. Section V.)

[b]OECD: *The Chemical Industry*, 1960-1, and 1969-70.

[c]1962 Little Report, p. 7. I assume that a constant price level was envisaged (not of course that all prices would remain static).

[d]OECD: *The Chemical Industry*, 1968-9, pp. 13-15.

[e]This is roughly two-thirds of the total European figure, not part of the OECD projection. It is based on the position in 1968. It is meant merely to give a scale of magnitude.

than in the United States and this continues. The formation of the EEC and EFTA consolidated most West European national markets into two free trade markets which might be merged into one. The key question for this study is to what extent, and how quickly, these developments will produce market conditions in the West European blocks, or in Western Europe as one block, which give the same scope for large-scale manufacturing and marketing in Western Europe, as exists in the United States as a result of the size of the American domestic market.

In 1962, at the time of the 1962 Little Report, the population of the EEC was only 6 per cent less than that of the United States, but GNP was nearly 60 per cent less. The EEC population was likely to grow more slowly. It would, the forecasters thought, be 20 per cent below that of the United States in 1975. But the GNP of the EEC was growing much faster. The population of EFTA was little over one half that of the EEC, and GNP less than one quarter that of the United States. If the EEC and EFTA merged, the combined market would have a population substantially larger than the United States—in 1975 the forecasters put it at nearly one quarter larger: the GNP of the area was already close on two-thirds that of the United States in 1967.[53]

By 1960 consumption of chemical products in the EEC was already almost half that in the United States[54] (though GNP was only 40 per cent as high) and the Little Report expected a further large relative increase in EEC consumption compared with that in the United States by 1970. The further growth of consumption in the United States has been considerably faster than was envisaged, whereas in parts of the EEC it has been slightly slower. An OECD statistical exercise made in 1968 projected that American consumption would on past trends still be substantially above that in the whole of Europe in 1975.[55] The figures are given in Table 20.

The aggregate demand for all the products of the chemical industry in the EEC was thus still in 1968 much below the aggregate demand in the United States and looked like being so for a decade or more. The position varied between sectors, as Table 21, giving figures for some particular sectors in 1967 and 1968, shows. Despite the forebodings of 1962 the American market for basic organic

[53]1962 Little Report, *op. cit.*, p. 7. For the population and GNP figures: *Basic Statistics of the Community*, Statistical Office of the European Communities, Brussels.

[54]See *The Chemical Industry, 1961* (Paris: OECD Secretariat, 1961), p. 109.

[55]The projection appeared to envisage that GNP in 1975, in terms of 1958 prices would be $980,000m in the United States and $600,000m in Western Europe. The bases of the projection were rather narrow. The Stanford Research Institute Report of 1967, *op. cit.*, gave a projection of output for 1970 and 1975 limited to petrochemicals: according to this, the United States output of primary, intermediates and "end" petrochemicals would exceed West European output by over 18 per cent in 1975, but West European output of polymer petrochemicals (largely plastic materials, elastomers and fibres would exceed American output by 20 per cent. Overall the United States output would exceed Western Europe's by 6 per cent. The United States *per capita* output would be over 50 per cent above the West European. United States net exports would exceed Western Europe's and exports were small in relation to home use, so that consumption and production in the areas were not very different. (Stanford Research Institute Report of 1967, *op. cit.*, Vol. II, Appendices I and R.)

TABLE 21

CONSUMPTION OF CHEMICALS BY SECTOR AND REGION[a], 1967-68

	United States	Western Europe	
		Total	EEC
Basic organic chemicals (m. tons)	20.0[d]	13.9[c]	10.3[c]
Sulphuric acid (m. tons)[c]	26.4	20.0	13.1
Primary ammonia (m. tons)[b]	8.9	7.3	6.0
Phosphoric acid (m. tons)[b]	4.3		1.4
Plastic materials (m. tons)[c]	6.5	7.6	5.5
Dyes ('000 tons)	111	130	80
$ million	454	407	260
Pharmaceuticals ($ m)[c]	5,376		3,100
Paint (kg per head)[c]	18.7	10.0	11.9
Soap ('000 tons)[c]	444	1,251	559
Detergent powders (m. tons)	3.02[e]	2.00[c]	1.35[c]
Glycerine ('000 tons)[b]	166	68	34

[a]The table does not cover all sectors, and for several sectors it covers a limited range of products only.
[b]1967. [c]1968. [d]Without Belgium. [e]1966.

chemicals was still far larger than the whole West European market and double that of the EEC and it was still supplied mainly from home production. The West European consumption of plastic materials on the other hand, according to the OECD figures, was larger than the American consumption, and the EEC consumption alone was 85 per cent of the American consumption. This largely reflected the high per capita use of plastic materials in West Germany which was one-quarter higher than the United States figure and double the British.[56] But this was exceptional: in most sectors consumption was substantially higher in the United States than in the EEC, and usually higher than in Western Europe as a whole.

The EEC market is not yet as free as the American market. Trade between member countries is still recorded as international and there are tax drawbacks to arrange. All this involves bureaucratic costs. Language and currency differences provide at least

[56]The consumption figures (Kg per head) for 1968 were: West Germany 40.4; the United States 32.5; the United Kingdom 20.4. The average for the other EEC countries was 21. In tables giving production details for particular plastic materials, the West German figures are said to include some materials used for fibres. Whether this enters into the consumption-per-head figures is not clear.

minor hurdles which involve costs in some sectors and there are important non-tariff barriers in pharmaceuticals. The national governments each have established controls intended to ensure that drugs which are on sale are harmless and effective and accurately described. The regulations differ, and in effect they all delay the entry of drugs from other member countries as well as from countries outside the EEC, and they add to the costs of the trade.[57]

It is of more general importance that, since most chemical products are sold to other industries as raw materials or process materials, the generally smaller size of firms and plants in Western Europe raises the costs in physical terms of distributing and selling chemical products in Western Europe above those in the United States. It would lower average added value per person. There is, as far as I know, no full or recent analysis of the comparative size of firms and plants in the relevant consuming industries, and no study at all of its effect on packing, transport and selling costs.[58]

To sum up:

(1) The aggregate consumption of chemicals in the EEC in 1968 was almost double that in EFTA, but it was more below American consumption than was expected in 1962. Forecasts suggest it may be a little over half the United States level in 1975.

(2) The EEC consumption of plastic materials (particularly the West German consumption) has been exceptionally high and in 1968 was almost as large as American consumption.

(3) The aggregate consumption of all chemical products (including plastics) in the whole of Western Europe was slightly over 12 per cent less than that of the United States in 1968, and current projections envisage that American consumption will remain as much or more above European consumption in 1975. West European consumption of plastic materials, however, was 17 per cent higher than American consumption in 1968, and this margin is expected to be maintained or increased.

(4) There remain more imperfections in the EEC market than in the American market and the average size of orders for industrial chemicals is almost certainly smaller.

[57]For a useful summary of the position in mid-1967 see *European Community*, Commission of the European Communities, Brussels, May, 1969, p. 20.

[58]The commonest comparisons are in terms of numbers employed per plant. These are irrelevant in this context—indeed in most contexts—since American outputs per worker are much higher, in virtually all industries.

It is not to be assumed that equivalence in size of market is necessary to give scope for maximum economies of scale. But clearly it would be a favourable circumstance.

Raw Material Costs

The American chemical industry has always had relatively cheap indigenous supplies of most bulk raw materials for industrial chemicals—such as salt, sulphur, phosphates, by-products of coal, non-ferrous metals. These have been cheaper than in the United Kingdom and probably cheaper than in West Germany and the European continent as a whole. There has been no recent change. The problem area, dealt with in the 1966 Little Report, and a year later in a report by Stanford Research Institute,[59] is in regard to feedstocks for organic chemicals, where the greatest expansion in output has occurred.

The petrochemical industry expanded dramatically after World War II, first in Texas and later in Louisiana, the major centres of the American oil industry. Its raw materials were the "waste" gases of the oil wells and refineries together with the vast natural gas resources of the area. The gas was rich in ethane, which became the principal raw material used for ethylene, which in turn became the main basic aliphatic chemical. Until the late 1950s the Texas and Louisiana petrochemical plants had cheaper raw materials than were available elsewhere. By 1960 the margin of advantage had been greatly reduced, perhaps eliminated, and many major American chemical firms thought that by 1965 raw materials for basic organic chemicals were now more costly in the United States than in either Western Europe or Japan. If this were so it clearly would be important for the impact of a free trade treaty arrangement.

By the mid-1960s the use of naphtha as a raw material had been developed to the point at which—according to the conventional way of assessing costs—ethylene could be made as cheaply in Western Europe and Japan from naphtha as it was made from ethane in the United States.[60] It was not a simple comparison, because ethylene is a joint product by all processes, but the proportion of products

[59]See Footnote 38, Page 180.

[60]W. A. Mason, of Imperial Chemical Industries, gave a good analysis of this question at the Frankfurt meeting of the Society for the Chemical Industry in April, 1968.

other than ethylene, particularly propylene and butadiene, is much higher from naphtha than from ethane. The economy of the process depends largely therefore on the prices at which *all* the products can be sold.[61] The market for these other products has been increasing rather faster than was generally expected, so that a process which would give more of the by-products had increasing attractions in the United States itself. The use of naphtha in the United States seemed, however, to be hampered by its market price there. This has been around $32 a ton, whereas in Western Europe naphtha could be bought for $19 a ton in 1965, and $21 in 1969. The difference basically arose from the fact that oil was easier, and therefore cheaper, to extract in the oilfields of the Middle East, North and West Africa, Venezuela and the Caribbean than in Texas and Louisiana. But the United States has restricted imports of cheap foreign oil and oil products by quotas. Petrochemical producers have succeeded in obtaining allocations to import about 7 per cent of their feedstocks: this would cover primarily imports of naphtha. (In fact they have *not* imported feedstocks, but have exchanged their quotas for domestic supplies: their quotas have been used for imports of crude oil.[62]) The United States cost prospect was further clouded by fears that the price of additional supplies of ethane would become much higher. In 1967 the average price of ethane sold was actually lower than in 1959—according to Tariff Commission figures.[63] But it is fairly generally accepted that because of competing demands for gas, and because the chemical composition of much of the gas from new wells makes extraction of ethane more costly, the price will increase. Some higher prices—up to 1 cent per pound—were being paid in 1968-69,[64] but some experts envisaged

[61]The "conventional" way is criticised as fallacious in the Stanford Research Institute Report of 1967, *op. cit.*, Vol. I, p. 97. If gas oil was used as raw material ethylene would cost less than nothing to produce.

[62]Stanford Institute Report of 1967, *op. cit.*, Vol. 1, p. 1.

[63]The figures (cents per pound) were:

1959	0.9	1962	0.8	1966	0.9
1960	1.0	1963	0.9	1967	0.8
1961	1.0	1964	0.8		

[64]In 1968-69 some firms were paying 0.9 per cent: one at least paid 1 cent. The spot price was no doubt above the long-term contract price.

prices rising in a year or so to 1.3 cents per pound,[65] compared with the average of 0.8 cents for 1967. If this increase occurred it would raise the cost of making ethylene by about 0.7 cents above the 1967 cost[66]—a substantial increase. The selling price of ethylene in 1967 was about 4 cents per pound; it was lower in 1968-69.

All this provides an impressive case for the view that the American makers are at a growing disadvantage competitively unless the import restrictions into the United States are relaxed. But there are conflicting views. The Stanford Research Institute in its report which was made for some oil-based chemical firms in 1968 concluded that "adequate supplies of domestic feedstocks will be available in the United States to 1975" (the terminal date of their study) "at slowly increasing but internationally competitive prices", and that American net exports of petrochemicals would continue to rise fast irrespective of the level of imports of feedstocks. It was pointed out, too, that although raw material costs were a large part of the cost of ethylene this component of ethylene cost was a relatively small part of the cost of the more finished products for which ethylene itself was a raw material.[67] Several chemical companies, chemical engineering constructors, and other consultants supported this view. The chemical companies who did so were subsidiaries of major oil firms.

Despite the forebodings widely expressed from 1965 onwards, American chemical firms continued to invest in new giant ethylene plants in Texas and Louisiana and in 1967-69 there was an investment boom. Some of the plants were based on ethane, some on mixed gases and at least one was based on light oil.[68] The choice of raw materials is not just simply between ethane and naphtha, although this is a convenient simplification. It is suggested—and it seems plausible—that chemical firms which are subsidiaries of major

[65]This was an estimate given to the author verbally.

[66]Following for convenience the convention of charging the whole cost of ethane to ethylene, although some by-products are also obtained.

[67]A rough calculation suggests that the cost or value of the input of ethane, propane, methane and light oils which provide the starting point for almost all United States organic synthetic intermediates and finished products (dyes, drugs, plastics, elastomers, plasticisers and so on) was about 5 per cent of the current selling value of the product. The average value of the products in 1966 was 18.9 cents per pound (*Report on Synthetic Organic Chemicals* [Washington: US Tariff Commission, 1966], p. 7). The average value of the input was below one cent per pound.

[68]The plant was built by the Shell Oil Company at Houston and started up in 1969. This company was the first to start chemical manufacture in Texas in 1940. It started making chemicals from refinery gases in California in 1929.

oil companies are better placed than "pure" chemical companies to spot the cheapest route for making ethylene at any given time, having regard to the price prospects both for raw materials and for the range of "by-products", which will have a much higher value if they can all be sold as chemicals and not as fuel.

To sum up at this point, then:

(1) The American industry does not have cheaper raw materials for most organic chemicals—particularly for aliphatic chemicals, notably ethylene—than competitors in Western Europe or Japan.

(2) It is not established by the published data that they have dearer raw materials—though there is strong support for this view, but it is also strongly disputed.

(3) The current situation appears to put American chemical companies which are subsidiaries of oil companies in a favourable position to get feedstocks at lowest costs.

(4) If American feedstock costs are now higher than competitors' costs this results largely from the protection of indigenous oil, and any disadvantage could be largely eliminated by administrative action—which has been contemplated.[69]

It should be added that the balance of raw material supplies is likely to be modified by the opening up of new natural gas fields and the cheap means now available of transporting liquid gas by sea—whether refinery gas or natural gas.[70] Some of the new natural gas, including all the gas found in Western Europe, is not rich in ethane. Such gas has a limited value only as a raw material for chemicals, although methane *is* a good feedstock for ammonia. But some gases valuable for chemical synthesis are likely to be found. In North America large new supplies of gas will come from Alberta and Alaska. North America is likely to have a stronger strategic supply of natural gas than Europe or Japan.[71]

The United States, then, has lower cost raw materials for inorganic chemicals than competitors in Western Europe and Japan, and need

[69]Proposals for replacing quotas by duties have had strong support in the Nixon Administration, but this has not yet been achieved.

[70]The indications are that large-scale imports of LPG have been moving into Japan from the Persian Gulf at landed costs of 5 to 7.5 cents a gallon, which is upwards of 1.1 cents a pound (1 gallon weighs 4.5 lb.), and from 52 to 78 cents a million BTU, or 5.2 to 7.8 cents a therm. Of the cost at the lower level roughly two-fifths is the freight cost.

[71]There is also cheap gas available in the Caribbean: the price of gas in Venezuela in 1968 was 1 cent per therm.

not be at a cost disadvantage in obtaining feedstocks for organic chemicals. Though she may therefore be regarded as having a net advantage in material supplies it is not a large factor in costs.[72]

Fuel and Power Costs

The American chemical firms have had much cheaper fuel and power than competitors in other countries. The gap is being lessened by the use of natural gas in Western Europe and by the cheap means of transporting this gas and refinery gas by sea as well as by land and possibly by increasing costs in obtaining primary fuels in the United States. It will be further reduced by the wider use of nuclear energy for generating electric power.

The prices of natural gas in Western Europe where they are available are above the prices in the United States. In Texas and Louisiana natural gas cost 2 cents a therm or less to large users in the late 1960s.[73] It was more costly to users remote from the gas wells, but often they had cheap coal. In Pennsylvania, for example, gas cost 3 cents a therm or more in the mid-1960s when used in power stations, but coal used by power stations near the mines cost from 1.5 cents to 2 cents a therm. In Holland in 1968 the price of natural gas was 3½d a therm; it was expected to be reduced, but not halved. In Britain the lowest price is not much below 3d a therm.[74]

Though the British price is much above the Gulf price in the United States it is much below the price of coal and somewhat below that of oil in Britain,[75] so that where it can be used for process

[72]It would be misleading in making the assessment to give great importance to the contrast between inorganic and organic chemicals: the two are very commonly used together (for example in PVC, acrylonitrile, etc.).

[73]Prices paid by utilities are published by the Federal Power Commission in *Steam Electric Plant Construction Cost and Annual Production Expenses: 21st Annual Supplement*, which gives the data for 1968.

[74]There is much obscurity about the price of gas for large industrial users, and contracts are often complex, price depending on characteristics of the load. Many of the chemical firms in the United States and some in the United Kingdom have their own gas wells; it is not possible to say what their transfer prices are, nor where they take their profit, although it is probable the prices of gas actually sold are some indication of relative costs. West Germany and Italy are both arranging to obtain gas by pipeline from Russia; here again the price is not published. Gas in some of the newer oilfields where there is no large local market is often much below the Gulf price in the United States. The price of gas in Venezuela was 1 cent a therm in the late 1960s; it was 0.2 cents a pound in Kuwait.

[75]The price of coal in the United Kingdom for power generation averaged about 4.3d per therm in 1964-5; 4.8d per therm, in 1968-9. The average cost in United States power stations in 1964 "as burned"; that is, after preparation, was 2.4 cents; it was much lower in the cheap coal areas.

heat and power it will lessen the gap between fuel costs in the two countries. The fuel cost for the same operation would probably still be one third or more less in the low-cost regions of the United States than in the United Kingdom—or the rest of Western Europe.

The cost of nuclear power could become approximately the same in all countries where the load makes it practical to use high capacity generating plants. In the United States the cost of electricity from nuclear plants now coming into use is expected to be almost as low as the cost in plants operating where the cheapest coal, or cheap natural gas, or cheap water power are available.[76] Prices for power for industrial users in low-cost coal and gas and hydro areas have been far below European prices.[77] As a result of nuclear power there will be a trend to more equal power costs both within the United States and internationally, but it will be gradual. Its impact on the chemical industry will depend partly on pricing policies. The West German chemical industry may be the first in Europe to benefit extensively—though this is less certain than it seemed in 1968. Two major firms, Badische Anilin and Farbwerke Hoechst, possibly in association with a utility, were planning to build their own nuclear plants to supply both process steam and power (as Dow Chemical is doing in the United States).[78] One plant might have operated by the end of 1975[79] but government concern over safety aspects delayed decision.

Expenditure on purchased fuel and power is a large part of costs in the manufacture of basic chemicals. Basic chemical manu-

[76]The Tennessee Valley Authority, for example, ordered four more nuclear units in the summer of 1970.

[77]The average price of electricity sold to industrial users was in many areas of the United States between 0.5 and 0.8 cents a KWh in the late 1960s. For *all* "large" industrial users (numbering 257,000) supplied by private utilities (this excludes therefore the low-cost Tennessee Valley Authority and Pacific Northwest supplies—where the average was below 0.8 cents) in high and low-cost areas the average price was 0.97 cents in 1968. The average cost of power for industry in the United Kingdom in 1968-69 was 1.55d (old currency) per KWh; the lowest *area* average was 1.3d (old currency).

[78]Badische Anilin have provisionally ordered a plant—a water reactor—but subject to reservation, because the Government might require safety precautions which would be too costly.

[79]The third major West German chemical firm, Bayer, can obtain exceptionally cheap brown coal locally, and has no immediate interest in nuclear power. Because no future market can be envisaged for brown coal it is being sold at prices which make no provision for the opening up of new deposits. There have been a few West German chemical plants which, through favourable contracts, have had exceptionally cheap electric power since the war.

facturing contributed about 3 per cent to total manufacturing output in the United States in 1963, but used over 12 per cent of the fuel and power purchased by all manufacturers. The total consumption of fuel and power for basic chemicals included much that did not come into these figures, because by-products were used as fuel, and many firms generated electric power in their own plants. This amounted to 13 per cent of total power used in the basic chemical industries in 1963. The production of inorganic chemicals involves the purchase of much more fuel and power than organic chemical production, because while the processes for the latter consume enormous quantities of heat and power, by-products and waste heat supply much of what is needed.[80] Expenditures on fuel and power in 1963 in the United States in the chemical and allied industries, and in a few sectors, are given in Table 22.

In the more finished product sectors the percentage varied around 1 per cent, not often above 1.5, often below 0.5 per cent. A high fuel and power content is normally contained, however, in the raw material costs of the more finished products.

To be able to buy cheap fuel and power is, therefore, of great competitive importance in some sectors. In basic chemicals, if fuel and power prices in Western Europe were 50 per cent higher than in the United States, then supposing the products made and the processes used were broadly similar, the higher European costs would have equalled roughly 3.4 per cent of sales value in 1963. It is probable that West European fuel and power prices were in fact *more* than 50 per cent above American prices in 1963. They may still be more than 50 per cent higher, but the margin will become less. All fuel prices rose sharply in the United States in 1969-70.[81] But if it remained overall at 25 per cent it would still

[80]Methane produced in making ethylene from ethane and propane, for example, is in some plants used as a fuel in the process. If it were not so used it would be saleable either as a fuel or raw material. In the organic chemical sector power generated in the plants supplied 40 per cent of total consumption in 1963. The contrast between consumption in organic and inorganic chemicals can mislead, because often organic and inorganic chemicals are used together in producing more finished products—as, for example, in PVC.

[81]The increase in spot coal prices in the United States during the latter half of 1969 and in 1970 was almost sensational. Prices had risen steadily by 10 per cent from 1965 to 1968. The price in June, 1970, was nearly 60 per cent above the 1965 price average. It had risen 35 per cent since June, 1969. (Figures from *Business Statistics* and *Survey of Current Business*, both published by the United States Department of Commerce, Washington.)

TABLE 22

EXPENDITURE ON PURCHASED FUEL AND ELECTRIC POWER AS A PERCENTAGE OF SALES IN THE UNITED STATES CHEMICAL INDUSTRY, 1963

	Sales $m	Expenditure as % of Sales	
		All Fuel and Power	Electric Power only
Chemical and Allied products	31,772	3.2	1.7
Basic Chemicals	11,109	6.8	3.9
Alkalies and Chlorine	783	10.6	5.0
Inorganic Chemicals[a]	3,845	9.7	7.0
Industrial gases	550	8.0	7.0
Organic Chemicals[b]	6,541	3.0	0.9
Plastic materials	3,523	1.5	0.6

[a]Excluding inorganic chemicals for which, as for alkalies and chlorine, details are given separately.
[b]Excluding organic chemicals for which details are given separately.

equal a cost differential of 1.7 per cent in basic chemicals—and 0.8 per cent for chemical and allied products all told.

Cost of Capital Equipment

Large refineries and chemical plants have cost more to equip and construct since the late fifties in the United States than in Western Europe. During the 1960s it seemed at times to skilled observers that the margin was getting wider and that the costs of obtaining new plants were rising faster in the United States than elsewhere. Available comparisons suggest that at least until 1968 the degree of difference has not varied greatly. Five comparisons covering the period 1959 to 1968 are collected in Table 23. The first was made by a major international oil company, based on experience as buyers. The second and third were made by the Little Reports of 1962 and 1965 based on their experience as consultants to chemical firms who were planning to buy plants. The fourth was made by a leading firm of engineer constructors. The fifth was made for an official inquiry (not in Britain) and was based on the experience of several large international chemical firms.

TABLE 23

INDICES OF THE COST OF CHEMICAL PLANTS IN DIFFERENT COUNTRIES

	1959[a]	*1961*[b]	*1964*[b]	*1966–7*	*1967–8*
United States	100	100	100	100	100–112[d]
United Kingdom	96	90	95	80	
West Germany	86	85	95	87[c]	89–93[e]
France	92	90	90	100[c]	
Holland	80				
Italy		85	85	78[c]	
Japan		80	80		85–97[e]
Canada					110–120

[a] *The Times*, September 19, 1959 (article on "The High Cost of Providing Capital Equipment").
[b] 1962 Little Report and 1965 Little Report (revised data).
[c] Final turnover taxes not included.
[d] The range is due to variation in cost at different locations. For the United States 100 represents the cost in Texas: 112 was the cost at the peak of demand at Baton Rouge, but shortly after, at Baton Rouge, the cost had fallen to 105.
[e] The range here is between costs of plants to make different products—ethylene, ammonia, elemental phosphorus: in each case the figures refer to 100 in the United States.

According to these indices the cost of a new plant in the United States was at most 25 per cent higher than the cheapest elsewhere and usually the difference was much less. The American cost was from 7 to 16 per cent above the cost in West Germany. In general, the British cost was conspicuously above that in West Germany or other West European countries and in Japan. The low 1966-67 figure for the United Kingdom is probably unrepresentative.[82]

[82] In 1966 the oil company whose 1959 experience is given in Table 22 confirmed that their experience in 1965 had been similar. United Kingdom costs were above costs for continental West European plants. But they said Continental costs were being pushed up by very heavy ordering resulting in delays and lower labour efficiency. They regarded it as a temporary situation. The Stanford Institute Report of 1967, *op. cit.*, Vol. I, p. 102, included figures for 1966 from a French source which put British construction costs 5 per cent below those in France and West Germany. The cost of much of the construction undertaken by the United Kingdom's chemical industry in 1966-67 turned out to be much above estimates. But this happens elsewhere as well.

These figures all refer to large units of plant where the design and practice has been essentially American. The comparisons are thus of fairly identical plants.[83] It is probable that the comparisons may be regarded as broadly representative for all types of plant.

The relatively small excess of the cost of new plants in the United States over competing countries reflects again much higher productivity in factor use, both in the manufacture of plant and equipment for the chemical industry and in construction. Wage levels are as relatively high by international comparison in engineering as in chemicals in the United States. In the construction industry American wages have been consistently not only much above the levels in other industries, but much more above those in competing countries than occurs in the chemical industry.[84]

The impact on production costs, and thus on competition, of the additional cost of acquiring new plants in the United States has fallen in the last decade because the cost of plants per unit of output has fallen—often remarkably. This has been due largely to increases in the size of plants, but also to radical changes or refinements in processes, the use of different catalysts, for instance, or new reactions, higher pressures or temperatures, newly developed materials for construction.

Table 24 provides some examples of the change in cost of plants per unit of output between 1962 and 1966. All are taken from data given by the two Little Reports for "typical" plants in 1962 and "averaged sized" plants in 1966.[85] The cost of plants per unit of output was lower in 1966 than in 1962 for all the products for which data are given in both reports by between 20 and 60 per cent—with two exceptions, one of which was almost certainly irrelevant.[86] The

[83]There are always differences arising out of the specific characteristics of the site, but also often differences in regard to feedstock, provision for varying degrees of flexibility in choice of what feedstocks to use and what products to make.

[84]The relative levels in 1967, comparable with those given for the chemical industry on Page 187, and taken from the same source, were: United States, 100; West Germany, 34; United Kingdom, 28; France, 27; Italy, 27; and Japan, 11.

[85]1962 Little Report, *op. cit.*, p. 72, and 1966 Little Report, *op. cit.*, pp. 61-4. In 1962, but not in 1966, the consultants gave the capacity of plants. The capacity of most of the 1962 plants in Table 24 is given later in Appendix III which sets out examples of increase in scale.

[86]The investment per pound for phenol was higher in 1966 than in 1962. But in 1966 (1966 Little Report, *op. cit.*, p. 70) the plant produced acetone as well as phenol. The 1962 process is not indicated. In the case of ethylene dichloride the investment per pound is small and the difference in absolute terms not significant.

TABLE 24

COST OF PLANTS PER UNIT OF CAPACITY AND PRODUCT PRICES IN THE UNITED STATES, 1962 AND 1966
(in cents per lb)

	1962		1966	
	Plant cost	*Price*	*Plant cost*	*Price*
Acrylonitrile	12.5	15	10	13
Ethanol	8.2	7	3.2	
Ethylene[a] (from ethane)	7.8	4.7	4.1	4.1
Ethylene[a] (from naphtha)	11		4.9	
Ethylene dichloride	2		2.5	
Ethylene oxide / Ethylene glycol	16.7	9	7	8
Methanol	7	3		3
Nylon			120	98–201[b]
Phenol	11	12	15	9
Phthallic anhydride	16	14	10	9
Polyester resin			13.3	30
Polyester fibre			80	72–167[b]
Polyethylene	28	21	21.5	17
Polystyrene			8	17
Polyurethane			22	59
PVC	16.8	18	10	17
SB rubber			15	21
Styrene monomer	11.7	10	5.5	8
Trichloroethylene	4.25	10	2.5	9
Vinyl acetate monomer	11.7	14	5	11

[a]Ethylene by both routes is a joint product. The investment in the table is for ethylene and other joint products. The volume of other products is larger from naphtha.

[b]The range is wide because nylon and polyester fibre are both made in staple and filament and yarn forms: the staple is the lowest priced, yarn the highest. There are quality variations also: the relevant average is certainly above the lowest figure in the range, although the prices were subject to discounts—especially for standard qualities.

drop in the cost of plant per unit of output in four years in the United States according to these instances was thus substantial.

The products in Table 24 are all organic chemicals or finished products based largely on organic intermediates. They are from the most expansive sections of the chemical industry, and they are also among the more capital intensive parts of the industry. It will be seen that for most products price per pound and cost of plant per pound of annual capacity were fairly close together in 1962, with the cost of plant per unit more often above than below the price. In 1966 prices had with few exceptions dropped, but costs of plant per unit had dropped more, and for most products was below, sometimes considerably below, the price.[87]

If it is assumed that 20 per cent is to be earned on cost of plant for depreciation and return on capital, then if the cost of an identical plant in the United States is 10 per cent more than in competitor countries the fixed capital charge will be 2 per cent higher in the United States than in the competitor countries. When price per pound and the cost of plant per pound of annual capacity are identical, this additional charge will be equal to 2 per cent of price. This percentage will vary in proportion to changes in the three components—the percentage to be earned on the investment, the excess of American cost of plant over competitors, the difference between price and cost of plant per unit of capacity.

The additional charge could be much more than 2 per cent. This is only likely if the cost of plant in the American rises appreciably more than 10 per cent above costs in competitor countries. Costs have been much increased in the United States, particularly by wage increases—but so they have elsewhere. With regard to the difference between price and the cost of plant per unit of capacity the table is slightly misleading—because most of the products are intermediates made from *other* intermediates (as vinyl acetate is made from ethylene) or "finished" chemical products such as PVC for which vinyl chloride is a raw material which in turn is made from ethylene. The ratio of price to cost of plant which is relevant for the calculation must take into account the cumulative influence of the higher cost of plant in the United States in the manufacturing costs of the intermediate (all stages) as well as of the finished product.

In the sectors of the industry producing more finished products the cost of plant tends to be—in varying degrees, but often con-

[87]Since in some the investment is related to one of a group of joint products the relation was even more often such that cost per unit of capacity was more below price than Table 24 shows. A notable case is ethylene from naphtha, where ethylene is only about 35 per cent of the saleable product.

siderably—below annual capacity turnover.[88] The addition to be made to this for the higher cost of plant used in making the intermediates is relatively small. If the cost of intermediates was as much as a third of the sales value of the finished product the addition would be from 0.5 to 1 per cent. This would put the additional cost due to the difference between cost of new plants in the United States and elsewhere at 2 to 2.5 per cent.[89]

The assumption so far is that plants in the United States and competing countries will be identical. How far this is valid in regard to scale, and even quality, will be considered in a later section. Two types of dissimilarity may, however, best be discussed here.

First, plants are built much faster in the United States than in Britain and possibly rather faster in the former than on the continent of Western Europe. In Japan the time taken is as short as in the United States. According to the Process Plant Working Party of the Economic Development Committee for the Chemical Industry, in a report issued in 1967, it took two to two and a half years (or even three years) to complete a plant in Britain, "whereas on a world-wide basis 15 months completions are not unusual". Because there was "an overload of work everywhere", eighteen months had become more usual in the rest of the world by 1967.[90] More recently, completions in the Benelux countries[91] and in North West Europe are said to take 21 months.[92] The "overload" around

[88]Turning to the 1966 Little Report, in forecasts of additional demand for petrochemicals, and the additional investment required to satisfy it, the sales income per dollar of investment which were used for different categories of demand were:

Organic Intermediates	1.0	Fibres	1.1
Plastics	1.4	Other	1.0
Rubber	1.3		

In some sectors—pharmaceutical preparations, for example, and paints, soaps, detergents and toiletries—the sales income per dollar of investment was much higher.

[89]This conclusion is consistent with the figures on the actual expenditure on new plant, which are below on Page 227.

[90]*Investment by the Process Industries* (London: HM Stationery Office, for the National Economic Development Council, 1967), p.12. The longer time taken to complete projects in the United Kingdom was not a recent development. But it had previously been more noticed in public discussion in connection with generating stations.

[91]Belgium, the Netherlands and Luxembourg comprise the Benelux countries.

[92]This was stated by Mr. Neil Iliff, as President of the Chemical Industry Association, on November 13, 1969.

Antwerp and Rotterdam is clearly exceptional. Delays also occur in boom conditions in the United States. But at the end of 1969 despite longer completion times elsewhere the still longer period required in Britain remained disturbing.[93]

When construction takes longer some costs are inevitably increased. Some expenditure will have to be financed for a longer period before there is any return for it and some overheads—supervision for instance—will be more costly. Some costs, overtime for instance, may be avoided (although commonly this does *not* happen). The important costs of relatively slow building, however, are not positive additions to the costs which figure in Table 23. The major real costs are (1) that the advantage of new output or lower costs begins later, (2) the development of new processes or new products is slowed down. These are both particularly important competitively in an industry characterised by rapid change. Competitors who complete plants faster will tend to keep ahead in development and earn the profits of innovation for longer. It is not possible to quantify this, but the disadvantage of the slow completion of plants in the United Kingdom could easily more than outweigh the advantage of having slightly cheaper plants than the United States. In competition with the rest of Europe the longer completion time is an additional drawback on top of having usually somewhat higher construction costs.

The second dissimilarity is in regard to financing the building of new plant. Differences in the cost of raising finance can affect the comparative cost of new equipment. It is not possible to explore this topic in detail on the scale of this study. More resources have been available from profits both in the United States and West Germany than in Britain and interest rates on borrowing have normally been lower in the United States than in Britain. Government assistance to investment has been a more conspicuous factor. In this respect British firms have had much more help, in various forms, than American or West German firms.[94] They have had most where they chose sites in development areas. The grant on plant in such areas rose to 45 per cent. Hence although this had often increased

[93] *Ibid.* The completion of one British plant, one of Shell's, was two years behind schedule.

[94] The Italian industry has had much government aid.

material or operating or transport costs the capital gains have been large.[95] According to the formula used earlier, the reductions in the capital charge on the production of ethylene would be close on 10 per cent of the price of ethylene. Policies of this kind, wherever they are pursued, are forms of subsidy which distort competition, which might not be popular in a multilateral free trade association.[96]

Shipping Costs

Shipping costs in the trans-Atlantic and trans-Pacific trades are high in proportion to prices for bulk "commodity" chemicals; relatively low compared with prices of more finished products and complex intermediates. The costs are being reduced by "containerisation" and analogous changes, though the extent of cost reduction is not well documented. Whatever the scale of the changes they are likely to reduce costs for the large competing firms in all countries fairly evenly. This section does not set out to assess the probable degree of change, but to give (in Table 25) some indication of the relative importance of shipping costs for a range of products excluding the most highly finished in the main trades between Western Europe and the United States.[97]

Thus for the chemicals covered in this table, shipping costs from Europe to the United States were upwards of 25 per cent of the price of products whose price was below 6 cents a pound, less than 12 per cent for products whose price was above 15 cents per pound, and usually between 5 and 9 per cent for products whose prices were from 15 to 25 cents a pound. Some of the differences are due to the nature of the product—some involve danger of explosion, or fire; some toxic gaseous products need to be compressed, which is costly. Aliphatic basic intermediates, notably ethylene, are costly

[95]The chief executive of the Brussels headquarters of Imperial Chemical Industries put it clearly in the *ICI Magazine*, April-May, 1967, p. 48: "Taken together with investment allowances and grants, our investment in bigger plants in the United Kingdom is beginning to give us a competitive edge in basic chemicals."

[96]They may lead, in the countries which pursue the policies, to a diversion of resources into less productive uses than would otherwise have occurred. But they would still have a competition-distorting influence in a free trade association.

[97]The figures deal solely with freights, including loading and unloading costs and port dues and insurance. Land transport is also required, but it is also required for domestic deliveries, and there is no uniform difference in this—nor is it necessarily always more for exports.

TABLE 25

FREIGHT AND INSURANCE ON VARIOUS CHEMICALS TO THE UNITED STATES, 1966[a]
(in cents per lb)

		From					
	United States price	*United Kingdom and France*		*West Germany*		*Italy*	*Benelux*
Product	*cents per lb*	*cents per lb*	*as % of price*	*cents per lb*	*as % of price*		
Soda ash	1.6	2.0	133	1.6	100	1.7	1.4
Ammonium sulphate	1.7	1.7	100	1.0	60	1.9	0.9
Acetone	5	3.4	68	2.0	40	2.9	1.8
Phosphoric acid and anhydride	5.6	2.3	40	1.4	25	3.2	1.3
Caustic soda	5.2	1.6	40	1.3	25	1.7	1.2
Ethylene glycol	8	2.6	32	1.8	22.5	2.9	1.8
Phenol	9	1.7	19	1.4	15.5	2.9	1.3
Styrene monomer	8	1.3	16	1.1	14	1.6	1.1
Phthallic anhydride	9	1.4	15	1.0	11	2.1	0.9
Hydrogen peroxide	17	2.2	13	1.9	11	2.2	1.7
Vinyl acetate	11	3.4	13	1.1	10	2.9	1.0
Zinc oxide	18	1.9	11	1.5	8.4	1.9	1.4
Titanium dioxide	25	2.1	8.4	1.6	6.4	1.9	1.5
Sodium cyanate	18	1.1	6	1.0	5.4	2.3	0.9

[a]When available the United States prices are average values of products sold; that is, average realised prices, from *Synthetic Organic Chemicals, 1966* (Washington: United States Tariff Commission, 1968). For the freights and insurance data the author is indebted to Horace De Podwin and Associates of New York.

for ship transport because they are gases. Ethylene can be shipped by land cheaply by pipe line.[98]

Shipping costs were notably lower for West Germany and the Benelux countries than for Britain and France—a reflection of the

[98]Stanford Institute Report of 1967, *op. cit.*, Vol. I, pp. 103-5.

high efficiency of Rotterdam and Antwerp. Shipping costs in these commodities for Italy were on average 17 per cent above British costs, but the differences were erratic—some Italian rates were below the British.

One regional differential does not appear in the table—but in fact shipping costs are in general lower from Europe to the United States than from the United States to Britain. The explanation is to be found in volume of traffic in the two directions, a "heavy excess of out-bound cargo over in-bound cargo" in the United States Atlantic trade—not in chemicals particularly, but in all the Atlantic trades.[99]

Table 25 does not include any high-priced chemicals. But fibres, dyes and drugs, to take three finished products, are much more costly than titanium dioxide, the highest priced product in the table. Dyes run at over $1 a pound; often over $2. An OECD pilot study of ocean freight rates in the North Atlantic showed that the average freight on cargoes whose average value was approximately $1 per lb was 3.3 per cent of the f.o.b. value of the cargo.[100] This included loading and unloading charges, but not all port expenses, and not insurance.[101] But with these additions it is likely the total shipping cost was below 5 per cent. With products of appreciably higher values the percentage would fall. Freights are raised for high-value products—the principle of "what the traffic will bear" is adopted—but there is competition between lines and tramp shipping, and, much more important for high-value chemicals, from air transport. Air transport can, moreover, reduce other costs—for instance, stocks of products which are required at short notice, as dyes may be, can be centralised and therefore reduced if fast trans-Atlantic transport is available.

To sum up: shipping costs in the Atlantic trade are high in relation to the price of primary basic chemicals, which limits the scope for trans-Atlantic trade in them, although it does not always rule it out. There have been large imports of ammonia into Britain from

[99]*Fairplay International Shipping Journal*, London, April 9, 1970, refers to a recent discussion on this topic in Ezra Bennathen and A. A. Walters, *The Economics of Ocean Freight Rates* (New York: Praeger, 1970) from which the phrase here used is quoted.

[100]*Ocean Freight Rates as Part of Total Transport Costs* (Paris: OECD Secretariat, 1968), pp. 11 and 30.

[101]For details, *ibid.*, pp. 7 and 14.

the Gulf, and it is believed to have been profitable. For intermediates, and plastic materials, products in general in the price range 10 to 20 cents per pound, shipping costs in the trans-Atlantic trade are mainly from 7 to 10 per cent of f.o.b. value.

Shipping costs to Western Europe are less than to North America. This can be important for low-price products, but much less so for high-price products (which are also normally high-profit products).

Size of Firms and Plants

The "internal factors" which are considered in the remainder of this section are closely interrelated. In the early 1960s reduction of costs by increases in the scale of plants and units of plant had entered a new phase. Illustrations of this were given above (see Pages 212–13 and Appendix III). Popular discussion has been concentrated largely on giant single-stream plants for making ethylene and ammonia. But dramatic changes in scale of operations, bringing remarkable reductions in cost and price, occurred (as seen earlier) in the making of a wide range of intermediates—and of more finished products, illustrations of which have been given in fibres and plastics. In the manufacture of dyes, pharmaceuticals and cleaning and toilet goods, large-scale production of basic constituents offers reductions in manufacturing costs and for many products packaging, labelling and stocking can be greatly cheapened by mechanising where the scale is large enough. To justify adopting large-scale manufacturing or packing methods the savings through these must be greater than additional costs in distribution.

There is still scope in the United States for further scale economies in manufacture—even in the giant single-stream units.[102] It is, however, in the later stages that scale economies are cumulatively much the most important. The value of the basic organic intermediates manufactured in the United States in 1966 was about \$1,600m, the value of *all* organic chemicals (including organic dyes, organic pharmaceutical chemicals but not pharmaceutical preparations, synthetic rubber and plastic materials, and the organic bases of detergents but not the finished detergents) almost \$10,000m.

The scale of firms and plants in different countries—if it were known—would be an indication of the relative extent to which

[102] It has become fairly small in such units, however, because in the 450,000-ton-a-year plants, raw material cost is often over 70 per cent of cost.

large-scale operations may have been developed. Unfortunately, the information available, as on most crucial points, is inadequate. Comparison based on census material can only be made for 1963.[103] If the main comparison is made between the United States, West Germany and Britain a sector analysis is only possible between Britain and the United States and this except in a very crude form only for firms, not for plants. Even for firms it is unsatisfactory. But it helps to give some idea of the extent of the gap. Table 26 sets out to show the contrast between the average size of the four largest "enterprises" in a dozen or so sectors in the American and British industries. The figures given compare average outputs—shipments for the United States and gross outputs for the United Kingdom. Many of the largest firms in both countries were engaged in many sectors. An "enterprise" in these statistics is not necessarily a firm but only part of a firm. On the other hand, an enterprise often had many plants or "establishments" within one sector. Thus the figures do not give the average size of plants. The American statistics are subdivided into more sectors than the British figures, and in a few cases the comparisons involve some hazards. The sectors are ranked with the organic chemical sector, in which the average output of the four largest American enterprises is largest, first; the remaining sectors follow in a descending order based on the average American outputs.

There is a close correspondence between the two ratios given in this table. The sectors in which the average output of American firms most exceeds that of British firms are, as a comparison with Table 18 shows, those where value added is highest and labour cost is lowest as a percentage of value added.

Table 26, provided the figures are reasonably comparable, shows that the average sales of the largest four American enterprises were more than three times the average sales of the four largest British enterprises in all except three of the sectors examined. In three of the sectors where the ratio exceeds 3 it varied between 3.3 and 3.7; in the remainder, responsible for nearly 47 per cent of American shipments, it was close on 5 or above 5. The gap between the average sizes of outputs in the two countries was thus substantial.

In one respect the average was highly misleading—because in

[103]The preliminary information for the 1967 and 1968 censuses does not extend to this.

TABLE 26
AVERAGE OUTPUT OF LARGER FIRMS IN 1963
$m

	United States		United Kingdom		Ratio B/D	A.V. per head in Sector in USA ÷ A.V. per head in sector in UK[i]
	Total value of shipments of sector	Average for firms 1–4	Total gross output of sector	Average for enterprises 1–4		
	A	B	C	D	E	F
Organic chemicals[a]	4,840	617	862	129	4.8	3.6
Soap and detergents	2,128	383	378	81	4.7	5.1
Organic fibres[b]	1.403	330	588	146	2.5+	2.3
Inorganic chemicals[c]	3,494	271	488	73	3.7	3.3
Plastic materials	2,571	225	459	77	2.9	2.9
Pharmaceutical preparations	3,314	186	574	39	4.8	4.8
Toilet preparations	1,793	170	228	19[g]	9.0	5.0
Intermediate coal tar products[d]	1,108	150				
Dyestuffs			204	47[h]	3−	2.9
Cellulosic man-made fibres[b]	732	150				
Paints and allied products	2,456	141	469	43	3.3	3.4
Synthetic rubber	764	109				
Acids and alkalies[c]	652	101				
Inorganic pigments[e]	485	82	106	16	5.1	4.2
Industrial gases	425	78				
Fertilisers[f]	869	74	403	58		2.3
Medicinals and botanicals	305	52	91	14	3.7	2.2

[a]The United States figure would be raised by the inclusion of part of the intermediate coal tar products. This, as seen earlier, was about 3/5 intermediates, 2/5 dyes and lakes and toners.

[b]The United Kingdom figure was for *all* man-made fibres. The United States average figures for a comparison would be higher because some firms made both non-cellulosic and cellulosic fibre.

[c]The United States figure would be higher because makers of alkalies and acids were included in the United Kingdom figures.

most of the sectors Imperial Chemical Industries (ICI), or to be more precise a part of ICI, was one of the four largest British enterprises, and often the largest. The British industry was in this respect markedly different from the American industry. ICI is one of the two largest firms in the chemical industry in the world, second only to Du Pont; but the other leading British chemical firms are, as chemical firms, substantially smaller and more limited in scope, although several are parts or subsidiaries of very large firms whose main business is outside the chemical industry.[104] By contrast, the United States had several very large chemical firms, so that the first four in any sector in that country were likely to be more balanced competitively than in Britain, and there are more than four powerful American companies competing vigorously in most sectors.

In West Germany there are three large firms, none as large as ICI but all strong in a wide range of sectors, and collectively much larger than ICI. Here again there is the basis of strong and evenly based competition.

Table 26 shows that in all save two sectors the four largest British enterprises supplied a larger proportion of the output of their sector than the four largest in the United States. There was a higher degree of concentration: this may be a token of the constraint exercised by the size of the market.

[104]In the lists of the world's largest chemical firms, Courtaulds and Unilever usually take high rank, but a major proportion of their business is outside chemicals. Instances of chemical companies which are part of much larger groups are Shell Chemicals and BP Chemicals (a large part of which, until the merger in 1967, was part of the Distillers Company).

---

[d]Of intermediate coal tar products the *intermediates* were produced on substantially higher scale than the dyes, lakes and toners. This is shown in Census Tables which do not give information on the size distribution of firms. But clearly the United States figure for dyes alone would be below 150.

[e]The United Kingdom figure includes organic pigments: in the United States figures these are in intermediate coal tar products.

[f]The United States gave separate figures for fertilisers, mixing only, and for agricultural chemicals other than fertilisers. The United Kingdom figure includes all these. A ratio between these figures would thus be meaningless.

[g]Average for firms 1–5.

[h]Average for firms 1–6.

[i]These are mainly the figures in column 3 in Table 9, but with some different sector groupings.

While there are no comparable figures showing the scale of enterprises in different sectors in West Germany, it is possible to compare the scale of the largest firms in the whole German chemical industry in West Germany in 1962 with the scale of the largest in the United Kingdom in 1963. This is done in Table 27, which also includes similar figures for the French industry in 1962.

TABLE 27

SIZE OF FIRMS IN CHEMICAL INDUSTRY, 1962-63

	Enterprises employing 25 or more (United Kingdom) or 20 or more (West Germany and France)			*Enterprises employing 1,000 or more*		
	United Kingdom	*West Germany*	*France*	*United Kingdom*	*West Germany*	*France*
Number of firms	793	1,336	1,237	66	84	34
Average number employed	500	384	201	3,615	4,448	3,179
Average net output (£m)	1	1.2	0.45	10.12	13.00	7.64

The figures are not perfectly comparable, but they show fairly conclusively that the average size of the big West German firms—not merely within the limit of the big three—was substantially above that of the United Kingdom and the average in both was much higher than that in the French industry.[105]

The American statistics show establishments as well as firms distributed into size categories; the British statistics do not. It is possible to make approximate comparisons for some sectors. When this is done it suggests that the comparisons of size of firms are a

[105]French statistics show the average size of enterprises in various sectors. The sectors appear to differ in definition from those used in the United States and Britain. But sector comparisons which can be made confirm that the scale of firms in the French industry was substantially below that in the United Kingdom in 1962.

reasonably good guide to comparative sizes of plants.[106]

Census figures do not allow international comparisons later than 1962-63; but the American series do show changes for the United States to 1966. There was a further substantial increase in the average size of the largest four firms in most sectors, although there was also in a majority of sectors a decline in the degree of concentration—the leading four firms contributed a smaller percentage of total sales. (See Appendix II for full details.) In most instances this change in concentration was small. But in organic chemicals, where the average of the sales of the four largest firms was by far the highest though it increased only slightly in these three years, the percentage of total sales contributed by the four fell from 51 to 40 per cent—a substantial increase in competition. In seven sectors

[106]While the American sector statistics usually give the shipments and added value of groups of establishments (broadly plants) grouped according to numbers employed, and it is therefore possible to get average net output of a small number of establishments which are the largest, in the British statistics it is only possible to get average outputs of establishments owned by the largest enterprises. It is often possible to find groups of firms which probably include most of the largest establishments. But the largest enterprises normally have several plants. To arrive at any comparison that seems valid it becomes necessary to compare relatively large groups as shown below. It is not possible to make comparisons of this kind in "General Chemicals" at all, because the American figures are much more fully sub-divided sector-wise in this group than the British figures. For what they are worth, the figures below are what the author deems to be the best comparisons of average sizes of plants which can be derived from the censuses for 1963:

	United States *$m*		*United Kingdom* *$m*		
	Plants (numbers) A	*Average sales per plant* B	*Plants (numbers)* C	*Average sales per plant* D	B/D
Man-made fibres	1–19	73.7	1–23	25.4	2.8
Toilet preparations	1–15	57.6	1–14	9.7	5.8
Pharmaceutical preparations	1–17	98.0	1–11	13.4	7.3
Paints and allied products	1–8 1–37	28.2 18.5	1–22	7.8	3.8 2.4
Soap and detergents	1–14	77.2	1–15	25.0	3.1
Plastic materials	1–13 1–29	98.6 44.5	1–19	6.8	14.5 6.5

the average *size* of the four largest firms rose by from 30 to 50 per cent in three years: in five others it rose from 19 to 29 per cent. These were high rates of increase,[107] and due mainly to internal growth, not to mergers.

The figures underline again the continuing vigorous development in the American industry referred to above. The team which was sent by the Economic Development Committee for the Chemical Industry to study the American chemical industry at the end of 1966 duly noted this vigour and it reported that "we found in nearly all cases that the basic unit of production was considerably larger than the corresponding unit in the British company (chosen as an opposite), in one case five times as large. Increased productivity depends not on jumbo works but upon jumbo plants." The team's report said nothing to imply that there had been any recent narrowing of the gap.[108]

But some "jumbo" plants were, as seen earlier, being built both in the United Kingdom and on the continent of Western Europe and in Japan; and major chemical firms in Western Europe often claimed that when they built a new plant it was on the American scale. However, as shown above, the total markets in the EEC, still more in Britain and the rest of EFTA, were for most products far smaller than those in the United States, and the EEC market was less completely integrated, remaining in part nationally divided, and production was less concentrated regionally. There was nothing quite the equivalent to the Texas development of basic organic chemicals with its enormous plants, great interchange of intermediates and remarkable external economies: though Benelux was an impressive shadow.

Thus, although bigger plants have been built in Europe, including some giants, it remains difficult to establish the rate at which the gaps shown by the 1963 figures between the scale of plants in the United States and in Britain and the rest of Western Europe have been or are being narrowed. Existing plants are in any event not changed overnight. For an assessment of the probable impact of a free trade treaty—whatever its scope—this rate is clearly one factor of major importance.

[107]A rise of 50 per cent in three years was a rate of nearly 100 per cent in five years, and nearly 15 per cent a year: a rise of 19 per cent was about 34 per cent in five years—6 per cent a year.

[108]*Manpower in the Chemical Industry, op. cit.*, p. 5 and *passim.*

Some indication is given by the scale of investment in new plant and by expenditure on research and development which are now examined.

Investment in New Plant

The United States' chemical industry has invested annually much more than the EEC countries—and still much more than any individual country. The broad figures are given in Table 28.

TABLE 28

INVESTMENTS OF MAIN PRODUCING COUNTRIES IN THE CHEMICAL INDUSTRY: 1958-68

$m

	1958	*1960*	*1964*	*1966*	*1967*	*1968*
United States	1,320	1,600	1,970	2,990	2,880	2,690
United Kingdom	401	334	529	723	592[a]	557[a]
Japan			703	513	824	1,206
West Germany	357	525	637	925	800	800
France	132	235	342	523	577	577
Italy	208	305	428	384	400	392
Belgium	42	50	91	191	240	240
Netherlands		90	167	349	344	360
EEC	739	1,205	1,665	2,372	2,361	2,369

[a]These figures are lowered by devaluation. In some contexts this is misleading.

Comparison with turnover and added value figures (see Page 134 above) shows that American investment is a substantially lower proportion of both of these than the investments of the larger West European countries (12.5 per cent compared, for example, with about 20 per cent). But it is substantially higher than the investment of these countries per person employed. This reflects the policy of developing methods which save both labour and capital per unit of output, which has been illustrated earlier. Productivity of both factors is increased, but in general (although it is not invariable) the reduction in labour cost per unit of output is percentagewise larger than the reduction in the cost of plant per unit of output. Therefore when the industry in one country is investing more per person employed than the industry in another it is probable that it is increasing the productivity of both factors faster than the other country. As usual there are difficulties of interpretation. Clearly if an industry is growing very fast, as is happening in the Benelux countries, the criterion would not apply and in different sectors the capital/labour ratio is necessarily very different. There is a further difficulty in that costs of plant, as has been seen, vary in different countries, so that some adjustment must be made in order to compare like with like.

FIGURE 6
INVESTMENT PER PERSON EMPLOYED
($'ooo per head)

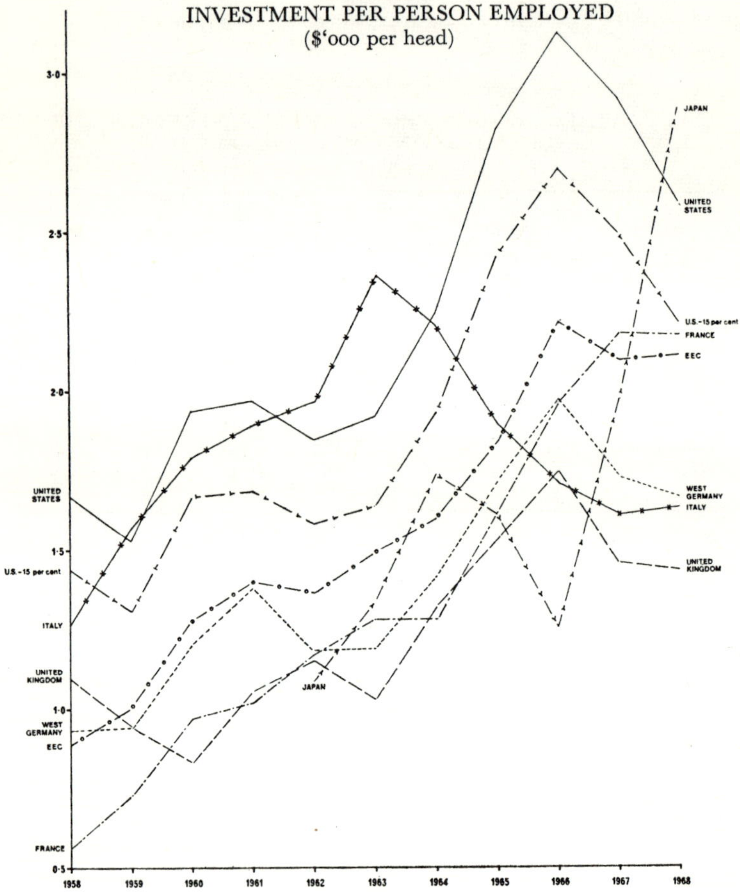

In Figure 6 investment per head in the United States, Britain and main continental West European countries and in the EEC and Japan are compared. In addition to the actual dollar figure for the United States a lower line is included on the assumption that all other countries could build plants 15 per cent cheaper than the United States. As seen above, on Page 211, this is an exaggeration for most countries. But the general conclusion to which this diagram points is that the United States has continued to invest more per head than the EEC countries or Japan (despite the fact that more of EEC and Japanese investment was for expansion) and much more than the United Kingdom which was expanding less—though here the diagram understates the British performance in 1967-68.

Research and Development

The problem here is whether, and to what extent, the output of successful research and development has been increased faster in the British, EEC and Japanese chemical industries than in the American industry. Here again the data are inadequate. One can only measure inputs, the money spent on research and development and the number of people who work on it, and not outputs, the results in products and processes; and the statistics on inputs come late and differ so much both in definition and lack of definition as to rule out precise comparison. Some broad conclusions, however, appear fairly firm.

The United States still spends much more and employs many more people, particularly qualified scientists and engineers (QSEs), on research and development in the chemical industry than any other country. The Japanese industry has increased its research and development faster than any other country in recent years, and now comes next to the United States in terms of employment in research and development. Apart from Japan the most notable increases have been in West Germany. Expenditure and employment on research and development in Britain are considerably less than in West Germany. Expenditure in Britain has possibly grown slightly faster (at its much lower level) than in the United States—employment in Britain, according to the most recent OECD guesses, did not increase at all between 1963-64 and 1966-67.

Table 29 includes these guesses. It is based primarily on OECD figures, but adjustments and additions have been made in order to use some later figures and to improve comparability.

The dominating position of the American industry in size of effort stands out in these figures, and clearly no rapid change was in progress between either the EEC or Britain and the United States. The difference in expenditure was greater, it will be seen, than the

TABLE 29

EXPENDITURE AND EMPLOYMENT IN RESEARCH AND DEVELOPMENT IN THE CHEMICAL INDUSTRY[a]

	Expenditure $m			*Employment* '000s			
	1964		*1967*	*1964*		*1967*	
				QSE and technicians	*QSE*[d] *only*	*QSE and technicians*	*QSE*[d] *only*
United States	1710[e]	(1,000)[b]	2,034[e]	74.75	47.1	75.8	50.5
United Kingdom[c]	192	(112)	236[f]	19.72	7.0	19.7[f]	7.0
West Germany	299	(175)	382	20.85	7.4	25.0	9.0
France	137	(80)	218	9.60	3.3	12.4	4.3
Italy	50	(29)		5.31			
Belgium	41	(24)		1.59			
Japan	159	(93)	263	32.25	13.2	43.6	17.0

[a]For these statistics the petroleum and petroleum products industry is included with chemical and allied products.

[b]The figures in brackets were given in *The Overall Level and Structure of R and D Efforts in OECD Member Countries* (Paris: OECD Secretariat, 1967) p. 52. I have quantified them, using the American figure published in *Research and Development in Industry 1967* (Washington: National Science Foundation, 1968), p. 27. The data for 1966-7 come mainly from *Science Policy News* (an article on "R and D in the British Business Sector", prepared by the OECD Directorate for Scientific Affairs, January 1970). But for the American figures in the article I have substituted the now available figures for the United States for 1967.

[c]The British figures are for 1963-4 and 1966-7.

[d]The OECD only gives estimates of QSE and technicians; but it gives data (*Science Policy News*, January, 1970, p. 79) on the proportion of QSEs to technicians in each country. My figures of QSEs are based on these except for the United States where the specific figures are available in the National Science Foundation's Report quoted in note b above.

[e]The United States expenditure figures are for current expenditure plus depreciation; the other countries' figures cover capital expenditure also. For the United Kingdom this was $38.6m, approximately one-sixth of the total. Depreciation would clearly be much less than this; hence for comparison something, possibly between 5 and 10 per cent, should be added to the United States figure.

[f]The United Kingdom figure was "by product field". The others were "by industry group". For the United States the "product field" figure was lower than the industry group figures, but omitted basic research, which was more extensive in the American industry than in the United Kingdom.

difference in employment. This is less so if employment of qualified scientists and engineers is taken as the best guide—as it probably should be.[109] It is probable certainly that the average level of training of scientists and engineers plus technicians was higher in the United States. More qualified engineers, as Christopher Freeman and A. Young have suggested,[110] were likely to be doing support work performed elsewhere by technicians, and together with the probable use of more labour-saving capital equipment in research and development this would make workers in research and development more productive in the United States, as would be expected.

American research and development was in most sectors highly concentrated. Of 1967 the expenditure for industrial chemicals ($1,006m) 92 per cent was by the first 20 companies, and 59 per cent —almost $600m—was by the first four: which is more than 2.5 times the whole British expenditure. Expenditure on plastic materials, resins, rubber and fibres amounted to $460m, twice the British expenditure on all chemicals. In pharmaceuticals the American expenditure ($354m) was seven times the British, and the four largest spenders spent $134m, compared with the total British figure of $49m.

To sum up, then: the available data on expenditure and employment on research and development appear to show that no change is under way which would rapidly change the relative competitive strengths of the American and West European chemical firms, although of course there are important research and development efforts in many West European countries. Britain is still second only in Western Europe to West Germany, whose research and development in chemicals is, however, growing faster, but not so fast as Japan's.

[109]The reason for lumping together qualified scientists and engineers and technicians in OECD statistics is because the boundaries vary in different countries. But in the chemical industry in the United States the qualified scientists and engineers were, for the most part, highly qualified. All save a trivial percentage of the chemists and physicists employed in industry, whether as operatives, managers or in research and development, had degrees in 1962 and over one-third had Ph.D. degrees. Of engineers employed in the chemical industry, 93 per cent had degrees; in the petroleum industry, 95 per cent. (These figures again covered all qualified scientists and engineers, whether or not in research and development.) The median earnings of engineers in the chemical and petroleum industries rose much higher than in most other industries. Cf. *Scientific and Technical Manpower Resources* (Washington: National Science Foundation, 1964).

[110]Freeman and A. Young, *The Research and Development Effort in Western Europe, North America and the Soviet Union* (Paris: OECD Secretariat, 1965), p. 40.

Quality of Labour and Management

Finally the discussion comes to the influence of differences in attitudes, abilities, skills, traditions and training. Sir Ronald Holroyd, in the impressive analysis of the economics of large plants referred to earlier, emphasised that "the degree of success achieved in almost identical plants but operated by different people and in different countries will nevertheless vary a great deal. Performance will increasingly be dependent on the quality, training and reliability of personnel of all ranks."[111] Performance in the United Kingdom in erecting and starting up new giant ammonia plants, he said, was clearly "worse than the average".

The number of men required to run and maintain plants can vary greatly according to local attitudes and practices. People can work more or less hard. There can be more or less care and foresight in observing whether all parts of a plant are working well, whether instruments remain accurate, for example, or leaks develop, and operations will be more discontinuous in some plants than in others. Marketing may fail to provide a satisfactory load—which may reflect bad original forecasting whether of sales possibilities or of costs and prices or a lack of skill in selling. Unexpected technical difficulties may arise in using particular raw materials, in maintaining yields and quality, which may reflect both lack of skill and lack of foresight in initial designing. Different methods of organising maintenance can involve both higher direct costs and higher indirect costs through loss of output.

The Economic Development Committee's working party report of 1967,[112] latest in the series of productivity reports which started for the chemical industry in 1952,[113] pointed again to the contrasts between British and American conditions and management and labour practices, which resulted, they thought, in the average output per worker in the United States being about three times the output of a British worker—a "real and disturbing difference", as they put it.

Differences were particularly significant in maintenance, but the team found American process workers also had a much higher

[111]*Chemistry and Industry*, London, August 5, 1967, p. 1315.

[112]*Manpower in the Chemical Industry*, *op. cit.*

[113]The first was a report by a team from the Anglo-American Productivity Council, London, on heavy chemicals, published in 1952. The British Productivity Council published further reports on visits to West Germany and Italy in 1961.

productivity than British workers. While much was accounted for by difference in scale of operations, the teams found the operations of American process workers, in specific comparisons, "about 25 per cent higher than in the British firms for reasons other than plant scale".[114] It is the same figure as Arthur D. Little Inc. gave in their 1962 report for the difference between productivity of *all* workers (not merely process workers) in the United States and the whole of Western Europe. American maintenance workers, however, according to the report of the Economic Development Committee—had an output 1.7 times the British output per man, for reasons other than plant scale. British firms, assuming no change in scale, would employ 36 per cent fewer people if they used American manning practices; operating on the United States scale, they would employ 60 per cent fewer.[115]

These are very impressive figures and so, too, is the analysis of the sources of difference. While detailed study is out of the question in assessing the prospects of change under the impact of a free trade treaty, it is necessary to identify the general nature of the sources emphasised by the Economic Development Committee's working party.

It was found that the American chemical industry attracted a better class of recruit than the British for hourly-paid workers—they imposed a high minimum educational requirement. Their workers were ready and able to take more responsibility and so there were no charge hands and sometimes, on night shifts, no supervision. There were no "mates". There was better job loading *especially in the labour-intensive sectors*; process workers had a wider range of jobs to do, which gave more job satisfaction, and they spent 10 per cent of their time on "first aid" maintenance. There were no demarcation disputes. Although they *did* more than the English process workers there was no sense of rush.

Much more care was taken in training foremen and refresher courses were run for them—the emphasis being on supervision and communication techniques, to make them effective channels in

[114]*Manpower in the Chemical Industry*, *op. cit.*, pp. 46-51.

[115]The Economic Development Committee for the Chemical Industry did not compare ICI practices and American practices, but the British company made a study of its own and Sir Peter Allen, as chairman of the company, confirmed the general statistical conclusions in saying that when the United States industry uses two persons, the United Kingdom industry uses three. This is close to the 36 per cent figure.

communication between management and workers, which was better than in the United Kingdom. There was better safety training in the United States than in Britain.

Maintenance was carefully organised to minimise loss of time. The practice of regularly scheduled maintenance, which in 1952 seemed to the Anglo-American productivity team the favourite American solution, had been largely abandoned; the work was done when there were signs of approaching trouble. It was carefully organised on a sort of PERT basis. Reserve plant for particularly sensitive stages was common so that maintenance involved minimum shut-down.

Managements worked as teams. There were no *prima donnas*. Responsibilities were clearly defined. Hourly-paid workers have secure jobs, but management is insecure, being judged by performance. No traditional methods of working are sacrosanct—costs are constantly being examined by a fine-tooth comb to discover means of reducing them. Capital investment to save labour was the normal means. The managements did not use the Harvard Business School for management training. Everyone was profit-conscious—and cost statistics are more readily available to staff than in the United Kingdom. *All* workers, of all levels, have the same hours and the same fringe benefits, including stock options, and they have better holidays than their counterparts in Britain.

It was a forbidding analysis, with a ring which has become familiar since World War II. Obviously much of the American practice was notionally transferable to the United Kingdom. But not all could come quickly. It was not possible, for instance, to overcome deficiencies in quality of entrants quickly; to make people quickly able and willing to work without supervision. The American industry, as has been seen and as the report of the Economic Development Committee showed, was a fast-moving target. It was significant that the practice of scheduling maintenance which seemed to provide an important lesson in 1952 was "out" by 1967.[116] Attitudes are more important dynamically than specific solutions, but not so easily adopted.

The report of the Economic Development Committee's working party gave an impetus to the designing of productivity agreements which promise to remove some of the obstacles to productivity that were identified. It may have contributed something to the improve-

[116] *Manpower in the Chemical Industry*, *op. cit.*, p. 22.

ment of productivity by 11.2 per cent in 1968—an unusual record for Britain, helped largely by a considerable, again unusual, reduction in the labour force. It was a considerably bigger increase of productivity than that in the United States in 1968, but it was still less than the increase in West Germany (13.3 per cent). It was not repeated in 1969, when again the West German increase was higher than the British.[117]

The team which reported on productivity in West Germany in 1961 was given little access to modern plants, perhaps due to a misunderstanding. Its report was limited therefore in scope. But it gave some signs that productivity might be advancing faster than in Britain. The system of training apprentices was better—as it appeared to be in Italy, too. In West Germany, training for process work included maintenance work; there were no demarcation disputes. Nor were there in Italy. In training, as in other ways, the West German industry, it was said, benefited from having larger works than were normal in the United Kingdom. The West Germans were more alive, it was reported, to the need for a sociological approach to rationalisation. Investing heavily, they put most into new *profitable* products: hence some of their plant for older products suffered. The new profitable products reflected extensive successful research and development—and were helped by conspicuous "applications research", discovering how to use new materials for as many uses as possible. Probably this accounted for the extraordinary development of the use of plastics in West Germany, which is more intensive than in the United States; and, as seen earlier, several times greater per head than in Britain. Despite devaluation in Britain and revaluation in West Germany, the latter's chemical industry still forged relatively farther ahead of Britain's industry, expanding output and exports faster in 1968-69.

To sum up, the quality of workers and management in the British chemical industry was less conducive to high productivity than that of workers and management in the United States and (in a lesser degree) in the West German chemical industry. The deficiencies in the United Kingdom were not solely in regard to the skills and response of workers, but in regard to most aspects of management—training of workers, for instance, the organisation of work, the

[117]The comparisons in Table 18, it may be worth noting, use 1968 figures for the United Kingdom; that is, they take into account the exceptional British productivity rise in 1968.

choice of projects and the erection, running-in and operation of new plants as well as the marketing of new products. While some practices adopted in the United States, or elsewhere, will be adopted with advantage, to reach a parity with the United States or other more vigorous developers would require radical changes of attitude, recruitment and incentives.

Profitability

It would be useful to complement the survey of cost and price trends with a close comparison of profit margins in the different sectors of the chemical industry in the main competitive countries and, in particular, profits from new investments.

The data for this is unsatisfactory and rigorous analysis of what exists would be beyond the scale of this study. Most important, chemical firms are large in many sectors; they do not attribute profits to their activities in separate sectors.[118] Firms which are predominantly in one or two sectors only are usually (as with Unilever and Courtaulds in the United Kingdom) largely engaged also in activities outside the chemical industry. Most of the large oil companies are important in petrochemicals, but their chemical industry profits are normally not shown separately, and would be of uncertain value if they were. Increasingly the major firms are international and it becomes harder to attribute changes in profits to activities in one country. Where profits statistics are published by governments these do not normally refer to particular sectors and, moreover, they cannot wholly escape the difficulties posed by the international activities of firms. In addition, there are the difficulties which arise in all international profit comparisons, arising from the different accounting practices used in different countries and different tax systems, different allowances for depreciation, different forms and degrees of investment incentive.

The indications are that profits in the chemical industry have been higher in the United States and West Germany than in Britain. Profits fell in the United States in the late 1960s and have varied greatly in different firms and, whereas they were for most of the 1960s above the all-industry average, they fell below it in 1967-68. Table 30 gives a comparison of profits after depreciation and "capital allowances" (but before taxation) as a percentage of turnover in the United States and Britain up to 1966.

[118]In recent annual reports ICI has given useful data on this point.

TABLE 30

PROFITS BEFORE TAXATION AS PERCENTAGE OF TURNOVER

Year	*United States*[a]	*United Kingdom*[b]	*Year*	*United States*[a]	*United Kingdom*[b]
1957	12.4	9.7	1962	10.7	8.3
1958	10.8	9.3	1963	10.7	6.6
1959	12.9	12.6	1964	11.3	7.8
1960	11.9	11.0	1965	11.5	8.4 est.
1961	11.0		1966	11.4	9.1 est.

[a]From United States Department of Commerce, Office of Business Economics, series: in Jules Backman, *The Economics of the Chemical Industry*, p. 348, 1970. The profits are after depreciation has been deducted.
[b]*Annual Reports of Commissioners of Inland Revenue*, 1962-1968. The figures are after deduction of capital allowances for tax purposes. The total allowances are slightly below the United States depreciation allowance as a percentage of turnover. The series has been discontinued, and the final figures are projections based on the trends of net profits (as given in the Blue Book on *National Income and Expenditure*) and of turnover in the chemical industry.

After 1966 profit levels dropped in the American chemical industry and rose in the British industry. If the figures are on a comparable basis they suggest that the level of return was normally higher in the American than in the British industry, but that the difference was possibly abnormally wide from 1963-65.

The only detailed comparison of world chemical companies, from a financial standpoint, known to the author—by C. P. Neidig[119]—covers the period 1961-66. It analyses the financial reports of some twenty-five major companies in the United States, Canada, Britain, the EEC countries, Switzerland and Japan. For the United Kingdom, Neidig takes ICI and Courtaulds: the former is the more important in this context, being much more purely chemical and in chemicals much more widely based. Neidig shows that ICI's rate of growth from 1961-65 was substantially faster than that of three of the four major American firms chosen for the comparisons, though less than two of the three main West German companies. Its percentage of foreign sales (that is, sales of exports and of products made in overseas subsidiaries) was exceeded only by one West German and two Swiss companies. Its investment per man, though

[119]C. P. Neidig, "Financial Comparison of World Chemical Companies". *Financial Analysts Journal*, New York, January-February, 1968, pp. 51-65.

much less than the American, was higher than in two of the West German companies, though less than in two of the Japanese. Its capital expenditure was 22.3 per cent of sales in 1966—a higher percentage than in any of the other companies. But the analysis of operating results confirmed the conclusion of Table 30. Pre-tax income as a percentage of sales was substantially lower for ICI than for either of the four American and three West German companies studied. It was lower than for the two American-owned Canadian companies and also for two Dutch companies, but above those for the French and Japanese companies.[120] A further table showed this from another angle; it showed that the increase of sales from 1961-66, as a percentage of capital expenditure, was comparable with that in the United States, although less than in West Germany. But the increase in pre-tax profits per dollar of capital expenditure in the same period was exceptionally low (4.9 cents—the American firms averaged over 11 cents, two West German companies over 10 cents).[121] ICI's "net profit per dollar of employee costs" was also much below that of the American firms and much below that of two of the West German firms and three of the Japanese.

These comparisons thus substantiate, in respect of ICI, the contrast shown in Table 30. But as the table shows 1966, though showing an improvement in profit level in Britain and a slight narrowing of the unfavourable gap, was within a period when British profits were lower than in the early 1960s. For ICI it was in fact an exceptionally bad year, and the profit comparisons would have been considerably more favourable if made two or three years later.[122] A rapid improvement in profits occurred which among other things reflected the delayed impact of heavy new investment in jumbo plants whose effects had been delayed by late completions and

[120]*Ibid.*, p. 56.
[121]*Ibid.*, p. 59.
[122]The changes are given below:

	Total assets employed	*Total sales*	*Profits before tax*
1966	1,208	885	86
1967	1,374	979	101
1968	1,487	1,237	153
1969	1,557	1,355	167

teething troubles, and the stimulus of devaluation. Export sales and sales by foreign subsidiaries grew faster from 1966-69 than home sales.

The OECD in a study of investments in the chemical industry, *The Chemical Industry, 1968-1969*, a supplement published early in 1970, gives the ratio for 10 countries of increases in turnover in the decade 1959-1966 to total investment in the decade. The United Kingdom comes bottom of the ten. The figures are given in Table 31.

TABLE 31

INCREASE OF TURNOVER AS PER CENT OF TOTAL INVESTMENT 1959-1966

Spain	194	Netherlands	82
Japan	137	West Germany	78
Italy	114	Sweden	77
France	108	United Kingdom	57
United States	97		

Such figures can be misleading: the proportions of investment which are for expansion and replacement, for instance, vary; and capital/output ratios are not the same in all sectors. These figures give a much less favourable view of the British position in this respect than Neidig's figures give for ICI alone. But if the United Kingdom profit as a percentage of turnover was relatively low, then the implication of these OECD figures would seem to be that the return on investment was probably lower in Britain than in competing countries, such as the United States and West Germany where profits on turnover were higher. It need not have been so, or in the same degree, in all sectors.[123] Again the series stops at 1966.

The position was likely to be changed after 1967 by devaluation and by this time, too, some of the heavy programmes of plant building of the mid-1960s began to contribute to expansion of output and profit—after irksome delays. Much of the building occurred in the years when returns on investment were falling. But although

[123] In general, it is to be expected that, other things being equal, the capital/output ratio will be higher in the heavy basic chemicals, and less for the more finished products. One would expect thus a higher investment/turnover ratio in countries where basic chemicals form a larger part of output, as in the United States and West Germany. This cannot of course be isolated in the OECD figures.

some improvements in the British/American profits ratio occurred, the change could be temporary and leading members of the British industry have indicated that the position is precarious. Profit margins on several major products fell in 1969-70—on plastic materials, such as polythene and PVC, fibres, dyes, paints, and fertilisers.[124] This was attributed primarily to inflation following wage increases and unofficial strikes and the smallness and exceptionally slow growth of the home market, although several other factors contributed. The wage agreements, according to the fashionable formula, were geared to increases of productivity which nominally would offset any cost increase. Many prices, however, were increased. Both ICI and Shell Chemicals said in April and July, 1970, respectively that conditions might lead to cutbacks in the further large programmes of investment in Britain that had been decided upon by both firms in 1968-69—because cash flows would not be sufficiently large, and returns would not be enough to attract outside capital.[125]

The Economic Development Committee for the Chemical Industry had discussed the position more generally in a report published early in 1970.[126] This gave no suggestion that existing capital commitments would be curtailed or delayed. But it emphasised the sensitivity of investment decisions in the chemical industry because all the large companies are international in their activities and they choose locations for plants—internationally—according to their "relative economic advantage". The report stressed the drawbacks of the British market, the high cost of electric power in Britain, the long construction times, the higher costs of shipping.[127] These and other disadvantages discouraged investment in the United Kingdom and, they argued, made government investment help essential. This was presented in rather curious terms:

> "The EDC concludes that assuming equal gross profit cash flows in different countries the discounted cash flow rate of return after grants and taxes is broadly equal as between the UK development areas and EEC countries. This underlines the importance of UK investment incentives to the industry."

[124] *The Times,* April 3, 1970.

[125] See the report of Sir Peter Allen's address at the annual meeting of ICI in *The Times,* April 3, 1970; and also Mr. Neil Iliff, as Deputy Chairman of Shell Chemicals, in *The Times,* July 8, 1970.

[126] *Economic Assessment to 1972, op. cit.*

[127] *Ibid.*, p. 21-3.

Whether equal gross profit cash flows were equivalent to equal margins on turnover, whether they were merely a convenient assumption or an experience and how, if they were an experience, the need for government grants emerged since grants were not normal in for example America or West Germany is not made clear. But the implication seems unmistakable that unless investment incentives on the development area level are provided in the United Kingdom an international company, at any rate, would prefer to invest in the EEC or in the United States. Put another way, if prices and output are equal, a better return is likely to be obtained on an investment in the EEC or the United States than in Britain, unless part of the investment is *given* by the State.

Summary of Costs Discussion

Some salient conclusions on cost trends and comparisons may now be summarised:

(1) The United States has some advantage over competitors in raw material costs for inorganic chemicals. Some experts have thought that it now has higher raw material costs for organic chemicals. This is disputed. But if it were so the disadvantage could be removed by freeing imports of raw materials for petrochemicals. Any difference in these costs is of relatively small importance in the cost of finished products.

(2) The United States has an advantage in cheaper costs of fuel and power. This is being reduced. If West European fuel and power costs remain 25 per cent above American figures (they have been more above) for chemical and allied products as a whole, this would mean a cost differential equal to nearly one per cent of sales prices. It would be much more for basic chemicals alone.

(3) The American industry pays more for broadly identical capital equipment than is paid by competitors, but the difference is not large. New plants are built faster in the United States—particularly faster than in Britain—and this probably gives the United States a net advantage in total cost. Firms building in the United Kingdom have the advantage of exceptional government aid in financing plants from capital grants and analogous assistance. But slow building shortens the period of premium prices and slows down the process of technical advance.

(4) Shipping costs in the Atlantic trade (which have been falling with the use of containers) are relatively high in relation to the value

of basic intermediates, but become a relatively small percentage of the prices of more advanced products. Although higher than transport costs to the Continent, they are not a high protection for the more highly priced chemicals which are also the more profitable ones. The United Kingdom is, however, at a disadvantage compared with the Continent in shipping to the United States, because British ports are less efficient and port costs are higher. Freights from the United States to Western Europe are above those from Western Europe to the United States because the demand for shipping space is greater.

(5) Major changes in relative costs, bringing costs in Western Europe and Japan below American costs for much output, were expected from the rapid spread of United States practices, facilitated by the creation of larger markets (the EEC and EFTA), international activities of American chemical and construction companies and analogous factors. In the event, changes in relative costs appear to have been less radical than were widely forecast and, at the end of the 1960s the American industry still had an impressive lead in scale and productivity. Added value per worker in 1968 was almost three times as high in the United States as it was in Britain, and more than double the level in Japan, West Germany, France and Italy. The ratios of earnings between the countries were almost as high as the added value ratios. Earnings in America were close on three times earnings in Britain. Nevertheless, in most sectors of the industry labour costs per unit of output in the United States were either approximately equal to or actually lower than those in the United Kingdom.

(6) Sectors in which British labour costs exceeded American ones, according to census figures, included general chemicals and dyestuffs; those where costs were equal included drugs and plastic materials, while those where they were lower included fibres.

(7) Markets had expanded less than had been expected in Western Europe, and more in the United States; the American market was not only much larger in most sectors than that of the EEC (and larger in most than the whole West European market), but more fully integrated.

(8) In the early 1960s in most sectors the average capacity of the four largest plants in the United States was probably from three to five times as large as in the United Kingdom. The average size of firms and plants continued to grow impressively through the decade

in the United States where statistics are available. Increased scale of units continued to result in large reductions in capital and labour costs. The gap in size between American and British plants remained large in 1969, although probably not so wide as in 1963. Figures are lacking, however, for Britain, as they are also for comparisons between Britain, the United States and the continent of Western Europe.

(9) The annual investment in new plant in the American chemical industry was more than that in the EEC throughout the 1960s, and from four to five times the investment in Britain. It was a smaller percentage of turnover, but a much larger amount per person employed than in the United Kingdom, West Germany, Italy or France: which reflects concentration on developing methods which save both labour and capital per unit of output.

(10) The United States spent much more money on research and development than the EEC plus Britain in 1967, and employed probably more people in that activity. There are no signs of a change in this field which would rapidly alter the relative competitive strengths of the American and West European chemical companies. Japan has gone ahead of West Germany in having the second largest number of research and development workers in the industry. The United Kingdom is second to West Germany in Western Europe in research and development expenditure and employment.

(11) The quality of workers and management in the British chemical industry was less conducive to high productivity than that of workers and managements in the United States and to a less extent in West Germany.

(12) The profitability of the chemical industry appears to have been less in Britain than in the United States or West Germany.

7 PROBABLE IMPACTS OF FREE TRADE OPTIONS

Attention may now be focussed on the central problem of this study: the effects which British participation in a multilateral free trade treaty, whether it embraces the whole of Western Europe and North America as well as Japan or is more limited in extent, would have on the chemical industry. The primary interest is in the United Kingdom's chemical industry, but naturally the impact on other countries must be considered.

The 1962 Little Report was in effect an analysis of the probable effects of a broad free trade treaty in an important segment of the chemical industry from the point of view of the American industry. It clarified the issues while probably overestimating the risk for the United States' industry. The chemical industry, growing fast in all major industrial countries, partly in response to markets, but partly creating markets (and creating new products), is growing faster in Western Europe than in the United States, although America has been, since the World War II, the leading force in the industry.

Implications of Import Trends

Growth in Western Europe is strongly based. West Germany had been, for long before the war, the technological leader in many major sectors. New wider markets provided by the EEC and EFTA, associated with the rapid general growth of most Continental economies, provide a stimulating environment. Helped by the readiness of American companies to license the use of their advances, and the establishment by their companies of West European subsidiaries, technology in the chemical industry has been mobile. Efficiencies in using capital, labour and materials are moving in Western Europe closer to American standards. Raw materials are not appreciably more costly (some are cheaper). New plant is cheaper. Earnings are still (in dollar equivalents) much below the American level. And, since the scale of operations approaches steadily closer to the United States scale, comparative costs in Western Europe have become increasingly competitive.

Growth in world production of chemicals has been accompanied by a still faster growth in imports of chemicals by major producing countries from each other. In this interchange West European countries have imported far more from the United States than it has from Western Europe (in 1968 the ratio was 2.4:1). As has been seen earlier, several factors have stimulated importing by major producers. Some are based on lower costs. Some are surpluses from high capacity units sold cheaply. Some represent a deliberate policy of international specialisation securing advantages of larger scale operations. Thus for instance some manufacturers of dyes import foreign firms' products to complete their range. Often demand for a product grows faster than indigenous supply. Also chemicals which are imported are often specialities and innovations. Sometimes firms who are subsidiaries of foreign firms import semi-products from the parent for further processing. Changes in import volumes are therefore not just a response to changes in relative costs.

The growth of imports has nevertheless clearly been helped by removals of quantity restrictions and reductions of duties, although until the Kennedy Round negotiations the duty reductions were only moderate. After the Kennedy Round agreement has been implemented the remaining import duties in all the major producing countries will be moderate, or low, with relatively few exceptions—conspicuously dyes (30 per cent) and to a lesser extent drugs (20 per cent) in the United States. The elimination of these remaining duties would substantially reduce the costs of supplying some imports and produce a competitive situation in which the import flows would change—and there would be changes in the balance of trade between various producing countries.

Trade Prospects under Free Trade Treaty

The 1962 Little Report envisaged a substantial gain—ostensibly a *net* gain—in West European exports to the United States if all duties were removed. As seen above, the American industry has expanded more vigorously than was expected and net exports to Western Europe have continued to grow vigorously, although not uniformly every year, but very strongly from 1967-68.[128]

[128]This presumably reflected to a small extent the first Kennedy Round tariff cuts. Imports into the United States from Western Europe have grown slightly faster. American exports to Western Europe doubled in 1961-68; imports from Western Europe multiplied by 2.6. But at the end the United States export figure to Western Europe, as noted in the text, was 2.4 times the import figure from Western Europe in 1968; and the net export of the United States in this trade

The experience of the 1960s suggests that in a free trade treaty embracing all Western Europe and North America the balance in trade between them would not be radically changed quickly. The elasticities used in calculating the effects of the Kennedy Round agreement would imply an increase in imports from Western Europe into the United States, if all remaining post-Kennedy Round duties were eliminated, of about \$140m to \$280m. If the low elasticity arrived at as a guess for the United Kingdom were applied to the whole of Western Europe, merely for convenience, the American imports from the United States into Western Europe would rise by between \$120m and \$240m.[129] These are very small figures in relation to turnover. The excess of additional West European imports from Western Europe to the United States over additional American imports to Western Europe is relatively slight. The other factors which result in higher imports could easily tip the balance the other way. These figures only refer of course to short-run effects—when the increase of exports would be limited by capacities. In the longer-run, investment would be stimulated to expand trades which, because of tariff changes, become profitable.

The experience would differ from sector to sector. One would expect American exports to Western Europe to thrive well in sectors where labour cost in the United States is a small percentage of added value, and less in sectors where it is a high percentage of added value. The difference between sectors in this respect are wide in the United States, as Table 18 on Page 192 shows. The developments in trade between Western Europe and the United States from 1966–68, shown in Table 8 on Page 143, accord well with this criterion. The American industry gained more percentagewise than the West European industry in the trade in general chemicals, pharmaceuticals, toilet preparations, soap and detergents, pigments and paint. West European industries gained more percentagewise and in actual values in synthetic dyestuffs; and more percentagewise in plastic materials, although here the United States exports were much larger in quantity and their increase in value from 1966-68 was almost equal to the total value of the import of plastic materials into the United States from Western Europe in 1968.

(excluding synthetic rubber and photographic chemicals) was \$650m compared with \$400m in 1961.

[129]There would of course be increases in imports of West European countries from sources other than the United States because of the shift to free trade in the EEC and EFTA.

In general, trans-Atlantic trade is unlikely to flourish in those basic products whose value is low in relation to weight. One would expect West European exports to do relatively well in sectors where the American duties after the Kennedy Round agreement has been fully implemented are still rather high—above all, in dyes (where the American duty will be 30 per cent). Here, indeed, West European exports to the United States already thrive: this is generally regarded as one of the least efficient parts of the American chemical industry. In other moderately high tariff sectors, such as drugs, photographic chemicals, agricultural chemicals, the position is more complex. In drugs, for instance, price competition is of relatively slight importance for much of the output: The American industry is exceptionally strong in research and markets the largest volume of significant new products. Where West European exporters may gain because of the current inefficiency of a particular sector in the United States—as in the dye industry—the American industry may of course react and become more efficient.[130] Reaction to competition in this way would of course be a gain due to free trade.

That West European competition might not be as disturbing in the United States as appeared possible in 1962 can readily be understood. The West European market has developed rather less fast, and the American market faster, than then seemed likely. In most sectors the United States home market is likely still for some time, to be more favourable to large-scale operations than the West European, which is not only smaller but much less fully integrated and homogeneous. The American industry has increased its efficiency more than was expected. It still spends much more than competitors on research and development and invests more per person employed; and the transfer of American management skills and labour practices and attitudes proves to be less easy than the transfer of plant and process designs.

UK Prospects under Free Trade Treaty

The impact of the removal of duties would be different in dif-

[130]It is claimed that this would probably happen in the dye industry. Small inefficient firms which proliferate in New Jersey could, it is said, easily raise their efficiency by reducing the range of products they manufacture, and presumably maintaining the range they sell by merchanting other manufacturers' products under their own name, which is commonly done in Western Europe. See *Synthetic Organic Dyestuffs and Organic Pigment Prices* (London: H.M. Stationery Office, for the National Board for Prices and Incomes, 1969), pp. 4 and 5.

ferent parts of the multilateral free trade association. Some parts of Western Europe would be less able than others to increase exports to the United States. The idea of the free trade association including all Western Europe and North America, as well as Japan and other developed countries, means that tariff barriers between the EEC countries and Britain would be eliminated: the British industry would face stronger competition both from American and EEC producers. The statistics of growth, added value, labour costs, overseas trade, and profits—all seem to show conclusively that the British industry is less strong competitively than the West German and possibly the Benelux industries and, in some respects, perhaps than the French and Italian industries. The Economic Development Committee for the Chemical Industry attributes this primarily, if not exclusively, to the British market, being relatively small and growing slowly; membership of a larger "domestic market" would be the way out. Their preference is for the EEC.

Before considering this preference, two reservations on the general proposition must be made.

First, if Britain became part of a larger free market, it would not necessarily mean that she was as well placed to exploit the larger "domestic market" as other member countries. She seems less well placed geographically than West Germany and the Benelux countries for selling directly to the major part of the Continental markets and moreover, she is not better placed geographically for exporting to the United States. Britain also is probably marginally less well placed to obtain cheap raw material supplies for organic chemicals than parts of the EEC—particularly the Mediterranean countries.[131]

Second, lower productivity in the United Kingdom reflects much more than the size of the market and it is deeply rooted. Lower productivity extends to service industries; port costs in Britain are higher than in Antwerp and Rotterdam, and construction costs are raised by the long periods required for completing plants. Deficiencies in organisation and judgment, in quality of labour and management, which have been discussed above and have been recognised and vividly illustrated in the industry's own discussions of its low productivity, may be more easily reduced in a wider market. But they are not due to the limited scale of the market and will not automatically disappear if the market is widened. Challenge under

[131]Oil and oil products from the Middle East and North Africa carry less transport costs to Italy and the south of France.

a free trade treaty may produce a response, but not necessarily an optimum response. To the extent that productivity remains relatively low in Britain as it well can in a larger free trade association, growth in the chemical industry would still be slower in the United Kingdom than in other parts of the area; exports—and possibly imports, too—would also grow more slowly.

UK Prospects in NAFTA (without the EEC)

Discussions of free trade options in Britain have focussed usually on the possibility of entering the EEC, contrasted (until recently) with the alternative possibility of a North Atlantic free trade association from which the EEC was expected to abstain. Entry into one of these would give the United Kingdom a larger area of duty-free trade, but could also provide an important new preference. Opportunities for expanding exports would be less than in the wider area including all Western Europe, but the cold winds of competition would be tempered.

The narrower version of the free trade treaty proposal would eliminate import duties between the EFTA countries and North America, but import duties would remain on EEC chemicals imported into the free trade treaty countries and on the products of those countries exported to the EEC. The British and Swiss chemical exports to the United States would have free entry, whereas exports to America from West Germany, the Benelux countries, France and Italy would pay the post-Kennedy Round tariffs.

This preference would be valuable in sectors where American tariffs would be high—especially, therefore, for dyes, where, to repeat the United States post-Kennedy Round duty will be 30 per cent and to a lesser extent for pharmaceuticals (where it will be 20 per cent), to mention some of the larger sectors. It would be of moderate importance for plastic materials and relatively unimportant for general chemicals. Where it would offer most—in dyes—the Swiss as members of EFTA would have the same new preference and would probably be able to make more use of it.

The sectors in which the preference would be helpful are also sectors in which the United Kingdom would be best placed in terms of relative costs to expand her exports, though, as has been seen, there are some difficulties in interpreting the cost comparisons. (See Pages 191 and 194 above.)

The analysis of labour costs per unit of output, which the census data for 1967-68 makes possible implies that in five sectors—general chemicals, toilet preparations, soap and detergents, polishes, and dyes and pigments—labour costs per unit of output were lower in the United States than in Britain. In five others—plastic materials, pharmaceuticals, adhesives and glues, fertilisers and paints—costs were approximately the same in both countries. In four sectors—fibres, agricultural chemicals, printing ink and explosives—Britain had lower labour costs per unit. It is likely that where the American industry had much larger units of production than the British industry capital costs per unit of output were probably also below the United Kingdom figures. But this has to be surmise.

The labour cost figures are, as shown earlier, least satisfactory where price levels in the United States and Britain are markedly different. This is so with dyes, where American prices are much higher, and for man-made fibres, where British prices are on balance higher.

One would expect the United States to expand exports to the United Kingdom most in sectors where her costs are lower: the sectors where labour costs are broadly similar would give scope for increased exports by both countries; the United Kingdom should be strongest where her costs are lowest.

Of the products where American costs are lower the American chemical industry would almost certainly increase exports to Britain of general chemicals, particularly of organic chemicals, which enter into international trade much more than inorganic chemicals much more successfully than the British industry would increase exports to the United States. General chemicals accounted for one-third of the total net output of chemical and allied industries in the United States in 1967. Despite the cost figures, the United Kingdom would initially at any rate almost certainly do better in dyestuffs: the cost comparisons are possibly distorted.[132] In the group where American and British labour costs are broadly equal, the probability is that, while both the United States and Britain would find more scope, the United States would gain most percentage-wise because of the larger scale of American plants. In plastic materials the United

[132]Britain's dye industry can probably reduce costs significantly. Much of the plant is old and its replacement is planned, according to the *Report on Synthetic Organic Dyestuff Prices* (London: H.M. Stationery Office, for the National Board for Prices and Incomes, 1969), p. 10.

States could export standard qualities; both would increase trade in specialities. In pharmaceuticals again both would be likely to gain, but here removal of import duties is likely to have a minor effect only—price competition, as mentioned earlier, is only important in a limited part of the trade, and the United States still contributes the major proportion of new products in this sector. Fertilisers and paints are not major factors in the export trades and are unlikely to be much affected by duty changes (the United States has no duties). In the group where British costs are lowest, fibres are most likely to be the basis of a big trade and here the prospect is that, despite the cost figures, removing duties would be of more help to American than to British exporters (though Du Pont and Monsanto already manufacture in the United Kingdom). Again price differences probably distort the cost comparisons, and the American industry is likely to continue to gain considerably from the use of much larger plants than would seem a practical possibility in the United Kingdom.[133] The British textile industry does not have a robust home market: it is disturbed by foreign competition, and vertical links between important parts of the manufacture of cloth and clothes and fibres may limit the development of economies of scale. Here again, the British makers would probably tend to concentrate on specialities, but of course the American makers are active in this too.

It was seen earlier that the elasticities derived from trade statistics implied that the increase of imports into both America and Britain which would follow the formation of a multilateral free trade association would be broadly identical. No precise forecast could be made; the elasticities gave the total increase of imports to be expected (in the case of the United Kingdom from £37m to £75m) if the whole chemical trade was free, and it is not logical to assume that a reduction of duties limited to a small number of countries would yield increases of imports proportionate to these countries' former participation in the trade. It is possible only to suggest a floor (in the case of a limited free trade association from £9m to £18m more

[133]Du Pont, for example, was contemplating a new polyester staple fibre plant to make 300m pounds weight a year. The capacity of ICI was 75m pounds. See *The Financial Times*, London, September 2, 1970. The present writer was told (in the autumn of 1969) that a plant to make 200m pounds would enable profitable sales at 30c a pound. The list price in the United Kingdom was then 62d, the discount price 55d to 58d. The United States list price was 42d.

imports into Britain) and a ceiling—the amount given above which removing all duties in all countries would induce.

If the same hypotheses for America and Britain are adopted, and the elasticities used for the United States are those adopted for the Kennedy Round negotiations, then the resulting figures suggest that imports into both countries would increase equally (see Page 163 above). This, however, seems unlikely. It is more probable in the light of the cost trends that the American exports to Britain would increase more than British exports to the United States. If this were so it would still be possible for the British industry to expand more than it would if the multilateral free trade association were not formed, and to specialise and increase efficiency more than it otherwise would under pressure of keener competition and with free entry to the American market. This probably would be the case.

UK Chemicals Prospects in the EEC

The preference of the Economic Development Committee for the Chemical Industry—and almost certainly of most British chemical firms—for the EEC rather than the free trade treaty option in its narrowest sense (which perhaps has never seemed a probable alternative) is readily explained.

First, the volume of trade with the EEC is larger than that with the United States and the balance is more favourable.[134] It offers much more expansion of exports, certainly in the short run—if, that is, one can assume broadly equal elasticities of import in the United States and the EEC which is not necessarily justified. It offers a larger increase in imports by the same token—roughly one-third more: but the additional export might be 125 per cent more by joining EEC than by participating in a free trade treaty confined to North America and EFTA on this crude type of figuring.

Next, the EEC market is closer. The American home market is larger than the EEC market and, in most sectors, larger than the

[134]The figures ($m) in 1968 were:

	United Kingdom exports to	*United Kingdom imports from*	*Net imports*
EEC	262	407	145
United States	116	290	174

whole West European market (though the West European market grows a little faster). But in a free trade association only embracing EFTA and North America, Britain would be more remote from the main part of her "large domestic market" than if she was in the EEC. It would be possible, because transport costs are lower to the Continent, to export goods with a lower value/weight ratio. This would be especially useful for firms who wish to supply early-stage intermediates, produced in the United Kingdom, to subsidiaries on the Continent—as Imperial Chemical Industries does, for instance.

In the EEC the United Kingdom's manufacturers would have a new preference over American manufacturers. This they would rate high; for they appear to regard the United States as the strongest competitor, partly because they think American costs are probably lower than British costs, partly because they believe the size of American operations and the smaller dependence of American firms on exports give an export advantage. On the Continent, by contrast, West Germany, the chief exporter, exports directly more of her output than the United Kingdom does.

If the fears expressed in the United States in 1962 were justified the British chemical firms should possibly expect EEC competition, especially West German, to become more penetrating than American competition. The extent of the gain from entering the EEC could clearly depend upon British competitiveness with West Germany and the Benelux countries—and to a lesser extent with France and Italy—both in producing and using chemicals. Access to Britain and other EFTA markets should be expected to stimulate more growth in the EEC chemical industries. British entry into the EEC would not in itself automatically change the relative trends in growth and productivity: as with a multilateral free trade association, it might stimulate faster British development while leaving the gap in growth rates and productivities broadly unchanged.

Impact on Foreign Subsidiaries

The international development of the chemical industry has been hastened by the setting up of foreign subsidiaries, wholly or partly-owned, by major chemical companies. One motive has been to avoid the import duties of the country in which the subsidiary is established, and to take advantage of any preferences enjoyed by that country—imperial preference or membership of EFTA or EEC. A free trade treaty would clearly remove this motive of firms to form subsidiaries within the free trade association and increase the attraction of direct exporting.

But there have been—and are—other motives. West German companies have established subsidiaries and partnerships in France and Italy, for example, since the EEC was formed, which will result in splitting their production of some products. The other motives fall into two categories. First, there are market factors. For some finished products it appears desirable to manufacture near the market. Customers may want special deliveries quickly. It is probably easier to adapt to local requirements and to organise technical advisory services where they are needed to promote a product. Second, it is possible in some situations to obtain cost advantages in a subsidiary, and to get the benefit of local skills. United States subsidiaries in Western Europe may not have found low wages a full offset for smaller scale operations and different labour practices and standards, but some American companies have said that with larger scale markets and operations in Western Europe, and rising raw material and plant costs in the United States, it might pay them to manufacture in Western Europe and export to the United States. For British companies the higher productivities of West German and other Continental workers may more than compensate for higher wages. It is indeed often stated that British management is more productive in other environments than in the United Kingdom.

The effect of a multilateral free trade association or membership of the EEC on policies in regard to subsidiaries could be important in their economic impact. At present the propensity to establish foreign subsidiaries appears to be growing—partly because more firms appear to prefer it as a means of promoting important innovations. Licensing probably gives quicker returns, but less long-term control. It seems likely the trend towards more investment in subsidiaries outside the home territory will continue. But formation of a multilateral free trade association may change the location of such investment. The formation of a free trade treaty confined to North America and EFTA would be likely to make Britain less attractive for American investment, and increase the incentive for United States firms to invest in the EEC. Such an arrangement might slightly increase the inducement to EEC firms to invest in the United Kingdom—but on a moderate scale, merely to participate in the British market against American competition enjoying a preference. If the United Kingdom entered the EEC the inducement to

American firms to invest in the United Kingdom would again presumably decline; location on the Continent would probably be more advantageous for supplying the bulk of the EEC market. Inducements to Continental firms to invest in the United Kingdom would also be less. The prospect of foreign investment in Britain would therefore be less with either NAFTA in its narrowest sense or EEC. The inducement to British firms to invest on the Continent or in the United States would, however, probably not be lessened. On the Continent there would be the attractions of closeness to the larger part of the market, plus local skills and efficiencies, and in some areas cheaper raw materials; in the United States, closeness to the large market and, again, local skills and efficiencies.

Impact on Canada's Industry

The Canadian chemical industry's approach to the free trade treaty option is illuminating, although it falls outside the main topics of this study. All save one of the major Canadian chemical firms are subsidiaries of non-Canadian companies, most of them of United States companies. One is a subsidiary of ICI. Most of the firms had growing difficulties in the late 1960s and a study of the industry's problems was made by the Canadian Government in close touch with the industry and the Canadian Chemical Industry Association. Unfortunately its results have not been published, but its main emphasis was made clear. This was on the need for operations to be on a larger scale. The American-owned firms had their parents' experience in the United States to guide them. In order to operate on a larger scale it would be necessary, most firms argued, to have larger markets in the United States. The Canadian domestic market was too spread out from east to west; a viable extension of markets must be from north to south. Further, in order to work on a larger scale, the Canadian industry would need to reduce the number of products it made. And this—the industry was increasingly inclined to believe by the end of 1968—could only be brought about by a concerted policy. They envisaged an arrangement with United States firms, sponsored by both governments, analogous in intention to the existing arrangement in the automobile industry (which was attracting a growing volume of American criticism). The Canadian Government did not show great enthusiasm for the proposal. For this study the two points of greatest interest are the emphasis on the need for larger scale required by recent technological advances and the claim for a transitional arrangement—which is based not merely on the excessive subdivision of current production but on the belief that the Canadian industry has certain relative disadvantages apart from small scale: its labour is slightly less good in quality, new plants cost more partly because they are further north than the United States plants and weather problems are more difficult, partly because capital is slightly dearer and taxation is a slightly heavier burden. Despite devaluation the Canadian industry has sold more imports and increased its net import to Britain in recent years.

Prospective Japanese Competition

The statistics of output, investment, research and development, and trade show that Japan is a growing force in the chemical industry. Her competition is still helped greatly by wages much below the West European, let alone the American, level. However, although Japanese competition is at times felt to be acute, and even menacing, it has not been a major force. It is likely to become one. A United States view was that whereas West Germany will be the major competitor for the 1970s, Japan might become so by the end of the decade.

Comparative Advantages in USA

If the American chemical industry's costs are substantially increased by further big increases in the costs of obtaining fuel and power, including prices of natural gas and electric power, and by further increases in the money cost of construction, this will be part of a general inflation which will raise costs in a wide range of United States industries. It is doubtful whether it will significantly reduce the comparative strength of the chemical industry compared with other American industries, though the chemical industry is one in which fuel and power costs and construction costs are particularly important. If the cost increase through inflation in the United States were seriously out of line with such cost increases in other countries it would presumably give rise to changes of a general character—such as changes of exchange rate parities.

Non-Tariff Barrier Problems

Non-tariff factors distorting competition which will require action if a free trade treaty is to be acceptable have not figured prominently in discussions on the proposal in relation to the chemical industry. The national regulations of pharmaceuticals and the analogous restrictions on the use of agricultural chemicals are the most conspicuous non-tariff factors which affect primarily the chemical industry alone. ASP might be regarded as such, but it is linked to the tariff; if a free trade treaty, with the United States participating, were formed ASP would be eliminated automatically within it. In a narrowly based free trade area—NAFTA as originally discussed—the persistence of ASP would in different ways, as shown earlier, increase slightly the attractions of the area both to the United States and United Kingdom industries. The national regulations of drugs and of pesticides which give rise to "unreasonable application of health and safety standards"[135] would certainly be subjects for negotiation, but the experience of EFTA where a partial elimination of the restrictions has only just occurred—after ten years[136]—suggests they would not provide a major obstacle for agreement.

But the treatment within a free trade association of several non-tariff factors not exclusively related to the chemical industry would be deemed important in the context of the chemical industry, whether within the industry or outside it, in establishing satisfactory bases for competition, and in eliminating resistances to the introduction of a free trade association.

Problems of origin would probably present relatively small problems, since they have been dealt with fairly effectively in EFTA and the rules adopted there could largely be retained. The problem would lessen in significance the wider a free trade association became.

State purchasing, direct or indirect, does not pose a major problem of discrimination in chemicals as it does in, for example, the heavy electrical engineering industry. State subsidies of all kinds would be subject to scrutiny as likely to distort competition. This might be disturbing from the standpoint of the British chemical industry which receives large support for its capital investment from the British Government, especially in development areas, and which

[135] *Future United States Foreign Trade Policy* (Washington: US Government Printing Office, 1969), p. 18. This was a report to the President of the United States (then President Johnson) prepared by his Special Representative for Trade Negotiations, Mr. William Roth, hereafter cited as the Roth Report.

[136] *The Times*, October 9, 1970.

has recently declared that such aid is needed to make large investments in the United Kingdom attractive. Britain is not the only country to assist investment, particularly in areas of high unemployment, but her scale of help has been particularly lavish; and although it is reasonable to argue that the resulting distortions have been bad for the United Kingdom, they may well prove unacceptable to other members of a free trade association. These large investment aids are available to foreign firms who invest in Britain, and firms in member countries who are interested in investing in the United Kingdom will doubtless welcome them. Their special interest, however, is unlikely to dominate policy decisions.

The principal firms in the chemical industry would clearly have a strong interest in securing satisfactory "rights of establishment" throughout a free trade association and satisfactory conditions for the flow of capital and income between member countries, in view of the international structure of most of the companies and the capital intensiveness of the industry.

Although the problem of added-value taxation, which has embittered EEC-American discussions in regard to chemical tariffs and ASP, would not be relevant at present in regard to a narrow NAFTA pact, it must be assumed that in any future negotiations for a free trade treaty to which the United States is a party, modifications of border taxes would be sought by the Americans. The American chemical industry has been prominent in raising the issue, and has argued that the West German replacement of a turnover tax by an added-value tax in January, 1968, largely offset the advantage which American exporters of chemicals to West Germany should have had from the first stage of the Kennedy Round tariff reductions. Estimates by the United States Administration put the effect of the tax change as equal to a devaluation of the Deutschmark by 2 per cent. American officials have been concerned with two changes: first, "the abandonment of a system under which domestic indirect taxes were only partially compensated at the border[137] and the adoption of a system under which full border compensation automatically occurs"—a change which "necessarily" restricts imports and stimulates exports; second, the tendency to increase the rate of indirect domestic taxation, which increased the effect

[137]Heinz Meisenberg, "Die aussenwirtschaftliche Wirkung der deutschen Umsatzsteuerreform" (mimeograph), 1968, gives figures calculated by IFO to assess the under-compensation in chemicals under the turnover tax.

of the first change. Both these changes "emphasised the trade disadvantage" which the United States suffered, it was argued, because it depended primarily on direct taxation. As a result the United States sought a review in the GATT of the rules whereby full border compensation is allowed for indirect taxes but no compensation for direct taxes, on the incorrect assumptions that indirect taxes are all borne by the consumer and that direct taxes do not enter into price.[138] American officials were less clear on the remedy to be sought than on the diagnosis. This tax issue would certainly emerge in a free trade treaty negotiation and the chemical industry would be much involved. The United States approach to border taxes rightly links discussion of the impacts of indirect and direct taxes. The latter, as Hans Liesner has emphasised,[139] are quantitatively the more important and since differences here affect the cost and supply of capital they are likely to be particularly significant for a capital intensive industry.

If special arrangements analogous to those in the United States-Canadian Automotive Agreement were sought by Canada for the Canadian chemical industry in a free trade treaty this would be a matter for negotiation with all member countries. An agreement could not be as the automotive agreement was—in intention and effect—bilateral, although other countries were nominally free to seek agreements on similar terms.[140] Nor presumably could the pattern of the automotive agreement, which freed imports of some United States cars and components into Canada but not all, be repeated. A new formula would be needed.

Finally, if negotiations were entered into for Japanese membership of the free trade association the apparently cartel-like structure of Japanese industry, and its discriminating price policies, would inevitably become an issue.

[138]Roth Report, *op. cit.*, p. 21-5.

[139]Liesner, *op. cit.*, p. 43.

[140]This was nominal only because the agreement allowed free entry into Canada of motor cars imported from the United States by manufacturers of motor cars. Almost all cars manufactured in Canada were manufactured by United States firms.

APPENDICES

Appendix I

INTERNATIONAL PRICE COMPARISONS

Despite the disparity between list prices printed in the journals and actual contract prices for a large proportion of sales, which have been referred to in the text, it is useful to analyse these list prices to see what conclusions might be derived from them. Although they are misleading guides to prices at which most sales occur they could indicate either the fluctuations in prices for particular products in one place or the differences between prices for the same products in different places. A rough analysis of all prices quoted in one issue of the *European Chemical News** to find out for how many products the American prices were lowest, for how many the West German prices, gave the following result:

	Numbers of Products		
	With lowest prices	*With middle prices*	*With highest prices*
United States	84	45	51
West Germany	70	58	46
United Kingdom	38	76	60

This is in accordance with the conclusion on Page 180 which applied, however, only to general chemicals, organic and inorganic intermediates, synthetic rubber, fibres, plastic materials and fertilisers.

The main sources apart from other trade journals used for price comparisons are:

(1) Reports of Census of Production for the United Kingdom

*The issue for February 22, 1965, chosen at random. The total number of products for which prices were given was 234. For several products prices were not quoted for the United States, Britain or West Germany. For some there were quotations for one of the three only (usually Britain). These were not used for the table.

(1958 and 1963) and Reports of Censuses of Manufactures for the United States (1958, 1963 and 1967).

(2) Tariff Commission Reports for the United States (average values of many products are published annually).

(3) Reports by Arthur D. Little on *The Impact of Proposed US Tariff Changes on Organic Chemical Imports*, 1962, and updating of the tables in this in 1965.

(4) Price data from individual firms, usually for limited periods only but including one long-term study. These have been particularly useful for the United Kingdom for the period after the 1963 Census—1964-7.

The period covered is from 1958 to 1969. There are no average value figures after 1967.

If the Arthur D. Little reports, which give comparative *contract* prices for a relatively narrow range of new materials and intermediates for 1962 and 1965 respectively, are taken first it is possible to construct a table analogous to the one given above for the *European Chemical News* price lists. The coverage is much narrower.

	Numbers of Products					
	1962			*1965*		
	With lowest prices	*With middle prices*	*With highest prices*	*With lowest prices*	*With middle prices*	*With highest prices*
United States	6	–	5	5	1	4
West Germany	2	8	1	3	7[a]	–
United Kingdom	3	3	5	2	4[a]	4

[a]In two products, West Germany and the United Kingdom had the same price.

The pattern is like that for the *European Chemical News* prices, except that the American industry is proportionately more often the one with lowest prices. Such loss in its lead as occurred according to these figures from 1962-65 was to the West German industry.

Comparison of average values and list prices for a number of products shows substantial but variable differences. The following examples are all taken from United States figures in 1966: the American list prices come from the *Oil Paint and Drug Reporter*.

	Quoted price cents/lb	*Average value cents/lb*
IPA	7	6
Acetone	6.5	5
n. Butyl acetate	13	10
Benzene	3·7	3·3
Methanol	4·1	3·0
Styrene monomer	12.5	8.0
Phthallic anhydride	9·5	9·0
High pressure polyethylene	15.8	18.0
Polypropylene	19	23

Thus in general the quoted price is above the average value. For the most part the variation in differences represent different market conditions. In the case of styrene monomer the list price refers to a special quality, but this became subject to exceptionally heavy discounts. The excess of the average values over list prices in the last two items probably reflects mainly variations in quality.

Comparisons of average values in United States and Britain where these are possible do not in general conflict with comparisons of list prices.

There is much more, and more continuous information on average values for the American industry than for the United Kingdom. This limits the scope for comparison, and there are other difficulties. The following table compares average values from the 1963 Census for 30 or so products.

This table again shows the American price—or rather average value—more often the lower when compared with the United Kingdom figure.

No "average values" were available when this study was made for the years after 1967. During this period price relations were disturbed by the United Kingdom devaluation and the West German revaluation: there were differing degrees of inflation, and acute divergences of price trends occurred in the first half of 1970. The general balance probably remained more favourable to Britain in 1969 than it had been in 1967. Nevertheless in the important expanding sectors of organic intermediates and plastic materials United States prices were as often below United Kingdom prices or approximately the same as above them in these years. The list prices

AMERICAN AND BRITISH PRICES
(cents per lb)

Product	*US Census of Manufactures 1963 or Tariff Commission Statistics*	*UK Census of Production*	*US price lower*	*UK price lower*
Caustic soda	2.4	2.7		
Soda ash	1.5	1.6		
Chlorine	2.5	2.9	X	
Sulphuric acid	0.85	1.04		
Nitric acid	3.3	3.1		
Phosphoric acid	6.2	10.9		
Ammonia—anhydrous	3.4	4.4		
Carbon dioxide	2.5	(3.5)	X	
Calcium carbide	4.7	(4.5)		
Ethylene	4.5	(5.4)	X	
Propylene	2.4			X
Ethyl alcohol	6.0	11.0		
Iso propyl alcohol } Propyl alcohols }	6.0	5.1		X
Acetic acid	7.0	13.0		X
Phenol	10.0	11.0		X
Methanol	3.0	(3.4)	X	
Acetone	5.0	6.2		
Styrene monomer	9.0	10.5	X	
Butadiene	10.7	(9.9)		X
Isobutylene	3.8	(5.4)		
Ethylene glycol	9.0	12.4		
Vinyl acetate monomer	13	15	X	
Vinyl chloride monomer	7	8.8		
Phthallic anhydride	10	10.1	X	
Acrylonitrile	14	(19)	X	
Polyethylene { high density	23 }	18.3	X	
Polyethylene { low density	18 }		X	
Polystyrene	19.3	19.7	X	
PVC	19	14		X
Synthetic rubber type-S	22			X
Synthetic rubber type-N	48	(50)	X	

for a number of them are shown in the following table; the writer has been told that they give a reliable view of the price relations, though in most instances not a precise view of the actual prices.

Product		United States cents/lb	United Kingdom cents/lb
Acetone	1967	6.75	7.4
	1968	6.75	6.75
	1969	6.50	6.75
n. Butyl acetate	1967	13.50	14.6
	1968	13.50	13.20
	1969	14.00	13.20
Methanol	1967	4.07	3.8
	1968	3.76	3.77
	1969	3.76	3.77
Benzene (nitration grade)	1967	3.67	4.2
	1968	3.66	3.63
	1969	3.40	3.86
Styrene monomer (polymer grade)	1967	9.00	10.50
	1968	8.50	9.00
	1969	7.75	9.00
Mono ethylene glycol	1967	13.50	13.2
	1968	13.50	10.60
	1969	13.50	10.06
Phthallic anhydride	1967	11.00	11.7
	1968	13.00	14.40
	1969	13.00	11.10
Synthetic glycerol 99.5%	1967	24.50	25.1
	1968	25.75	23.60
	1969	24.25	23.60
Methyl ethyl ketone	1967	12.5	11.5
	1968	12.5	10.39
	1969	11.5	10.39
Polyethylene* (low density)	1967	17.00 (13¼)	18.6
	1968	17.00 (11¼)	16.0
	1969	13.00 (?11¼)	16.0 (13.5)
Polyethylene (high density)	1967	18.0	24.4
	1968	18.0	21.5
	1969	18.0	21.5
Polypropylene (general purpose)	1967	27.0	27.4
	1968	19.5	24.25
	1969	19.5	24.25

Product		*United States cents/lb*	*United Kingdom cents/lb*
PVC (general purpose Mech. grade)	1967 1968 1969	15.0 15.0 14.0	14.0 11.5 11.5
Polystyrene (general purpose)	1967 1968 1969	14.50 15.50 15.0	15.7 13.50 13.0
Phenol formaldehyde (moulding)	1967 1968 1969	21.50 21.50 21.50	17.50 15.00 18.50
Polyisoprene rubber	1967 1968 1969	23.0 20.5 20.5	22.2 19.0 20.00

*Here actual prices diverged greatly from quoted prices and the figures quoted in brackets are an indication of this.

This is not comprehensive, and it has not been practicable to obtain authoritative assessments of price comparisons in all sectors. But these figures suggest that price movements may be leading to an equilibrium where American prices for individual chemical products will again be more often than not lower than the British prices.

Appendix II

CONCENTRATIONS AND SIZE OF FIRMS UNITED STATES, 1958-66

Sector	*Total % of Sales by four largest Companies*			*Average shipments by four largest Companies (in million dollars)*				
	1958	1963	1966	1958	1963	1966	% *Increase* 1958-1963	% *Increase* 1963-1966
Agricultural chemicals and fertilisers		33	36		40	60		50
Pharmaceutical preparations	27	22	24	170	182	265	7	46
Toilet preparations	29	38	40	73	171	243	134	43
Fertilisers	34	34	34	46	74	99	61	34
Biological products	44	36	46	6	9	12	50	33
Synthetic rubber	60	57	56	79	101	133	32	32
Industrial gases	72	72	79	46	76	99	117	30
Cellulosic man-made fibres		82	85		150	194		29
Organic fibres		94	85		329	420		28
Alkalies and chlorine	64	62	63	78	101	125	60	24
Intermediate coal tar products	54	54	52	105	150	182	73	21
Paints and allied		23	23		145	174		20
Plastic materials	40	35	32	181	237	282	31	19
Inorganic pigments	69	68	64	69	82	93	·19	13
Soap and detergents		72	72		383	432		13
Organic chemicals n.e.s.	55	51	40	424	605	654	54	8
Inorganic chemicals n.e.s.	34	31	29	222	272	277	23	2
Medicinals and botanicals	64	68	70	48	52	50	8	−4

Appendix III

INCREASE IN CAPACITY OF PLANTS IN THE UNITED STATES, 1962-66

	"Typical Plant Capacity Data" for 1962[a]	*Capacity of Large Plants completed or ordered 1966*
	tons/year	tons/year
Acrylonitrile	18,000	125,000
Chlorine-caustic soda	80,000	350,000
Ethylene	90,000	450,000
Formaldehyde	9,000	40,000
Methanol	47,000	240,000
Phenol	20,000	150,000
Phthallic anhydride	10,000	62,500
PVC	25,000	100,000 (UK)[b]
Styrene monomer	20,000	50,000 (UK)[b]

[a]Based on data in the 1962 Little Report; the figures probably refer to 1960-62.
[b]Figures given as "minima" in United Kingdom projects and for products for which United States figures were not at hand.

INDEX